SOCIAL EXPERIMENTS

Volume 131, Sage Library of Social Research

RECENT VOLUMES IN
SAGE LIBRARY OF SOCIAL RESEARCH

social experiments

methods for design and evaluation

LEONARD SAXE
MICHELLE FINE

Introduction by DONALD T. CAMPBELL

Volume 131
SAGE LIBRARY OF
SOCIAL RESEARCH

 SAGE PUBLICATIONS   Beverly Hills   London

For information address:

SAGE Publications, Inc.
275 South Beverly Drive
Beverly Hills, California 90212

SAGE Publications Ltd.
28 Banner Street
London EC1Y 8QE, England

Printed in the United States of America

Library of Congress Cataloging in Publication Data

Saxe, Leonard.
    Social experiments.

    (Sage library of social research; v. 131)
    Bibliography: p.
    1. Sociological research—United States. 2. Evaluation research (Social action programs)—United States.
3. Social policy—United States. I. Fine, Michelle.
II. Title. III. Series.
HM24.S322   301'.072073   81-13606
ISBN 0-8039-1710-4   AACR2
ISBN 0-8039-1711-2 (pbk.)

SECOND PRINTING, 1982

CONTENTS

Section IV: Conclusion

Preface

This book represents our commitment as social psychologists to the value of social research and its application in the understanding and amelioration of social problems. We hope to demonstrate how a rigorous and rational approach to social problems can be used to further their understanding and solution. The book is designed for professionals and students interested in social research and public policy, activities often referred to as evaluative or applied social research. Our hope is that we have contributed to the use of social science methodology to improve social programs and the delivery of human services.

As with any creative endeavor, this one embodies each author's biases, along with our best efforts to be fair and objective. Our view of evaluation research has been heavily influenced by Donald Campbell and his view of an "experimenting society." In an experimenting society, amelioration of social problems is achieved through systematic development and evaluation of social programs and theories. Realization of an experimenting society—the conduct of rigorous applied research—requires collaboration between those who study and research social problems and those who design and implement social programs. The present volume attempts to model a collaborative relationship by discussing social experimentation both in terms of the scientific research process and the pragmatic process of implementing social research. It is for this reason that we hope both researchers and practitioners will find this volume useful.

The book consists of four sections: the first section, "Social Experimentation and Society," discusses the concept of social experimentation and places it in context with the study of social problems and applied social research. The role of social science methods and theories in the amelioration of societal problems is discussed and examples of social problems amenable to such rigor are presented. The second section, "Social Experimentation: Principles," summarizes methodological principles relevant to applied research. This section includes four chapters, each of which balances the presentation of methodological and conceptual material with illustrative experiments. The content of Section II is similar to traditional research methods textbooks (including research design, measurement, and analysis), although the focus of the material is on "real world" research. Experiments in education, health care, criminal justice and various social problem areas are used as illustrations. In a third section, "Social Experimentation: Practice," the chapters parallel those in Section II. Each chapter describes the application of social research principles in actual experiments. Section III describes issues encountered when social programs are established as part of research efforts. The conclusion attempts to provide perspective on the feasibility and future of applied research and experimentation. Its focus is a critical discussion of the assumptions and use of experimental principles and methods.

The book has been written for those interested in applied research and social planning. Although it may seem unusual to develop a book intended for both researchers and nonresearchers, this focus follows from our analysis of the collaborative requirements of social experimentation and applied social research. Since most students in fields such as psychology and sociology (as well as other fields) do not go on to research careers and become involved in various human service programs, the focus on applications of research methods seems appropriate. Our belief is that an understanding of social experimentation will prove both relevant and beneficial to a broad spectrum of such students. The book should also be useful either as the principal or supplemental text in a research methods course or, perhaps, substantive courses in social problems. In addition, the book may serve as a primer for students in specialized courses dealing with evaluation research, public policy, and applied social research.

Acknowledgments

While cognizant of exhibiting *hubris,* we would like to acknowledge publicly one another's contributions in writing this book. We struggled over ideas, but also shared a common vision of the usefulness of social science. At times the process became more important than the substance, yet we hope that the final product represents the truly collaborative effort that underlies its development. We continue to believe that this was a project that neither of us could have completed on our own and we hope that the fervor and excitement of our intellectual journey will be transmitted to readers.

We are pleased to acknowledge the contributions of our friends, colleagues, and students who helped in developing this book and provided critical feedback. The number of these individuals is embarrassingly large.

Initial encouragement was provided by Larry Wrightsman and the staff at Brooks/Cole Publishing; in particular, Claire Verduin. Our friends and colleagues, Faye Crosby, Clara Mayo, Rick Hardin, and Timothy Elig provided feedback on several of the chapters in their early form. Comments on the full manuscript were provided by Ross Conner, Ruth Garner, Meredith Miller, and Susan Solomon. Particular appreciation is expressed to Larry Wrightsman and Howard Gardner, who provided extensive comments on drafts of an early version of the full manuscript. Thanks are also expressed to students at Boston University and staff of the Community Services Administration who, during a two-year period, read and commented on various portions of the manuscript as part of classroom assignments. The individuals involved are too numerous to note, but that should not diminish their contribution.

The support of our institutions should also be acknowledged. During 1979, the first author was a Congressional Fellow at the Office of Technology Assessment (OTA), which gave him both an opportunity to witness the policy process and to be part of an important intellectual undertaking. The staff of OTA's Health Program, including David Banta and Clyde Behney, deserve special thanks. The support of Boston University, which has been the first author's "home" since 1975, should also be acknowledged. The Boston University graduate program in social psychology provided many of the personal and material resources necessary to accomplish this project.

We would also like to acknowledge the tremendous assistance of several individuals who worked with us directly in preparing the many drafts of this book. Susan Keator-Tierney typed the initial chapter drafts. Mary Palasak and Andrea Basinait typed many of the later drafts. Mary also served as a research assistant to the first author and was responsible, along with a myriad of other duties, for verifying most of the references included in this volume. Robert Karen and Denise Dougherty, both of Boston University, assisted greatly in providing editorial feedback and suggestions. Their critical eyes and sharp pencils greatly improved the manuscript.

The first author would also like to thank his wife, Marion Gardner-Saxe, whose love and understanding has been central to his ability to function as a writer and thinker. And, Michelle Fine thanks David Surrey whose warmth, intelligence and humor endured *Social Experiments,* as it gradually permeated every corner of our lives, and helped us see beyond the Experimenting Society. For all those skeptics who thought the book would never end— Thanks for waiting.

Leonard Saxe
Boston

Michelle Fine
New York City

INTRODUCTION

Introduction: Getting Ready for the Experimenting Society

Donald T. Campbell

Authors' Note: Our debt to Donald Campbell is enormous and in order to acknowledge his contributions, we asked that he provide a preface for this volume. Campbell's most complete statement of his views on social experimentation are contained in a 1971 lecture, "Methods for the Experimenting Society," prepared in response to the 1970 award of the American Psychological Association's Distinguished Scientific Contribution to him. Unfortunately, despite the fact that publication in the American Psychologist *was at one time guaranteed and a 60-page manuscript was prepared (which has been widely distributed), the paper remains "stubbornly unpublished." Campbell continues to believe that the paper needs revision. Nevertheless, he has allowed us to reprint an overview of his 1971 address that was initially presented to the Fall Commencement of the University of Michigan (December 15, 1974). Although Campbell may not concur, we believe that his ideas are as clear and relevant today as they were in the early 1970s.*

We live in a period of exceptionally rapid social change, and must discover new methods for adapting to change if we are to survive. One recommendation that rings true to me is that we must spend more of our time "living in the future," giving detailed consideration to a number of "alternative futures." This strategy calls for the detailed development of multiple alternative "scenarios" of possible courses of action and reaction. It includes the deliberately utopian invention of ideal future societies, differing from such classics as Plato's *Republic,* More's *Utopia,* and Bacon's *New Atlantis,* primarily in paying a great deal more attention to scenarios as to how one could get from the present social system to the future ideal. The alternative futures we should be considering include not only utopias, but also "dystopias," undesirable futures that may be implicit in current policies and trends. Huxley's *Brave New World* and Orwell's *1984* are examples. In recommending that we spend more time living in the future, I am recommending that each of us become expert on a range of alternative futures, both utopias and dystopias, and use the perspectives so gained in guiding present political decisions.

The "experimenting society" is one alternative future that I propose we seriously consider. It is an image of the future that emerges from using social science in the service of society and government. Is *the experimenting society* a utopia or a dystopia? I appear before you as an ambivalent advocate. But it is near enough and plausible enough so that, utopia or dystopia, we should carefully think it through.

The current name for my own specialty in applied social science is "Program Evaluation Research." In this new field social scientists work with government, or the critics of government, in trying to assess the impact of governmental programs designed to cure social ills, such as Head Start, Job Corps, Model Cities, welfare reform, the 55-mile per hour speed limit, Phase 1 wage and price controls, and the like.

Two aspects of Program Evaluation Research push us towards speculating about an experimenting society. On the one hand, as we try to implement high quality program evaluations, we meet with continual frustration from the existing political system. It seems at times set up just so as to prevent social reality-testing. This leads us to think about alternative political systems.

On the other hand, if we look at our own recommendations to government regarding how to implement programs so that their impact can be evaluated, one can see that we evaluation methodologists are in fact often proposing novel procedures for political decision-making. We are in fact designing alternative political systems. If we were self-consciously aware of this, we would, I believe, often make different recommendations.

Out of these influences comes the imagery of an experimenting society, one that would vigorously try out possible solutions to recurrent problems, would make hard-headed, multidimension evaluations of outcomes, and, when the evaluation of one reform showed it to have been ineffective or harmful, would move on to try other alternatives. There is no such society anywhere today. While all nations are engaged in trying out innovative reforms, none is yet organized to adequately evaluate the outcomes of its innovations.

The values of an experimenting society can be drawn both from our present democratic ideals and from the values that govern science itself, for science is an admirable self-governing social system.

The experimenting society would be a *scientific society* in the fullest sense of the word "scientific." The scientific values of honesty, open criticism, experimentation, willingness to change once-advocated theories in the face of experimental and other evidence would be exemplified.

It would be a *nondogmatic society*. While it would state ideal goals and propose wise methods for reaching them, it would not dogmatically defend the value and truth of these goals and methods against disconfirming evidence or criticism.

It would be an *honest society,* committed to reality testing, to self-criticism, to avoiding self-deception. It would say it like it is, face up to the facts, be undefensive and open in self-presentation. Gone would be the institutionalized bureaucratic tendency to present only a favorable picture in government reports.

It would be an *accountable, challengeable, due-process society*. There would be public access to the records on which social decisions are made. Recounts, audits, reanalyses, reinterpretations of results would be possible. Just as in science objectivity is achieved by the competitive criticism of independent scientists, so too the experimenting society would provide social organizational features making competitive criticism possible at the level of social experimentation.

It would be a society committed to *means-idealism* as well as *ends-idealism*. As in modern views of science, the process of experimenting and improving would be expected to continue indefinitely without reaching the asymptote of perfection. In this sense, all future periods will be intermediate and transitional, rather than perfect goal states. Ends cannot be used to justify means, for all we can look forward to are means. The means, the transitional steps, must in themselves be desirable improvements.

This statement of ideals may make the experimenting society seem wholly desirable. There are, however, many methodological problems to be solved before it can be implemented. Working on solutions to these problems is in itself an exploration of that future society, and may uncover undesirable features that would lead us to advise against it.

Let me raise four illustrative problems.

First, the issue of randomized experiments. A new program is often tried out as a pilot program, with the status of participants being measured before and after. But the changes thus found may be due to the many other events that have happened, or simply to growing older. We need to know what the participants would have been like without the program. This leads to collecting similar data on "control groups" not getting the program. But such groups are usually different to begin with and very likely to have different patterns of growth. To solve these problems, the statisticians recommend randomized assignments of persons to experimental or control conditions. This requires sufficient social control over participants to insure that each ends up in the randomly assigned treatment. Research in social psychology laboratories also shows that experiments are most valid when participants are unaware that an experiment is going on. For scientific inference in theoretical social psychology, experiments are still being implemented in these ways. *But* when a social experiment is testing a proposed governmental policy, it is a political process.

As such, under the ideology of the experimenting society, it should be accept-able as a regular political process. In the mode of science it should be charac-terized by openness, honesty, accountability, equalitarianism, and volunta-rism. Under the requirement of "means idealism" it has to be a political process we are willing to live with. It cannot be justified as a temporary expedient en route to an ideal state. The voting booth rather than the experi-mental animal laboratory becomes the appropriate ethical model. Just as people should know what issues they are voting on, they should know what experiment they are in.

This policy has great costs in clarity of scientific inference, known to some of you as Hawthorne effects, guinea pig effects, selection bias, and the like. We must live with these limitations and turn our methodological skills toward solving the problem in other ways. For example, experiments using volun-teers who are informed of the treatment and control group alternatives and agree to accept whatever random assignments they draw—such experiments seem to me well worth doing. On some problems, such as public housing versus rental vouchers, they might be as informative as disguised experi-ments, but even if not, the experimenting society may have to make do with them. In the New Jersey Negative Income Tax Experiment, the most famous recent social experiment, participants were told about the particular treat-ment they were asked to volunteer for, but were not informed of what others would be getting. Should the control group have been told of the thousand dollar supplemental income it was missing? Perhaps the experimenting soci-ety of the future will decide it should have been. However, today's methodolo-gists regard the envy and resentment that might thus be generated as too great a threat to experimental validity to tolerate. Here is a tangle of problems we should be working on right now.

A second problem area:

Opinion surveys would be centrally important in an experimenting society, as "social indicators" of the effects of new programs. Treating opinion surveys as an ideal political decision-making process akin to voting, would require great changes. Here are a few: Interviewees would be told who had paid for the questions and how their answers would be used. They would know what programs were being evaluated by their answers. They would be given the results of the survey, just as they are given voting results. They would be allowed to use these results in political debates. They would be "co-owners" of the opinions they had created. From the point of view of present day social science methodology, these changes would make opinion surveys less valid. Respondents would distort their opinions in deliberate efforts to influence governmental decisions as to which programs should be continued or which regions were most in need of more resources. There would even be campaigns to get people to answer interviews in certain ways.

These costs in "validity" are probably unavoidable. Opinion surveys, how-ever, would still be useful and informative, just as are votes now, once we got used to these new conditions of meaning. The methodological problems involved are ones we should be working on right now and indeed are ones best researched in the transition period.

A third problem area:

The social indicators that are now being used include public records as well as opinion surveys—records of deaths, diseases, crimes, accidents, incomes, and school achievement test scores. In the experimenting society of the future, these would probably be used even more as indicators of how programs are doing. It might be thought such records would be more resistant to bias than are interview data. More resistant, yes, but still subject to a discouraging law that seems to be emerging: *The more any social indicator is used for social decision-making, the greater the corruption pressures upon it.* Measures that have been valid for describing the state of society become invalid when they start being used for political decision-making. Moreover, such use often leads to a destructive corruption of the social process that the indicator was designed to measure. Thus the U.S. war on crime of 1968-1971 achieved its results by downgrading the seriousness of crimes as recorded. Thus scoring police departments for their efficiency in solving crimes, combined with plea bargaining, has led the burglar who confesses to the most unsolved crimes to be given the lightest sentence. Thus achievement tests once valid for describing educational status have become less valid when used as the basis of rewards to students or teachers. Thus in the Russian five-year plans, setting quantitative quotas for factories produced wasteful distortions of production, as in the nail factories that overproduced large spikes when the quota was set by tonnage, and overproduced small nails when the quota was set by number of items turned out. Thus the U.S. Army reform in reporting enemy casualties in terms of body counts rather than subjective estimates, and in using body counts to evaluate the effectiveness of field commands, created an immoral and irrelevant military goal in Vietnam. Thus census data for Chicago are more to be trusted than voting records, not because the census-taking is more protected against fraud—quite the contrary—but because the voting data are so much more used in political decision-making.

In the experimenting society, such social indicators will be more used than at present, and the corruption pressures will thus be greater. This problem seems to me so serious that while I believe it is solvable, it provides one more reason why we should not rush forward into the experimenting society until it is solved. We need social-system inventions, and studies of how some high-pressure indicators, such as the cost of living index, remain so free of distortion.

A fourth problem:

One solution to bias is to use multiple indicators of the same problem each of the indicators being recognized as imperfect, but so chosen as to have different imperfections, different susceptibilities to distortion. This produces a variety of estimates of program effectiveness, benefits, and harms. The judgmental task of pooling all of these indicators is one more appropriate for an elected legislature than for a committee of social scientists. Furthermore, in an experimenting society we would be doing scientific evaluations on many more programs than we are doing now. With *multiple measures* on *multiple programs* we will have created a monster of measurement, a formidable information overload. How to reconcile our need for facts with democratic decision-making is another problem we must solve before we welcome the experimenting society. New institutions will be needed, such as an auxiliary legislature of quantitative social scientists, each appointed by one real legislator. Such an auxiliary legislature could process advisory decisions, with full attention to the scientific evidence. The real legislator could then guide his own decisive vote by the auxiliary legislature's actions and the issues raised.

I hope these samples have conveyed something of what an experimenting society would be like, and the kinds of problems that you and I should be thinking through in getting ready for it, either to welcome it or to avoid it. My own vote is still in favor, based on the faith that we have the ingenuity to solve the problems it will present.

In my daily work I continue to be appalled at how regularly we lack any interpretable evidence of the effectiveness of new programs costing millions of dollars. Again and again, we program evaluation methodologists see where just a little more advanced planning, just a little more scientific method, just a little more political willingness to face the facts, could have made things so much better. What I have done here is to look ahead to the kind of society we might have were our advice to be taken up on a large scale, and were we to recognize that in our advice we were designing political decision-making processes. This perspective has raised problems which both methodologists and concerned citizens must think through before we welcome the experimenting society.

SECTION I

SOCIAL EXPERIMENTATION
AND SOCIETY

CHAPTER 1

PERSPECTIVES ON SOCIAL EXPERIMENTATION

> *the line it is drawn, the curse it is cast*
> *the slow one now will later be fast*
> *as the present now will later be past*
> *the order is rapidly fadin'*
> *and the first one now will later be last*
> *for the times they are a changin'*
>
> Bob Dylan, "The Times They Are A Changin'"

As Bob Dylan's lyrics illuminate so poignantly, our society is undergoing rapid change. One of the most significant aspects of the future, as social commentator Alvin Toffler (1970, 1980) has noted, may be the rate at which change occurs. Dealing with change has become increasingly important to each of us and we seem to have entered a period in which fundamental changes, such as new roles for men and women, and alterations in our lifestyle, are commonplace. Some of these changes are planned, some just seem to happen and, in the case of almost all change, there exists a great need to understand their implications. Increasingly, social scientists are being asked to provide society with understandings and ways to deal with the problems associated with these changes. The purpose of this book is to indicate how social science can contribute to the development of understandings about social change and, in particular, how the methodology of social science can be applied to the systematic development and evaluation of social programs.

NOTE: The above quote is © 1963 WARNER BROS. INC. All rights reserved. Used by permission.

Social Science and Social Policy

The chapters that follow describe the theory and practice of science applied to understanding social change. The approach here is conceptual, in that a systematic application of social science methodology is developed. Numerous examples illustrate the ways that social science methods can be applied to study and evaluate programs designed to ameliorate social problems. Although a variety of approaches are described, the view of social science emphasized involves the systematic testing of social innovations and the use of experimental methods.

Although some form of testing ideas and social interventions has always been a part of the response to social change, only recently has this been done systematically. The conduct of social experiments represents an extension of methods developed in psychology, sociology, and related disciplines. Social programs are designed as research studies where comparisons are made among groups who have been exposed to the innovation or to some variation of it. The comparisons use carefully selected measures of the impact of innovation. Because social experimentation involves the integration of research with social innovation, it is a multidisciplinary activity that requires collaboration across social science fields and among social scientists and those responsible for social planning.

An increasing reliance exists on such applications of social science at all levels of government and in the private sector. The methods of social experimentation and the scientific logic which underlie its application are useful anywhere that rational decision-making is required. The information generated by social experiments documents the effects of social changes and influences the design of innovations so that they build on experience. Research conducted as part of the development of compensatory education programs, police patrol practices, homes for troubled youth, and ways to finance health care services reflect the areas in which social experiments have been conducted and which we will use to illustrate social research principles. Almost any social intervention can be designed so as to permit a systematic study of its effects. The conduct of such research requires a commitment to understanding the treatment and its possible impact, to specification of outcomes, and to systematic implementation of the innovation. It is necessary to specify the objectives of the program, the expectations of the program, and to implement the program according to a prespecified design. A social experiment delivers a service while it generates meaningful information about the problem and the impact of particular solutions.

Social Problems and Experimentation

The chapters that follow provide an introduction to the concepts and methods of social experimentation. On one level, the book will serve as a methodological guide in the application of social science to real-world problems; it is also an introduction to the development of planned social change. The connection between social research and policy offers an important theme. In order for social science to have an important impact on society (that is, to conduct useful research), the relationship between social science and social policy must be improved. Those responsible for the design and implementation of social policy need to understand the impact of their programs. A corresponding need is for social scientists to study problems as they exist in the real world, and to investigate the impact of interventions-as-solutions.

This book has been written to provide future participants in what Donald Campbell (1969, 1971) has called the "experimenting society" with an understanding of the scientific approach to the remediation of social problems. We are not, as yet, a society in which social experimentation is a natural feature, although the increasing reliance on social research portends a shift in this direction. Throughout the text, a great number of social experiments are used to illustrate the potential for and the process of such studies. These social experiments, however, are prototypical, not necessarily characteristic of current modes of conducting research of making social policy decisions. Whatever the actual use of these procedures, the methods should not be viewed simply in terms of their value for responding to social problems. Rather, social experimentation represents a way of viewing social problems and interventions that relies on social science principles and theory. This "way of thinking" is relevant and useful to employ whether or not actual experiments are conducted.

At various points in our discussion it may seem as if the experimental approaches to developing social problem solutions that are described are not different from current practices; at other points, it may seem as though a radically different type of social science is promoted. Probably, both interpretations are correct. Social science disciplines, such as psychology and sociology, are making important contributions to our understanding of social problems (Weiss, 1977b). Present applications of social science, however, lag behind the needs of society (see Cronbach et al., 1980; Lindblom & Cohen, 1979). Social scientists have not demonstrated that they have useful knowledge for society, although social scientists are involved in studying a prodigious number of problems and a vast literature has emerged.

There are a variety of reasons for the unfulfilled promise of social research. Our belief is that one of the central problems is that the methodology of science has been inadequately employed. Scientists know how to conduct good research, but more often than not such research is put to theoretical rather than practical use. This problem arises in applied settings not only because of the attitudes of social scientists, but because others (that is, nonscientists) do not understand their approach—and cooperation is essential.

In terms of the attitudes of social scientists, one difficulty is that a number of divisions exist within the social sciences. A principle division is the bifurcation of basic and applied research (Mayo & LaFrance, 1980; Saxe & Fine, 1979), even within specific social science disciplines. Different methods have been seen as relevant for theory-driven research and problem-driven research (see Kruglanski, 1975; McGuire, 1973). Unnecessary distinctions hinder the development of useful understandings of and solutions to social problems. The view to be developed in this volume is that an experimenting society—where social science and social policy formulation are integrated processes—can be both problem-oriented *and* theoretical. Although our view by no means represents a unique statement of what social science can accomplish (cf. Kidd & Saks, 1980), our goal is the same type of unequivocal statements of causal processes for which traditional basic research strives (see Hendrick, 1977; Schlenker, 1974).

Although most social science claims to be socially relevant and to provide a perspective from which social problems can be understood and solved, it rarely meets this test. A chasm of sorts has developed between social science as it exists in principle, and social science as it exists in practice. In addition to the inaccurate views of basic and applied research, the gap also results because of insufficient collaboration between social policy makers and social scientists. Those who are responsible for the design and implementation of social programs are not coordinated with those who theorize about social processes and conduct research on social problems. Because of this division of labor, many social programs are inadequately understood and much social research is irrelevant or inadequate. We hope to demonstrate the need for better collaboration between social scientists and social policy makers, both to improve research and to develop more realistic understandings. Such collaboration forms a central theme of this book.

In this regard, it should be noted that the authors are writing from their experiences and perspectives as social science researchers and theorists. Both authors come from the discipline of social psychology—the subfield of psychology having to do with relations between individuals and their environments. The authors are methodologists interested in the development of new research models, and also conceptualizers interested in understanding complex social interactions. The authors are committed social activists and believe strongly in the need for wide involvement in the development of social policy. Social activism is indirectly related to all themes of the book. It may explain why this book exists and why social research and policy are viewed as intimately connected. Although the authors are *not* social policy makers, we have tried to understand the view of those responsible for social programs.

Because the integration of social research and policy is emphasized, it is hoped that this book will be useful to those interested in social research and also to those interested in the planning and management of social and human service programs. To the extent possible, research strategies have been presented in a way that "makes sense" in terms of actual problems and policy. The goal has been to develop a joint perspective, driven by the nature of problems rather than a particular discipline, that incorporates a rigorous view of social science with an appreciation for the difficulties inherent in bringing about social change. In order to develop this shared perspective, the discussion of the methods of social experimentation has been coupled with examples of social programs.

In the present chapter, our view of social experimentation and the development of an experimenting society is introduced. Initially, the nature of social problems is discussed—how they are to be regarded and how our society has attempted to deal with them. The concept of an experimenting society is also developed here. Next, social experimentation is further explicated through several illustrations of social experiments. Finally, the plan for the book is described and a brief summary of some ideas detailed in later chapters is presented.

THE NATURE OF SOCIAL PROBLEMS

Our discussion of how social science can be applied to real world problems will focus on the use of research methods and the development of understandings of social problems. A number of assumptions have been made about the nature of social problems. These assumptions are important to articulate in order to understand the conduct of social scientific research and the development of an experimenting society.

At the outset, it should be noted that a very broad view of social problems has been adopted. A social problem, for present purposes, will be regarded as any problem that arises from the interaction of individuals or that can be ameliorated by other individuals' intervention. Problems here will tend to be viewed as problems of people, rather than as problems of a technology being employed. Although, for example, medical, legal, and educational technologies are used frequently to illustrate principles of social experimentation, the focus will be on the individuals interacting with and affected by these technologies, rather than their technical features. Within this framework, specific health care, legal and educational interventions are viewed as social programs (or sets of programs). The problems that these systems and their numerous programs address—crime, disease, ignorance—are obviously complex and everchanging. Although substantively different, the problems require social remedies. Social research aims to determine the effects of these interventions and to enable the better design of future programs.

Although the term "social problems" will be frequently used, it should be obvious from the broad definition that the analysis here will include much that is not traditionally considered a social problem. Thus, for example, social innovations introduced at the work place to improve the quality of worklife will be considered. References to social problems reflect the tradition out of which much of the social scientific approach was developed and are not intended to delimit the application of this logic to problems such as education and poverty.

One reason that social research needs to be applied to the study of social innovations is that the nature of social problems is becoming ever more complex. It was possible, perhaps as recently as a hundred years ago, for an individual or a family to be relatively self-sufficient. For all practical purposes, that ability has disappeared and we are dependent on others to provide us with food, clothing and protection. Our personal and work lives involve increasing amounts of interaction with and dependence on others. Western society now represents a complex system of interdependencies involving the government, the community, social and economic institutions, and friends and family. Applied social research can be viewed as a way of obtaining feedback on the systems we develop to manage and deal with our interdependency.

As we have grown more dependent on others, it is not surprising that governments have assumed an increasingly active role. Although the pendulum may swing in the opposite direction and the next decade may witness a reduction of governmental activity—especially at a centralized level—this does not lessen the extent of interdependency. It does mean, however, that the responsibility for developing effective solutions to shared problems (that is, those problems that have direct or indirect consequences for each of us) may be placed on a more local level.

Solutions to social problems may be primarily social or technological, or reflect both social and technological components (see Ellul, 1964). In effect, it may be impossible and unproductive to separate the two. The energy crisis, for example, which has only recently been recognized as a serious problem (see Stobaugh & Yergin, 1979) has both such technological and social components. Although the problem of more efficient use of available energy resources represents, in part, a problem of physical technology (such as making dwellings, automobiles and other mechanical devices more efficient), the energy problem is also a significant social problem (see Stern & Gardner, 1981). How individuals use energy and their ability to adapt to changes that may be necessary by current resource technology limitations are crucial to society's ability to deal with the energy crisis problem. Research and experimentation with social solutions to the energy problem are ongoing.

Another example of the social aspect of technological problems can be seen in our health care system. The past 50-100 years have seen great advances in medical science (although for a contrasting view, see Illich, 1976). Improvements in health notwithstanding, while the features of our health care system have purely medical components, some of the most important problems of health care may be independent of medical discoveries. Thus, for example, medical technologies which are efficacious when applied by university-based specialists may not be similarly effective when used by medical practitioners not associated with such centers (Banta, Behney & Willems, 1981). In addition, physicians and others concerned with health care systems are increasingly recognizing the need to make decisions about the use of medical procedures as part of a broader context of social policy (see Fineberg & Hiatt, 1979). Decisions to employ a medical technology have a variety of social, economic, and ethical implications, and the use of a technology not only yields particular effects, but may preclude its use (or the use of other technologies) with other individuals.

In the education system, the social nature of problems is similarly striking. There has been a knowledge explosion within recent years (generated, of course, by people), and claims are now made that the amount of information doubles or triples every few years. How the educational system copes with preparing students to understand the complexities of the current world and to function as useful society members is a critical question (see, for example, Shostak, 1981). There are indications that the educational system, at least in the United States, has not coped well. In addition to problems such as violence against teachers, truancy, and other problems historically present in some form, available evidence indicates that present-day students have poorer basic skills than earlier generations. The College Entrance Examination Board (1977) has found a relatively steady decline in Scholastic Aptitude Test (SAT) scores among students who graduated from high school 5, 10, and even 20 years ago. Although there are problems interpreting such evidence as "proof" that schools have failed (as will be discussed in Chapter 3), great concern has developed about the situation. A variety of methods have recently been tried to improve schools' ability to provide both basic skill education and training appropriate to society's new complexities.

The problems described here should be familiar to all readers. Each has been the subject of extensive public debate, and governments and private groups have long struggled with the best approaches for solutions. There seems to be agreement that current responses to these problems are not totally effective and that new solutions must be developed. Although it is probably futile to discuss solving these problems in any absolute sense, "benign neglect" (Moynihan, 1970) is not tolerable. It should be possible to reduce the crisis nature of the energy problem, improve health, and increase the ability of schools to educate students with the basic skills necessary to function in society. While this book promises no solutions to these social problems, the social research methods described should provide ways of developing solutions and understandings. An ongoing and systematic program of testing new ideas and solutions to these social problems is necessary for our continued ability to respond effectively and knowledgeably.

THE EXPERIMENTING SOCIETY

The thrust toward a "testing" or "experimenting" society, where social innovations are systematically tried and evaluated, at present appears more in the minds of social scientists than those who have responsibility for social policy. It does, however, have harbingers. Ever since President Johnson decided during the 1960s to harness federal resources in an "attack" on poverty and its concomitant social problems, systematic testing of social innovation has been recognized as a necessity (see Lynn, 1978). Within recent years, evaluations of the new programs have been institutionalized such that Congress authorized many government agencies (such as the Public Health Service within the Department of Health and Human Services), to allocate a specific portion of their budgets for program evaluation studies. Information for decisions about direction of social programming is routinely generated.

As the reader will discover through our discussion of specific social programs, neither the programs nor the research studies conducted to understand the programs are always effective or without controversy (see Congressional Research Service, 1976). In particular, evaluation research studies of Federal programs have often been post hoc and poorly conducted, subject to criticism on methodological grounds (see, for example, Bernstein & Freeman, 1975; Gordon & Morse, 1975) as well as substantive grounds (see Aaron, 1978). Some criticism of research applied to studying social interventions may be inevitable, given it may refute "common wisdom" and suggest that a new program was not worthwhile (see Gilbert, Light & Mosteller, 1975). Criticism may also represent the "growing pains" of society trying to utilize social research and researchers becoming attuned to practical problems.

Throughout the text, a number of successful and unsuccessful social experiments and evaluations will be presented. In some cases, such as the initial evaluation of the federally funded Head Start program (a preschool program for disadvantaged children; see Chapter 3), the study generated disagreement about the study's usefulness and the program's success (Cicerelli et al., 1969; Datta, 1976). In other cases, a study shows negative program results (see Ross & Blumenthal, 1975), but is considered a successful research effort because it results in our learning what does not work. To be sure, cases exist where an intended research study does not get done or is so poorly executed that no useful information is obtained (see Michelson et al., 1977). There are also a number of examples of successful tests of effective programs. Probably the best tradition of such tests is represented in health care. Thus, for example, one of the most extensive experiments was conducted in 1954, to test and validate the effectiveness of the Salk poleomyelites vaccine (Meier, 1972). Of a more social nature, early tests of televised educational programs such as *Sesame Street* (Ball & Bogatz, 1971; Cook et al., 1975) showed that the programming had positive effects and, in part because of these data, additional funding was made available.

The pressure for conducting evaluative research studies of social programs, particularly those that are government funded, seems to be increasing from a variety of sources (Levitan & Wurzburg, 1979). Although such research should not be the sole basis for deciding among policy alternatives, we have entered an era where there are clear limits to the resources available for any problem (Thurow, 1980) and where decision processes are necessarily complex. Because resources are constrained and need to be appropriated more thoughtfully, and because research techniques are available to provide information that can be used in this process, their use likely will expand. In the following chapters, the uses of social research as ways to improve policy-making and the interrelationships between research and policy will be developed.

Social problems and policy form the basis of this book, but no attempt has been made to describe either process comprehensively. Instead, the book offers an approach to changing and studying social innovation. Readers are provided with a guidebook to the *process* and *methods* that can be used by social planners and researchers to respond to social problems. As we hope readers will come to appreciate, methodology is more than a collection of specific techniques (Kaplan, 1964). Methodology represents a particular application of scientific logic and a way of thinking about social change. Learning this logic is important, whether or not you become a direct utilizer (for example, as a social researcher or planner). Each of us participates in a society which uses this approach and struggles to develop solutions to complex social problems.

The experimenting society represents a social system in which research is systematically applied to testing ideas and solutions to social problems. It is a society in which social planners collaborate with others, variously called social researchers or evaluation researchers, in order to design and analyze social innovations. Real-life problems of groups and individuals "drive" the system, although scientists' search for generalizable understandings are an important aspect to what kinds of designs and analyses are employed. Social experimentation represents a systematic way to respond to social problems and, as such, differs from typical (arbitrary, politically expeditious, unplanned) ways of dealing with such problems. Three examples of

significant social problems and the use of social experimentation are provided below to help clarify the interrelations of social research and policy.

Illustrative Programs and Social Experiments

As a way of introducing the concepts of social experimentation, this
section describes a series of problems that have been subjected, in varying
degrees, to experimentation. Although these cases are not intended to indicate the range of problems suited to systematic experimentation nor the
range of available methods, each illustrates some important issues in developing and using social experimentation.

HOW TO POLICE MORE EFFECTIVELY

An interesting social experiment demonstrating both the complexity of
conducting such tests as well as their potential utility is a program and
research study carried out in Kansas City during the early 1970s. Commonly
known as the Kansas City Preventive Patrol experiment, this study examined the impact of different approaches to police patrolling (Kelling et al.,
1976). A group of social researchers from the Police Foundation worked
with the Kansas City Police Department to test a common assumption of
crime prevention—that the presence of police "patrols" deters crime and
aids in the apprehension of criminals. According to the traditional and intuitively substantiated principles of police practice, patrolling creates an impression of police omnipresence. The number of police on actual patrol is
assumed to be directly related to the ability of police to control crime. Based
on this belief, almost all police departments in the United States allocate a
significant amount of their resources to patrol functions.

The Kansas City experiment put to a test this common belief about the
effectiveness of patrolling. The study adopted the alternate hypothesis that
preventive patrolling does not deter crime. The implications are important
should the alternative hypothesis be accepted, because they suggest that
police time could be better used. The experiment involved testing a suspen-
sion of routine patrol in selected police districts. As part of the experiment,
patrol practices were altered so that in specific districts, police were available only in response to calls for assistance or crime reports. Fifteen patrol
districts in Kansas City were divided into five groups of three, according to
criteria that matched the areas according to demographic characteristics
(such as average income of residents, density, and so on). Within each
group, one patrol beat was designated (through a random sampling procedure) as a *reactive* beat, one a *control* beat, and one a *proactive* beat. In the
five reactive beats, officers were instructed *not* to enter the area unless there
was a specific call; in the control areas, no change was made from the

standard procedure of a police cruiser being available at all times; in the proactive beats, police presence was increased two to three times normal (partly with the aid of police units that were previously assigned to the reactive areas).

The designers of the experiment, in collaboration with police officials (particularly Police Chief Clarence Kelley, who later became the Director of the Federal Bureau of Investigation), worked to insure the maintenance of experimental conditions. This involved making sure that police officers followed their experimentally assigned patrol beats. (Although at one point early in the study the experiment had to be suspended because of violations of the patrol rules, these problems were later overcome.)

Several types of information were collected to test hypotheses about the effects of the patrol changes. Three primary sources of information were used: (a) surveys and questionnaires of residents, (b) interviews and observations with the police, and (c) police department and court records. The surveys determined if community members recognized changes in police presence and measured the amount of reported crime. If only police data on crime rates were used, the rates may have been artificially low because there were not police available to whom crimes could have been reported. Interviews with patrol officers and observations of police behavior assessed how officers' behavior was affected by the change in patrol policy. Finally, Kansas City Police Department statistics—indicating the number of reported crimes, number of arrests, and so forth—were utilized to determine the impact of the new patrol policy against standard police criteria of effectiveness. The use of a variety of data sources guarded against some information being affected by the experimental change.

The results of the experiment are interesting and somewhat supportive of the initial hypothesis. The findings, however, are not totally unambiguous or without controversy (see, for example, Larson, 1976; Risman, 1980). On almost all of the measures used to assess the patrol program, the data showed no significant differences between reactive and proactive patrol districts. Increased patrolling did not drastically reduce criminal activity, nor did a lack of preventive patrol activity lead to an increase in crime. At least during the period of the experiment, changes in police presence did not seem to affect crime rates within the community.

However, before one decides that police departments should reduce patrolling activity on the basis of this study, the experimental procedures should be carefully examined. Two important aspects of the study stand out as potential threats to its utility (see Fienberg, Larntz & Reiss, 1976; Larson, 1976). First, the essential treatment condition—the reactive beat condition—may not actually have been implemented as intended and there are some suggestions that a great deal of similarity existed among the actual patrol levels across conditions. Because police did patrol the outskirts of the reactive beats and because special police units (such as emergency services units) continued to patrol the districts normally, police presence may actually have been maintained in the reactive condition. Second, conclusions from the study are based on essentially negative results—a finding of no differences between conditions. Unfortunately, results that indicate the absence of effects are not convincing tests of hypotheses—they may only indicate insensitive measures or an inadequate implementation of the treatment. If this experiment were replicated, it would be desirable to make the conditions even more dissimilar so that any actual differences would be obtained.

Although the conclusions of this study remain vulnerable to different interpretations, that in itself may not suggest a poor result. If the study focuses attention on the assumptions underlying police practices and provides some evidence of the impact of alternative ways of policing, it has probably served an important function. From the perspective of applied social science, the study also illustrates the applicability of research methods to a problem that had not been subjected to scientific scrutiny. It suggests the potential for other studies to be conducted in order to understand and improve the functioning of the police and criminal justice systems. The fact that such studies can be conducted as part of the delivery of police services and yield findings that are not obvious or intuitive indicates the potential usefulness of the experimental approach. In addition, it should be noted that the use of a random selection procedure for deciding where patrolling should be changed leads to confidence that differences among the conditions were actually due to patrol alterations, rather than other factors.

The Kansas City experiment, while a local project, offers potential implications for many other areas. Determining the generalizability of such studies is one of the analytic problems with which social researchers must be concerned. Whatever its value, however, it illustrates the range of both settings and problems for which social experimentation techniques may be applicable.

TREATING THE MENTALLY DISABLED

More typical of programs subject to systematic social research are programs for treating the mentally disabled. Mental illness is traditionally considered a social problem and has long been the subject of research to understand and develop improved treatments. Although it turns out that far less knowledge exists about mental health treatments than might be assumed (especially about psychotherapy treatments), a prodigious amount of research on mental health interventions has been conducted (Saxe, 1980). Perhaps more importantly, many changes have been introduced to the mental health system during the past several decades, and despite the large number of studies, the conditions under which psychotherapy is effective, and how this should be measured remain unclear (see, for example, Parloff, 1979).

One important study of efforts to treat mental illness was an investigation of behavioral and psychoanalytic therapies conducted by Sloane et al. (1975). This experiment involved a group of about 100 outpatients at a Temple University psychiatric clinic. Patients who came to the clinic within a specific period and were diagnosed as having an anxiety neurosis or personality disorder were assigned to one of three categories: behavior therapy, psychoanalytic therapy, or a waiting list (no therapy). Assignment to the conditions was random (patients had an equal chance of being in each of the conditions) and waiting list patients were kept out of therapy for four months. Those on the waiting list learned that there would be no openings in the clinic for possibly four months, but the clinic would maintain contact with them during this period.

The purpose of the experiment was to determine whether therapy could be shown to have a more positive impact on patients than no therapy and to determine if behavior therapy and psychoanalytically oriented therapy had differential effects. The impact of therapy was measured by a paper-and-pencil social adjustment test and by ratings of adjustment by therapists who were "blind" to the type of treatment received by the patient. These measures were assessed after four months of treatment (or after being on the waiting list four months) and after one year.

Sloane et al.'s results were relatively clear-cut. After 4 months, both of the actual treatment groups showed significant improvement compared to those patients on the waiting list. After one year, during which time the waiting list patients received therapy, no differences were found among the three groups. No differences between the group who had received behavior therapy and psychoanalytically oriented therapy emerged either at the four-month checkpoint, or after one year.

Although the results are relatively clear, their implications are not as clear. As will be the case with about every experiment to be described, limits to the generalizability of any set of findings constrain the implications. In this case, the fact that patients were not severely impaired and the short duration of therapy limit the kinds of situations to which the findings might be applicable. In addition, the study used very limited measures of impact and it is unclear, for example, whether measures such as therapists' ratings, actually indicated better social adjustment.

A more difficult problem is that it may not be correct to assume that therapy, per se, was responsible for the change. The specific advantages of therapy notwithstanding, improvement shown in the two therapy conditions may have been the result of receiving any form of treatment or attention. The study also is not a definitive test of two types of therapies. It may be, for example, that psychoanalytically oriented therapy needs to be conducted over longer periods of time, or it may be that behavior therapy is only effective for a narrow range of problems. Since these aspects of the situation were not systematically varied, it is difficult to make conclusions about them. It should be noted, however, that the experimental design utilized by Sloan, et al. does make it possible to accept, with some confidence, the finding that currently practiced therapy does help individuals. Because patients were randomly assigned to the waiting list, improvement in the treatment conditions is difficult to explain without acknowledging the impact of therapy.

The Sloane et al. experiment, while typical of some types of applied research, differs because it was set up explicitly as a research study and utilized a rigorous design. Although there are advantages to the design employed here (as will be described in later chapters) the situation of this clinic may not be representative of other situations. A variety of ethical and pragmatic problems are related to withholding treatment (even temporarily) which may not be possible in other settings. This study does, however, illustrate one type of experimentation that has been successfully carried out on a significant problem in a real-world environment.

VIOLENCE IN THE HOME

In both of the previous examples, the "treatment" tested was relatively circumscribed and involved improvement of current practice, whether patrolling practices or a mental health treatment. In the next example, the nature of the most effective treatment is, as yet, not clear and consideration of the problem is in a somewhat primitive state. The social problem concerns wife battering, a type of domestic violence that has recently gained increasing attention from the public and from social scientists. Media coverage has been exhaustive and articles about battered wives have been prominent in newspapers, magazines, and on radio and television. Wife battering, a social problem historically hidden from public scrutiny (Doron, in press), has not only come to the fore in the media, but has been the focus of intensive legislative and judicial scrutiny (Eisenberg & Micklow, 1977). As an important social issue, wife battering provides an example of a problem that potentially could be addressed through the methods of the experimenting society. As efforts along this line are only beginning, it would be useful to examine how social research might deal with the problem.

The first step in developing a solution to any social problem, the determination phase, has already occurred through the extensive media and governmental attention to wife battering, generated largely by feminist and other women's groups. It is now acknowledged that between 28 percent (Strauss, 1977) and 54 percent (Gelles, 1972) of all U.S. marriages are characterized

by domestic violence. The relationship between child abuse and wife battering heightens public attention to the issue of domestic violence (Roy, 1977;
Varna, 1977). The problem has become more intrusive and, as such, more
demanding of public and governmental attention. The federal government
has responded to battering with a series (albeit inadequate) of intuitively
designed social programs, many of which create more problems for the
victims and their dependents. For example, the Law Enforcement Assistance Administration (LEAA) allocated $1.3 million during 1978-1979 for
the establishment of hotlines, counselling, and shelter services for battered
victims (New York Times, 1977).

No doubt the establishment of shelters plays an important role for battered
women, yet this isolates the victim. Many are inaccessible or unsafe; and
most are restricted by time, eligibility requirements (such as unwillingness
to shelter drug abusing women) and/or services (such as access to housing,
job opportunities, child care) (Fine, 1981). Although shelters need to be a
component of any comprehensive package to combat battering, there is
danger that resources will be directed at reactive rather than preventive or
investigatory solutions. The problem can be summarized as follows: intuitively, women's shelters appear to meet the needs of battered victims. Although very few shelters exist today to service an estimated 15 to 28 million
victims (and even these few are currently in fiscal jeopardy), the shelter
solution is still favored. Although shelters may satisfy the immediate residential needs of some battered victims, they in some ways obscure the
need for a comprehensive economic and social response to the problem.
Not all battering victims are in need of shelters. Shelters are not the only
responsive intervention. Alternate treatment programs such as vocational
training and subsidies might equally aid some victims in their flight from
domestic violence.

The shelter approach reflects the development of an intervention that
directly ameliorates the symptoms of the problem but, unfortunately, may
blind us to the social forces which sustain the practice of battering. Before a
solution is developed, even one subject to testing, the social problem must be
better understood. This probably entails a study of the incidence of battering
and the context in which it occurs, as well as an understanding of what
women need to enable them to leave such situations. After the problem is
better understood, a more comprehensive treatment package more applicable to the varied needs of the battered population might be developed.

Once the problem has been clarified, the task of generating and selecting
social responses to be tested can begin. One must consider, however, the
assumptions which underlie proposed "solutions." An example of a mis-
guided policy can be seen by the following exchanges that occurred in the
Israeli Knesset (the ruling government body of Israel). In response to an
increase in the number of reported rapes, a member of Knesset suggested

that an evening curfew be imposed on Israeli women. Golda Meir, then the Prime Minister, was outraged and reminded Knesset members that rape was a crime committed by men. If anyone deserved a curfew, men, not women, should be restricted, according to Meir (Chapman & Gates, 1978). Although restricting women's freedom might have been an "effective" solution, such a solution is obviously unacceptable and represents a "punishing the victim" approach (Ryan, 1972).

The experimental testing of solutions has been virtually absent from the current response to wife battering. What would such studies in an experimenting society look like? Assume for the moment that after extensive conceptual work, it was hypothesized that battered women are unlikely to leave violent homes because of the inadequacy of their options (Fine, 1981; Gelles, 1972). They may be financially unable to subsist independently, and, as a consequence, live with the terror of physical violence in their homes. From this vantage point, a number of possible treatments, including counselling programs, vocational training and job placement, income subsidy programs, and shelters might be appropriate (Fine, 1978). At this point, only minimal attention has been paid to what these women need.

In order to test adequately the effectiveness of these solutions, women who have been identified as battering victims, perhaps by coming to a shelter, would be enrolled in one of the treatment programs. If 100 women came to the shelter, 25 might be assigned to counselling, 25 to vocational training and job placement, 25 to a combination of the services, and 25 to the standard shelter program. In order to test the effects of the program, after a set period of time, various information would be collected on employment, relations with children (when appropriate), financial status, self-confidence, independence, mental and physical health, and self-reported ability to cope. Such information could be collected on a regular basis in a follow-up study to determine which women stayed away and which returned to the battering homes. This is important, because according to both Burdick (1978) and Gayford (1975), many battered women are forced to engage in a cycle of leaving and returning to their battering homes. Such experimental information could determine which programs are more effective for whom and provide information about better directions for policy formulation.

Imagine one learns that a combination of vocational and income subsidy programs are most effective in aiding battered women during the transition period. A governmental agency might then develop this idea into a policy proposal and allocate funds to implement an aid program formed on such principles. Of course, this does not mean the end of the research or alternative interventions. It may not be the best solution, and it may have unanticipated effects. Data must be collected regularly and systematically because it can be expected that the nature of the problems will change due to social events and the very institutionalization of the treatment programs. New problems may emerge that will require amelioration (such as finding jobs for newly trained women), or old issues may become new problems (for example, research might indicate that adolescent girls exposed to violence between their parents anticipate and, in turn, tolerate some violence in their future marriages). Assuming that new problems do become apparent, the cycle of problem definition and solution development will need to be recycled. Social science thus provides a perspective and a methodology for ongoing participation in social policy.

The approach to solving the wife battering problem outlined above is not overly complex. It is merely a systematic way of analyzing a problem and developing information to support the effectiveness of a solution to the problem. The role of scientific inquiry in the amelioration of such problems requires planning and coordination at a number of levels. Hypotheses will probably not develop solely for those who are involved in providing services or from those interested abstractly in problems of family violence. Hypotheses, as well as planned interventions, will evolve through the joint work of researchers, planners, and activists. The outcome of such systematic social innovation should be better understandings of serious social problems and improved policy responses.

Conclusion

In the experimenting society, new programs and ideas about programmatic responses are subject to systematic tests and evaluation. Social policy is formulated on the basis of research findings and social research becomes an integral part of the development and implementation of social policy. As we have tried to demonstrate in this chapter, the need for an experimenting society relates intimately to the rate of social change and the ever increasing need to develop and redevelop solutions to social problems.

The central feature of the experimenting society assumes the conduct of experiments to generate information that tests ideas and social innovations. At the national level, this involves systematically experimenting with large-scale social programs. On a more local level, it involves testing out variations of existing programs in order to determine the most effective treatments for particular problems. We obviously have not as yet achieved an experimenting society; faced with an increasing array of problems and potential responses, it may be inappropriate for us *not* to experiment systematically.

THE PLAN OF THE BOOK

As stated earlier, this book will be an introduction to the process and methods of social experimentation. It is based on an assumption that a gap exists between what social science knows about solving social problems and what is actually applied. An important emphasis of the book will be to synthesize these two perspectives. By the end of the book we hope that readers will have learned to appreciate the perspective of an applied social researcher and of a social planner.

The book comprises four sections. Section I consists of this chapter, and has been designed to provide a general perspective on the concept of an experimenting society. Section II consists of four chapters and provides a review and synthesis of the methodology of social experimentation. These later chapters have been written primarily from the point of view of the social researcher and attempt to translate theoretical social science practices into procedures that can be understood in an applied context. Section III, also composed of four chapters, parallels Section II and presents a review of issues in the experimenting society from the point of view of social planners and implementers. The issues of research design are presented as they are implemented to study actual problems. Finally, Section IV, consisting of a single chapter, summarizes and discusses the potential for an experimenting society.

Although the attempt here has been to organize the concepts and problems of social experimentation as neatly as possible, issues are not always clear-cut. There is an important interaction between principles and practice in the experimenting society which makes it difficult to present complete discussions within any chapter. In order to reflect the interactive nature of the issues, discussions will often refer to other chapters. In addition, to maintain continuity in our discussion, the examples described in this chapter are referred to throughout. These examples and the others to be utilized should serve to remind readers of the central goal of our endeavor: to be better equipped to understand and solve the critical problems of our social world.

SECTION II

SOCIAL EXPERIMENTS: PRINCIPLES

CHAPTER 2

SOCIAL EXPERIMENTATION AND SCIENCE

> *"The real purpose of the scientific method is to make sure that Nature hasn't misled you into thinking you know something you don't actually know."*
>
> Robert H. Pirsig, *Zen and the Art of Motorcycle Maintenance*

During the early 1940s, a method was developed to prevent brain damage in premature babies. The treatment consisted of placing premature infants in an incubator environment of high concentrations of oxygen during their first few weeks. The treatment seemed to be effective and, within a short time, incubators in many hospitals had been modified to allow oxygen to be made continuously available. Soon the routine treatment for all premature babies, it steadily gained in application from the end of the 1940s until the early 1950s. During this period, although physicians did not recognize the connection, the incidence of a form of blindness called retrolental fibroplasia elevated dramatically. It became almost epidemic among premature infants during the early 1950s. Our account of this medical crisis is based on an article by William Silverman (1977) in *Scientific American* which described the search for a cause of this disease and its implications for medical research. Although a medical problem, it illustrates a number of features of the scientific approach to social change and innovation.

Retrolental fibroplasia, a disease of the retina, occurs when blood vessels in the retina develop abnormally. In some cases reversible, many who are affected become totally and permanently blind. The sudden occurrence of this disorder stimulated a number of researchers to investigate the problem. They eventually discovered high oxygen therapy to be the cause of the disease. An experimental study was developed (in 1953) to test what was then a hypothesis about the cause of retrolental fibroplasia. The study involved almost 800 infants in 18 hospitals. Infants in this controlled study, in sets of three, were randomly assigned to one of two conditions which required that they receive a certain amount and concentration of oxygen. A routine treatment group received 50 percent oxygen for 28 days, while a curtailed oxygen group received oxygen only when their clinical condition indicated it was absolutely necessary.

As Silverman (1977: 103) noted, "the results were dramatic. Retrolental fibroplasia occurred in 23 percent of the infants in the routine oxygen group and in seven percent of the group that received curtailed amounts." Since all other facets of the treatment of the routine and oxygen curtailed groups were the same, the difference between the 23 percent and 7 percent rates of occurrence appear to be due to the use of high concentrations of oxygen. The important question why seven percent of the infants in the curtailed oxygen condition developed the disease may be asked, and its answer may affect the need to search for other causes. As it turns out, when one examines the study in detail, babies were not entered into one of the conditions until 48 hours after birth. Before that time, infants in both groups had been treated routinely (that is, with high concentrations of oxygen); according to Silverman, this placated the nurses who thought it was cruel to restrict oxygen to premature babies.

The retrolental fibroplasia example provides testimony to the danger of implementing a new procedure without prior experimental validation of its safety and effectiveness. High oxygen incubators, with little systematic pretesting, were assumed to be safe devices that would prevent mental retardation in premature infants. From a scientific standpoint, however, this hypothesis should have been subjected to a systematic test in order to ascertain its validity. Unfortunately, methods to test medical techniques exist, but are employed infrequently (see, Banta, Behney & Willems, 1981; Wortman & Saxe, 1981).

Although a medical example, the retrolental fibroplasia case parallels other more distinctly social problems. Just as the previous chapter described examples of systematic efforts to study new programs, examples of problems which have not been subjected to research abound. Unfortunately, the latter set of examples is much larger than the list of scientifically conducted studies. In the remainder of this chapter, some of the principles underlying the scientific study of social problems and innovations are described. The problems which occur when one does not apply this scientific perspective and the principles of science embodied in social experimentation are detailed.

As a rigorous form of applied research, social experimentation incorporates the principles and logic of science into a collaborative applied science endeavor. Most readers are probably familiar with these concepts and the logic that underlies them. Our emphasis concerns the relevance of these principles and their relationship to the understanding of social interventions. The chapter has three sections. The first section discusses the philosophy and logic of social science. The second section discusses concepts, such as randomization and validity, which are central to understanding the conduct of social experiments. The final section integrates some of the previous material by describing the relationship between social experiments and scientific principles. In broad terms, we attempt here to translate ideas about science into a framework useful for understanding their application to solving social problems.

The Logic Of Science

Science represents a system, of sorts, for establishing relationships among changes in the environment and in particular outcomes. Although an extensive discourse on the logic of science can be found elsewhere (Kaplan, 1964; Nagel, 1961), an underlying thesis of this book is that some of these basic principles of logic must be understood if science is to be employed effectively in the social policy arena. To be sure, science already is utilized as part of the social policy process; however, the commonly employed version lacks the necessary rigor and, therefore, usefulness. It will be argued that rigorous research is as possible in the real world as it has been in the laboratory; furthermore, such rigor will lead to a more useful social science.

One difficulty is trying to present scientific concepts so that they might be applied is the negative image many people have about science. All too often, science is characterized as an ogre that dehumanizes human problems. Three misconceptions seem to disenchant many with scientific endeavors. First, science is frequently typified as a cold, hard discipline, antithetic to "human interests." Second, science is often shrouded in a cloak of intellectual mystique, portrayed as an arduous and complex sequence of events beyond the intellectual capabilities of the lay person. Third, science is often mystified as the method for learning the truth—for determining what is right and wrong. Aldous Huxley's (1946) *Brave New World* is a caricature of a society ruled by science.

We disagree with these popular characterizations of scientific inquiry. The perspective adopted here is that the methods underlying scientific practice can be utilized to further social or "humanistic" ends, by providing evidence and tests of ideas about how to improve social conditions. It is certainly a rationalistic approach but one that can lead to useful understandings. Of course, science can be, and has been, used for a variety of less desirable ends. But as the retrolental fibroplasia example illustrates, the absence of scientific testing of the treatment obscured the identification of a harmful outcome. Once this outcome was known and weighed against the benefit of the treatment, a judgment about the most humane path could be developed. In our description of social experimentation, we hope to convince readers of the ways in which social science can be used to cultivate and promote more, socially beneficial responses to social problems. In the absence of scientific data, pragmatic responses are not likely to be any more humanistic than those established empirically; and in fact are likely to be less responsive to the actual groups suffering the problems.

As a logical system, science does not require specific technical expertise and is distinct from the image of science suggested by test tubes and computers—the hardware often associated with scientific research. Social science is merely a way to determine and understand the nature of our social world, helping us to identify the impact of social interventions. The scientific approach provides one systematic way of unearthing information about social policy problems and serves as a basis for inferring the effects of particular social changes. Although not the only way to understand social change, science nevertheless provides an important and unique perspective.

BASIC PRINCIPLES

Scientific logic is at the heart of what we have called social experimentation. Kaplan (1964), a prominent philosopher, has argued that in order for people to understand their world, they must be able to stand outside of that psychological world and observe it from a detached vantage point; in essence, science represents this perspective. Social experimentation, as a collaborative effort, reconnects science and experience by linking researchers and program personnel. Knowledge is most commonly the result of accumulated personal experience and naive intuition. Our social understandings have, until recently, been subjective rather than objective. More recently, however, methods based on the logic of science have been used to develop valid—accurate and generalizable characteristics of many—understandings. We now employ scientific logic to test our naive assumptions and to integrate objective and subjective experiences. Science involves the generation and cumulation of empirical evidence, evidence based on experimentation, research, and experience (Popper, 1968).

In the following description of scientific principles, our emphasis will be a reconstructed logical view (Kaplan, 1964). That is, we will present the idealized form of the logic, rather than what Kaplan has referred to as "logic-in-use." Science does not have inflexible rules of procedure, although particular scientific disciplines subscribe to agreed-on procedures. By presenting reconstructed logic, we hope to provide a basis for describing particular implementations of social science.

Experimentation, the principal scientific method to be emphasized here, involves at a simple level the comparison of groups or individuals who have been differentially exposed to changes in their environment. Experimentation provides a way to check intuitions and assumptions about why certain social phenomena occur, and why certain social programs do or do not work effectively. For example, researchers used experimental comparison of premature infants treated by high oxygen incubation and a group not treated by extra oxygen to determine the treatment's negative side effects. Similarly, in the Kansas City Patrol Experiment (see Chapter 1), a comparison was made among experimentally constructed patrol conditions in order to determine the effects of regular police patrols. Some scientific outcomes are, perhaps, obvious, while others seem counterintuitive. The most unequivocal way to assess such practices is to experiment: to alter the procedure and collect data about the effects of the change. The concepts described below are important to understanding the development of experiments.

Theory. The role of theory in social research should require no justification for its import (Kaplan, 1964; Merton, 1957). Although there are many different types of theories which vary widely in their scope, they share the common purpose of conceptualization. Theory involves the coordination of ideas about a social intervention and allows for the prediction and/or explanation of behavior as a function of the presence or absence of specific variables. Implicit in the design of any social program, a theory in simplest form justifies the program. Although the word theory is often associated with high-level intellectual activity, one person's theory can be held by another as lightly as a passing thought.

Theory, in the context of social experimentation, provides a starting point for developing hypotheses about connections between a treatment and its effects, which can be tested in social experiments. Theoretically, the high oxygen environments were associated with reduced risk of brain damage in premature infants. While the test ultimately confirmed this connection, it was also learned that the treatment was related to risks of blindness. The results of the experiment modified the theory. Social experimentation has been described as the "Cadillac" of applied research methods (Acland, 1979). It generates policy relevant information that is scientifically rigorous and expands the limits of social theory.

Empiricism. The gathering of data—most often in our case, information derived about the process and impact of a social program—underlies the logic of social science. This orientation, referred to as empiricism, demands that impressions be confirmed by accumulated information before they are accepted. Concepts, or a set of ideas connected in a theoretical framework, require experimental tests and empirical confirmations to be considered factual. An intuitive "sense" of a connection is a necessary, but not sufficient, basis for scientific confirmation. As a number of the earlier examples suggest, intuitions can often be grossly inaccurate. Intuition needs to be put to the test, via experimental investigation, in order for it to be useful in developing theory and, ultimately, effective social policy.

The need for empirical evidence underscores the logic of the scientific model and differentiates social experimentation from politically expedient policy-making. Empiricism involves collecting systematic and comparative information about programmatic responses to a social problem. In most cases, social policy derives on the basis of unsystematic data about the nature of a social problem (see Aaron, 1978). Empiricism goes beyond the intuition that a problem exists, and strives to verify the presence of the problem through observable and confirmatory proof. Until a social problem is empirically determined, its existence, prevalence, and solution are questionable, at least as far as scientific standards are concerned.

Operationism. Operationism involves the procedures by which theoretical concepts are translated into concrete entities that can be tested. It represents the transformation of theoretical concepts into programs or treatments which can be manipulated, with outcomes that can be measured. Operationalization is the process by which an educational innovation is defined as special courses on sex-role stereotyping for school children in grades 4-6; a social response to domestic violence becomes a short-term shelter with provisions for children; or a juvenile offender diversion program becomes a job development project in which juveniles can work to compensate victims of their crimes.

The concept of operationism is central to understanding social experimentation. Traditionally, social planners respond to problems with ideas that sound like sensible resolutions to the problem. The ideas are then refined, distilled, and operationalized. But there is generally some slippage between the theoretical concept and its operational counterpart. For example, the designers of the Police Patrol experiment were dismayed when the actual reactive patrolling arrangement differed radically from the original concept. It was theoretically assumed that the reactive patrols would be visible only in response to calls for assistance. Operationally, the intended limited visibility was undermined by the presence of special police units. The test of the idea did not adequately represent the theory.

Most social programs and innovations are already operationalized by the time social researchers become involved. Ideally, social researchers would be involved in social experiments from the point of conceptualization and guide the process from theory to operationalization. But this is usually not the case. Social researchers, who come on the scene once a program has been designed and/or implemented, have two types of responsibilities. First, they must help planners move backwards to derive the theory which underlies the operational program; that is, from operation to concept. Second, the social scientist must help the program personnel to operationalize program goals and effects and determine how they should be measured. By operationalizing both a theoretical construct and its presumed effects, the impact of a social program can be measured and the relationship of the program to its consequences fully understood.

Consider a social experiment designed to reduce the incidence of high school illiteracy. A group of teachers argues that if motivated, students will learn more. A group of school administrators argues that motivated teachers induce greater learning. To test both sides of the argument, a social experiment is designed. Student motivation is operationalized so that students are given financial rewards for grades: $100 for a C, $300 for a B, $500 for an A. Teacher motivation is operationalized in a similar way—a $7000 bonus for the highest average class scores on a standardized test. The concept of motivation has been operationalized into financial incentive. Although this way of operationalizing motivation may seem extraordinary, such an approach has actually been proposed (Hughes, 1979). The media executive who described this in a column in the *New York Times* suggested that this plan would be less expensive than the total of federal and local monies now expended on remedial education. The assumptions of Hughes's argument are questionable. They illustrate the importance of selecting operations that accurately reflect the theoretical perspective being tested. In this case, the operations reflect external motivations (money). An alternative operationalization might have introduced internal motivators for students and teachers (such as self-esteem); or targeted the intervention at changing school *structures,* not people. The operations selected to test a theory require substantial thought; once implemented, they cannot be modified easily.

Once the operationalization of a program is determined, it is necessary to operationalize the goals and expected outcomes of that program. For example, the goal of the program might be to improve students' attitudes about the educational system and to provide them with basic skills. Operationalization involves specifying independent (treatment) and dependent (outcome) variables, determining how these should be measured, and specifying particular achievement and attitude tests to be used in the measurement.

Causality. Basic to the rationale underlying social experimentation is determining the relationships among independent and dependent variables. Most often these connections are causal relationships; that is, does a change in one variable *cause* a change in another? If social programs are designed to respond to and/or prevent social problems, it is assumed that there must be an empirically confirmed relationship between implementation of the treatment and reduction of the problem. This search for causal relationships is, if you will, the scientist's way of operationalizing the goal of understanding. The confirmation of causality between a treatment and its effects is a central feature of social experimentation.

An unambiguous cause-effect relationship is impossible to determine. One aims to document the conditions under which a treatment and an effect are related—and to what extent changes in one influence changes in another.

Does reduced oxygen treatment diminish the probability of retrolental fibro-plasia? Do income subsidies to battered women reduce their rate of return to violent homes? Those factors assumed to influence or cause the effects constitute independent variables. Those factors which are caused or effected by the independent variables constitute the dependent variables. In a social experiment, the independent variable is presumed to elicit a variety of effects in the target population. Employed as an independent variable for the purposes of conceptualizing an experiment, the social program is expected to have impact on a set of dependent variables.

To establish a cause-effect relationship between independent variables and dependent variables is the objective of scientific endeavors. Of course, no linear relationship between a simple "cause" and effect is possible. Does reactive patrolling reduce crime? Does compensatory education help disadvantaged children maintain high educational standards? Do community mental health centers change peoples' access to mental health services? Developing completely unambiguous cause-effect relations through a process of experimentation is aspired to but never fully achieved. All social problems have multiple causes and require multiple responses, many of which social programs do not provide. Independent of patrolling patterns, unemployment affects levels of crimes, inadequate nutrition interferes with children's abilities to learn, and a lack of transportation may obstruct help seeking from mental health agencies.

Despite the multicausal nature of social problems, the programs suggested for social experimentation are assumed to have major impact. The extent to which they do, or not, is measured by criteria of causality. To approximate causality between treatment and effects, Cook and Campbell (1976) identified three criteria sufficient to infer a causal relationship between independent variable X (treatment) and dependent variable Y (programmatic effects, such as reduction in the incidence of a problem):

(1) X and Y must *covary* in the environment. If X is present, so is Y. When a treatment is administered, the effects are more likely to emerge.
(2) A consistent temporal sequencing exists between X and Y, such that X precedes Y across time, circumstance, and persons. The effects emerge in greater proportion only after the treatment has been administered.
(3) Alternative explanations cannot explain the covariation. Other factors cannot be implied to account for the emergence of expected effects.

The logic of these statements should be easy to follow. If, after participating in an individualized educational program, students improve their test scores and attitudes towards learning, the program may have *caused* this improvement. The program was implemented and higher test scores reported in the same semester, and participation in the program preceded the test score increase. If no other explanations for the findings can be specified (for example, the best teachers were selected to implement the special program), the program could be accepted as the cause. Alternative explanations, as thorns in the side of causality, usually abound. The "game of science" (McCain & Segal, 1977) involves figuring out the possible rival explanations and collecting other evidence which reduces their plausibility.

As an example of how complex this process can become, consider the medical researchers investigating the cause of "Legionnaire's disease." The disease is often fatal and struck a group of individuals who were primarily members of the Pennsylvania American Legion conventioning in Philadelphia in 1975 (Fraser & McDade, 1979). What kinds of independent variables might explain the epidemic? Age: this particular group of older individuals had a higher probability of dying from natural causes; food: this group may have suffered from food poisoning; environment: the air conditioning for the rooms of this group may have dispersed an infectious bacterial substance; stress: an event at the convention may have stressed certain participants to the point of death. Experimentation aims to disprove as many *alternative explanations* as is possible through experimental control of the conditions which may have produced the disease. To eliminate all alternative explanations is impossible. We proceed "as if" alternative explanations were eliminated, and "as if" extraneous factors have been controlled, but remain aware of uncontrolled influences on the research (Blalock, 1964).

SUMMARY

Scientific logic structures our observations of people and the environment, facilitating the establishment of causal relationships. Scientific inquiry involves a number of critical steps: developing a theoretical framework from which hypotheses are derived, developing empirical proof of the existence of a phenomenon, operationalizing independent and dependent variables being tested, and searching for causal relationships which will contribute to our understanding of social processes. Social experiments, through scientific logic, translate experience into science through the process of formalizing and testing the degree to which naive understandings of the world can be confirmed. Other means are available for gaining knowledge and insight about our social environment (Snow, 1963). We hope to demonstrate in the following section the logic that science provides: a systematic way to understand, predict, and influence aspects of our environment.

Key Concepts For Assessing Social Experiments

The abstract ideas of science are not really very far from our own experience. Each of us uses data (observations) about our social world; we think in concrete (operational) terms, as well as in the abstract (theory); we also—if the recent research of social psychologists is to be trusted—think in causal terms. Attribution theory (Heider, 1958; Kelley, 1973) explains how each of us "makes sense" about what causes the behavior of others. We see a man running down the street with a pocketbook under his arm. We are likely to infer that he may have stolen the bag. Such judgments form an important basis for how we react to others. Although it is not necessary to understand attribution theory in order to understand social experimentation, it may be helpful to relate some abstract ideas about social experimentation to your own experience.

In the following section, the concept of social experimentation is further described through the presentation of some key principles. Most important, the text focuses on a precise description of what is meant by experimentation and how it relates to the logic of science. In addition, some elements will be described that distinguish experimentation from other forms of science: randomization, control groups, and hypotheses. Finally, the concept of validity is discussed in terms of its use in assessing the efficacy of social experiments. This discussion introduces concepts that will be discussed in the next three chapters.

EXPERIMENTATION

Empirical inquiry generates the least ambiguous data and dispels the greatest number of alternative explanations when the experimental method is employed (Campbell, 1957; Cook & Campbell, 1976). The experimental method enables researchers to research systematically the differential consequences of various forms of social intervention. This strategy permits the testing of causal relationships between treatments developed to reduce social problems, and their actual impact on those problems. The experimental method (which uncovered important information about the effects of high oxygen incubation on infants, for example) structures research so that important comparisons can be made. True experiments, in contrast to quasi- and nonexperiments, represent a very special form of empirical research and controlled observation. They involve the use of rigorous procedures for testing hypotheses about the effects of social interventions. Social experimentation rests on relatively simple logic. The process of experimentation, however, can be complex. It involves substantive understanding of the problem, as well as methodological skills. For this reason, we repeat the importance of collaboration between social planners and researchers.

Experimentation involves formal and planned, rather than random, observation; hence, it is more objective than nonscientific observation. Experimentation also consists of controlled observation of human behavior in situations where the experimenter actively varies a treatment. In simplest terms, some individuals receive a treatment, or participate in a social program; others are placed in a no treatment or control condition. In some cases, others may be placed in a variation of the program. The experimenter chooses the circumstances and indicators for observation and controls critical variables between the conditions so that a determination can be made of how treatments are related to outcomes. If too many variables are free to vary, attributing observed differences to the treatment becomes impossible. As will be described in more detail in a later section, a key element of experimentation is comparison—comparison of outcomes between the different conditions.

The opportunity to examine the impact of treatment under controlled circumstances is the *sine qua non* of scientific experimentation. Examination of these influences is the way in which experimentation provides a testing ground for experience-based "hunches." As John Dewey (1957: 224) noted:

> Experimental science means the possibility of using past experiences as the servant, not the master of the mind. It means that reason operates within experience, not beyond it, to give it an intelligence of reasonable quality. Science is experience becoming rational.

In testing the impact of a juvenile offender program on subsequent court appearances and school attendance, researchers and program planners decided to use an experimental design. Contrary to predictions, juveniles in the program did not improve on either outcome measure. They did not have fewer court apperances or better school attendance than previously. But because an experimental design was used, it became possible to learn that the juveniles in the control group got *worse* over time: their court appearances and truancy increased. Hence, the treatment succeeded in that it halted further deterioration. The effectiveness of the program could only be determined with a comparison group using experimental methods (Kushler & Davidson, 1979).

RANDOMIZATION

A central criterion for true social experiments—and a key method for improving our ability to make valid comparisons—is the application of randomization procedures (Cook & Campbell, 1976). Each participant bears an equal chance of being assigned to any one condition. If a social experiment involves one experimental and one control condition (a simple type of experimentation), each participant has a 50 percent chance of assignment to a condition. If the experiment involves two experimental conditions and one control condition, each participant has a 33 percent chance of as-

signment to any one condition. Randomization is the best way to insure that
the distribution of participants in any condition is unbiased, that there is an
even distribution of characteristics across the conditions, and that comparisons across conditions are valid.

Imagine that students are *not* randomly assigned to different conditions in
a study of the effects of a new "skills awareness" program. The program is
offered to school districts in a large city, and approximately half of the
schools *volunteer* for the program. An effort is made to determine if students
at volunteer schools where the project is implemented do better academi-
cally than students at the other schools, and if this improvement can be
linked to the program. Achievement scores of students at volunteer schools
are compared to students at the other schools. After six months of the new
program, children in volunteer schools rate at much higher levels than
children in other schools. The "skills awareness" program seems a success.
Or is it? Based on the limited information given here, one can generate a
number of plausible interpretations. Gains in academic achievement may be
due to the program, or they may have had more to do with characteristics of
the faculty at the volunteer vs. control schools. If the schools which selected
the program were also more educationally progressive than the controls
(which would be reasonable, since they volunteered for the program), the
improved scores may not be due to the particular program but to some other
factors related to the schools' philosophy, structure, or faculty.

Without additional data, it is difficult to know which interpretation is most
valid. However, if randomization of schools (to condition) had been used, it
would be possible to circumvent these interpretation problems. Randomization requires that for any sample of participants—in this case schools—each
participant is given an equal chance of being selected for any of the conditions. In this situation, each school would have an equal chance of being
placed in the treatment condition or control condition. If participants in this
experiment had been randomly assigned to conditions, differences among
the schools should have been distributed equally across all conditions. Individual characteristics (in this situation, school characteristics) should influence all conditions equally. Randomization reduces the possibility that one
condition will consist of a group of schools that are highly discrepant from
schools in the other condition(s). Randomization accomplishes this by con-
trolling the assignment of schools or individuals to a condition of the experiment.

An ideal experiment might involve control over all variables that are
thought to be important. This is impossible to achieve. In our illustration of a
new educational program, full randomization would involve such variables
as the social composition, size, and philosophy of the schools and create an
artificial context. The number of variables which may have an influence is

infinite, and obviously can neither be predetermined nor controlled. As R. A. Fisher (1960: 19) commented,

> Whatever degree of care and experimental skill is expended in equalizing the conditions, other than the one under test, which are liable to affect the result, this equalization must always be to a greater or lesser extent incomplete, and in many important practical cases will certainly be grossly defective.

By using randomization procedures, investigators are in a better position to attribute condition differences to the treatment than to an extraneous variable. Randomization reduces the likelihood that findings of between-condition differences are actually due to particular characteristics of the setting, the experimenter, or the population exposed to that condition. Each condition constitutes a subject group which reflects proportionately the distribution of characteristic found in the greater population.

Take, for example, the juvenile offender program described above. All of the juveniles involved were randomly assigned to a condition. This design strengthened the findings. If juveniles were not randomly assigned—and the best-chance-of-success children were placed in the treatment program and the lowest-chance-of-success children placed in the control group—one could not determine if the results were due to a successful program or to a successful group of juveniles. In an experimental design, the latter explanation is disconfirmed. That juveniles were randomly assigned to conditions substantiates the impact of the program.

Randomization can nevertheless camouflage important findings. Characteristics that are randomly distributed may be those characteristics most likely to be affected by the treatment. For example, if a new school program is most effective with slow learners and slow learners are randomly assigned to a condition, the relationship between the program and this particular group may be masked. In this case we would find no difference between conditions, and erroneously assume the program to be ineffective without realizing the specialized impact on slow learners.

CONTROL GROUPS

In any discussion of experiments, the idea of control groups should be considered. In its simplest form, a control group provides the experimenter with baseline data that can be compared to the treatment condition. Data from a control condition informs the experimenter what the treatment would be like were the program not implemented. Assuming that control and treatment groups differ only in the presence or absence of a treatment, comparisons to a control group enable unequivocal assessments of treatments.

Without a control group, the understanding of the impact of a program suffers. Imagine the "skills awareness" program is applied systemwide and, thus, no schools are exempt from participation. No control group could then be formed. Now assume the results indicate that from September to January, achievement scores increase an average of 10 points per student. Can we infer program success from this finding? No. An increase might have occurred even if the program had not been implemented. After all, students learn over time no matter what educational program they are in. Control groups provide information about what would have happened had no program been instituted.

Now assume the same information, but that control schools have been added to the design. If students in the control school increase by approximately eight points per child, the impact of the treatment diminishes. It must be statistically determined if the two-point difference is reliable and significant. Alternatively, what if the control group showed a mean increase of only two points per child? This might suggest that the new program did, in fact, exert a strong effect on learning (the difference would be 8 points). Often the term "control group" implies that no treatment is administered, although that is not always the case. Frequently, the control group condition of an experiment involves participation in a program that is a variation of the treatment. It is virtually impossible to set up a condition where "nothing" happens. In our example of a new educational program, even in schools that choose not to adopt the new program, teachers are always innovating and altering their curricula. Unstructured changes have unmeasured effects on the outcome of the experiment.

Without control group data, we would assume the juvenile diversion program was ineffective (that it had no effects on the participants). Because no reductions in court appearances or truancy were found, those interested in using the results might suggest terminating the program. However, the inclusion of a control group permitted the determination that although the treatment did not reduce court appearances or truancy, it did prevent a worsening of deviant behavior. Without control group data, this insight could not have been extracted from the study.

In summary, a control group makes it possible to gather information about how the experimental group would have progressed had the treatment not been instituted. It provides a context, with no treatment or a different one, against which treatment condition results may be compared.

HYPOTHESES

Rarely are successful experiments conducted without serious consideration given to anticipated outcomes. Hypotheses involve a series of predictions of causal or correlational connections which are tested (Kaplan, 1964; Popper, 1968). Experiments are the vehicles through which the validity and durability of hypotheses are tested. It follows that hypotheses direct the flow of experimentation.

In most situations, an infinite number of ways of operationalizing and testing a program exist (Satin & Saxe, 1979). Theory-based hypothesizing narrows down the number of possibilities and guides observation of the treatment outcomes. Without a plan of what to look for, attention often gets paid to inconsequential outcomes or outcomes that have appeared to be significant by chance.

Each of the experiments described earlier tested a particular research hypothesis:

(1) High oxygen environments will reduce mental retardation in premature infants.
(2) Reactive police patrolling will affect rates of crime as well as proactive patrolling.
(3) Involvement in a juvenile offender diversion program will reduce the number of court appearances and truancy.

These hypotheses guided the research. The first hypothesis suffered from an incomplete understanding of the impact of the intervention; in that a major outcome of the treatment (that is, blindness) was unanticipated. The second guided the research but lacked precise implementation. The treatment was implemented in ways that differed from the original idea. The third hypothesis was overzealous and exaggerated the expected outcome. It did not account for the fact that a program might be successful if it could halt deterioration of behavior rather than reduce the absolute amount of deviant behavior.

Hypotheses are useful to guide research and explain findings. When experiments show no effects (that is, no difference between the treatment and control conditions), researchers may:

(1) Assume the theory and hypotheses are wrong and redevelop the research;
(2) Assume the methods or implementation are inadequate and replicate the design; or
(3) Assume the indicators are insufficient and broaden their scope.

Even when hypotheses are confirmed by preliminary results, the experiment might be repeated, that is, *replicated,* to determine the extent to which the findings may be generalized to different populations, circumstances, and times.

VALIDITY

Validity is the process by which one confirms the true and enduring relationship between treatment and effect. It is the concept which allows us to determine the quality of an experiment and its findings. A valid study establishes an unequivocal association between a treatment and effect(s). Problems that interfere with our ability to establish unequivocal relationships pose threats to validity. By designing social experiments to get around these threats, a powerful tool, a validity analysis, can be developed to assess and improve experiments.

The logic of validation has been worked out by Donald Campbell and his colleagues (Campbell, 1957; Campbell & Stanley, 1966; Cook & Campbell, 1976, 1979). Campbell and his colleagues propose four criteria to serve as guideposts to establishing a valid study:

(1) *Internal validity*. This refers to the process of determining a causal relationship between treatment (program) and effect. Threats to internal validity occur when variables other than the treatment may have influenced effects. If the police and teachers decide to be especially supportive of juvenile offenders in a special diversion program and treat the control group juveniles less supportively, a threat to internal validity would be introduced. Did the program or the extra support reduce subsequent delinquency? These threats are usually uncontrolled aspects of the situation in which the experiment is conducted.

(2) *External validity*. This refers to the degree of generalizability of the results of a social experiment across time, settings, and persons; that is, the degree to which findings from one social experiment apply to the effects of a similar program implemented in another setting, at another time, or with different groups of participants. One of the most critical threats to external validity results when experimental program participants are significantly different from future participants. This is often the case. Experimental program participants frequently are volunteers, or the pilot sites are often "special," more interested or better financed than the norm for program innovation. Trying to generalize findings about police practices from Kansas City to New York City might be a mistake, for example.

(3) *Statistical conclusion validity*. This refers to how appropriately statistical tests have been applied to the observations conducted as part of the experiment. A common threat to statistical conclusion validity occurs when researchers utilize numerous outcome measures, only a few of which reflect any significant differences between groups exposed to the program and groups that have not been exposed. Although the researcher may be tempted to attribute great meaning to the few outcome measures which do show differences, this would be an inappropriate emphasis on "success," the results of which may be better explained by chance factors than by treatment effects.

(4) *Construct validity.* This is a complex type of validity which refers to the theoretical labeling of the program or treatment. While a program may demonstrate effects, the cause of these effects may be misattributed. The fact that the reactive patrolling pattern varied in operation from the original concept is a construct validity problem. In many social programs, the treatment is multifaceted and discerning the element(s) responsible for the effects is difficult, if not impossible. A treatment may appear to be effective because of an unintended or unmeasured aspect that has been unsystematically added to the program. One must be sure, especially if generalizations are to be made about program efficacy, that the true reasons for treatment effects are determined.

Social Experimentation in Practice

So far, our discussion of social experimentation has been primarily conceptual. In addition to having their own logical system, social scientists have developed a detailed language about their work. We hope to make clear through the present discussion that the logical system and its accompanying language offer necessary tools for understanding the experimental approach to social problems.

We would also like to make clear a distinction between types of social experiments as a way of organizing this discussion. Up to this point, we have only alluded to different forms of social experimentation. At least two types of social experiments, true experiments and quasi-experiments (Campbell & Stanley, 1966; Cook & Campbell, 1976) can be distinguished. These forms of social experimentation, though closely related and in some cases difficult to distinguish, represent different levels of control over independent variables. Each type of social experiment generates data, different in terms of their validity. Much of the material in the next several chapters reviews how such experiments yield different types of information.

TRUE EXPERIMENTS

The form of research represented in most of the examples presented earlier is *true* experimentation. Designed to produce data high in internal validity, true experiments involve the random assignment of program participants (or other units) to treatment and control groups. The ability to compare across groups assumed to be equivalent is the advantage of using true experimental designs. Examples of true experiments have, in the past, been difficult to find outside of laboratory settings. They were infrequently done because randomization and control group procedures were often seen as impossible to implement in applied settings. However, the recent use of "true" experimentation characterizes many fields including health, police patrolling and education (Boruch, McSweeny & Soderstrom, 1978).

An example of a classic true experiment was begun in 1939. The Cambridge-Somerville Youth Study experimented with a mental health treatment program for adolescent boys. The treatment program consisted of long-term counselling and supervision, designed to minimize the probability of delinquency. A total of 650 boys referred by social service agencies and social institutions (schools, churches, police) were matched in pairs according to similarity of background and then *randomly* assigned to either a long-term counselling program (the treatment) or a control (no treatment) condition. One noteworthy aspect of this study is its duration. Boys who participated in the program (both from the treatment and control conditions) were tracked from 1939 to 1976 on a variety of psychological and social dimensions (McCord, 1978; McCord & McCord, 1959, Powers & Witmer, 1951).

For those who believed that delinquency and criminal behavior were treatable and preventable through individual-targeted interventions as opposed to structural intervention, the outcome is unfortunate. None of the data collected about the efforts of the program demonstrated that youths in the treatment conditions fared better than those in the control condition. In fact, the most recent data (collected in 1975-1976 by McCord) indicate that men in the treatment condition were more likely to have committed a crime and to show signs of alcoholism and serious mental illness than the controls. Information was obtained from 95 percent of the original study participants. Among those who critiqued the study, several (for example, Sobel, 1978) have explained the results in terms of the relative ineffectiveness of counselling in the 1930's compared to its effectiveness today. Despite this explanation — which essentially questions both the external and construct validity of this study — the randomized selection of participants makes it difficult to challenge the finding that this program was ineffective.

Although the results of the follow-up evaluations of the Cambridge-Somerville Youth Study are relatively clear-cut, a variety of important questions about the study persist. Aside from external validity questions (that is, how generalizable it is to youth offenders today) and constant questions about a program developed 40 years ago, one might also want to explore whether the treatment was successful for some participants while harmful or without impact for others (thereby masking program effects), and whether the outcome measures were appropriate. Additional questions about the agreement of the conclusions with other studies of similar treatment programs (a type of construct validity) and the correctness of statistical tests (statistical conclusion validity) also must be asked. True experiments, though rigorous in design, must be accountable to all four validity criteria.

QUASI-EXPERIMENTS

Quasi-experiments represent variations on a theme. They share many of the characteristics of true experiments (such as careful observation and comparison of the effects of a treatment), but do not randomize participants to treatment and control conditions. They entail comparisons between groups that cannot be assumed to be equivalent. Nevertheless, quasi-experiments provide a suitable basis for assessing causality and are frequently employed in applied settings because they are easier to carry out and do not require control of treatment to the extent required by true experiments.

Quasi-experiments engender greater numbers of internal validity problems than do true experiments. Such problems may be compensated for by the greater likelihood of conducting a quasi-experiment in a real-world setting, thus making research more possible. Sophisticated ways of ruling out alternative explanations (that is, establishing internal validity) may be applied to quasi-experiments. For many purposes, carefully analyzed and presented quasi-experiments can provide data as meaningful as true experimental data.

An example of one type of quasi-experimental study is represented by the early national evaluation of the Head Start program (Cicirelli et al., 1969). Head Start is a compensatory education program implemented in the 1960s to prepare disadvantaged preschool children to cope successfully with school. Head Start formed one of the cornerstones of President Johnson's War on Poverty. Because of a series of political constraints (McDill, McDill & Sprehe, 1972; Williams & Evans, 1969), an evaluation of the program was carried out on an ex post facto basis during 1969; that is, after the program had begun. Investigators were essentially interested in determining if children who had previously participated in Head Start and were then in the first, second, or third grade performed better in school than children who had not participated in the program. In order to study the program, a group of children who had participated in a selected set of Head Start programs were matched with a group of children who had not participated in Head Start. The children were compared on a variety of cognitive and affective tests.

The design for this study was quasi-experimental in that children were not selected randomly to participate in the treatment program. Although control group subjects were later selected because they were similar to experimental subjects (matched), this matching procedure did not produce equivalent groups. The results of the study created a tremendous controversy. Findings indicated that Head Start students did not do better in school than their non-Head Start counterparts. Any gains that did occur in cognitive and affective development seemed to be transitory. The only noticeable effect was a "marginal" improvement in cognitive development for students who participated in the Head Start preschool program for an entire year—despite the fact that parents and others expressed much enthusiasm about the program.

In addition to political implications of the results (over release of preliminary findings, for example), a controversy arose about how the program was assessed. Campbell and Erlebacker (1970) provided a detailed critique of the study that tried to refute the claim that the matching procedure produced groups which were equivalent. Campbell and Erlebacker argued that control students (those who didn't participate in Head Start) were initially better prepared for school than were those students who participated in Head Start. They argued that the program succeeded in attracting students who needed it the most, and suggested, therefore, that the scores of the Head Start students may have indicated an improvement which would not have occurred if they weren't enrolled in the program. While our discussion overlooks some complexities of Campbell and Erlebacker's arguments (in particular, the claim that statistical attempts to equate the groups were inappropriate), principally, they confirm that it is impossible to know post hoc how students in the control and treatment conditions differ.

Despite the methodological problems of the study, it did generate useful data and provided a focal point for discussions about Head Start. While the comparison group may, in fact, have been more competent initially than the treatment group, the evaluation may have been correct in noting that affective and cognitive gains were not as had been anticipated.

If more of the problems with the ex post facto design had been noted earlier, perhaps it would have been possible to correct them; in particular, to collect more data about the similarities and differences between the treatment and control groups. The collection (or use) of additional data is the principal method for improving the sophistication of quasi-experimental designs. If, in this example, additional cognitive and affective data had been available, the actual impact of the program on the children's lives could have been more broadly assessed. Data collected at a variety of time points would permit the elimination (or acceptance) of alternative explanations of the data based on pretreatment differences. This entails, as will be described in later chapters, fairly complex statistical analyses which help one to make sense of the data and to discover patterns among variables.

Conclusion

We have attempted to demonstrate, through the examples provided above, how the abstract concepts of science apply to social experiments. Recall the admonishment early in this chapter that science is more than a set of rules. True and quasi-experiments, though they can be viewed as two distinct forms of research, represent related types of scientific inquiry based on a single conceptual framework. It is less important to be able to categorize such experiments as it is to understand what types of information can be generated using the different methods. Such understandings are essential to the ultimate goal of improving social interventions.

This chapter was intended to guide you along a quick journey through the logic and conduct of social science and social experimentation; to offer a framework, a conceptual lens through which social science and social experimentation could be viewed. The concepts of science certainly require far more detail than has been provided here (we have no pretensions about having done science any justice in this brief overview). It is hoped that you now have gained familiarity with the options available to researchers and thinkers who seek to generate the most meaningful and unambiguous data possible about social problems and programmatic responses. The next chapter provides a more in-depth exploration of the issues involved in viewing social programs as independent variables. In doing so, we will consider issues of how to assess research designs and how to design programs that lead to understanding of their effects.

CHAPTER 3

THE DESIGN OF SOCIAL EXPERIMENTS

*"The mind of the most logical thinker goes so easily
from one point to another that it is not hard to mistake
motion for progress."*

Margaret Graham, *Gift & Givers*

The *raison d'être* for conducting social experiments is to generate understandings of the effects of social programs and interventions. Although
social experiments and social programs are closely related to one another
(both include the delivery of a specific treatment), a social experiment goes
one step further. Social experiments are designed to offer a treatment *and* to
assess the impact of such a treatment. Assessing the impact of a treatment
involves the collection of information about its intended and unintended
effects and the develpment of understandings about the reasons for effects.
Determining the presence or absence of treatment effects involves comparisons of groups or individuals who have been exposed or not exposed to the
treatment.

Such comparative information does not naturally "fall out" of a social
program or intervention; rather, the program must be carefully designed so
that such comparisons can be made about the effects of the intervention. Our
goal, as social experimenters, is to construct tests of social programs that
yield valid information about the programs, information that can be used for
understanding and improving the treatment. Such information can offer
paths to understanding why programs are successful or unsuccessful; and
whether they should be modified, discontinued, or expanded. The requirements for developing understandings of social interventions differ from the
requirements for developing actual interventions and programs. These differences will be noted throughout the chapter.

Treatments and research designs. In order to generate valid information about program effects, social experiments must incorporate both a treatment design and a research design. The treatment design is the way in which the intervention is organized and targeted to a particular population; in effect, the treatment is the substantive component of the program. The research design is the plan for systematically varying implementation of the treatment. The research design typically involves some program participants (or groups) receiving one version of the treatment, while others receive no treatment or some alternate treatment. The research design is developed both to be practical and to generate scientifically valid information about social interventions (see Chapter 2).

Social experimentation, incorporating both the treatment and research design, combines social action with research. The goal is to develop understandings of social interventions which can lead to improving their responsiveness to social needs. Social experimentation offers a way for generating utilizable, scientifically credible, social research. To integrate social action and research requires collaboration of program administrators, who develop and run the treatment, and social researchers, who design the research aspects of social programs. A social experiment thus lies at the intersection of the delivery of services and the scientific study of social interventions.

The present chapter focuses on research design issues that underlie the development of social experiments. The presence of a research design distinguishes social experiments from those lacking in systematic development of a social intervention.

Criteria for social experiments. The term "social experiments" has been applied colloquially in ways which might be misleading. Many endeavors considered "social experiments" would not qualify in terms of our more technical view of experimentation. Some people, for example, might view the women's liberation movement as a social experiment in the sense that women (and men) are urged to try different roles. Changes in men's and women's roles have not, however, been implemented on a systematic experimental basis. Actual social experiments involve projects such as the Cambridge-Somerville Youth study (McCord, 1978), the Kansas City Police Patrol experiment (Kelling et al., 1976) and the Sloane et al. (1975) study of mental health treatments. Each of these efforts includes both a treatment program and an empirical test of treatment effects. What makes these programs social experiments is that an intervention was systematically implemented and evaluated. A variety of such experimental efforts have taken place, especially during the recent decade (Boruch, McSweeny & Soderstrom, 1978; Riecken & Boruch, 1978). Although not all of these projects were experimentally conducted, the range of social problems for which experiments are being designed is increasing (Sechrest et al., 1979; Stromsdorf & Farkas, 1980).

The recent literature is replete with examples of social innovations that have been the objects of experimentation in education, mental health, economics, criminal justice, race relations, health care, and labor. As more innovations submit to experimental tests, there is an increasing likelihood that positive effects will not be established (Gilbert, Light & Mosteller, 1975). Often, research evidence indicates that these innovations are not as successful as they are presumed and that misleading expectations are held about a program and perpetuated in policy. Research finds that some programs are indeed successful despite reputations to the contrary, or that an intervention is most useful for particular groups. It is also the case that research may provide equivocal information about a program; the value of the research is then in raising important questions and highlighting spurious assumptions about social problems.

Social experiments provide a unique way of developing information about social interventions. Their goal is to help to understand and develop more responsive social policies (as will be discussed in Chapter 9). They also help to correct false assumptions on which social policy may be developed. Underlying social experimentation is the use of a systematic research design which enables comparisons among groups exposed to different forms of the treatment. These comparisons contribute significantly to building the basis for a logic of social experimentation. Guidelines for developing comparison groups are discussed next, emphasizing the concept of validity.

VALIDITY AND DESIGN

The spectrum of research designs suitable for social experimentation appears to be infinite. Despite the number of design variations which might be employed, the focus of most can adequately be explained by a handful of design principles. These principles rest on the concept of validity (Cook & Campbell, 1979), and our goal is to demonstrate how research can be designed to obtain valid information about social interventions. Three of the four types of validity, introduced in the previous chapter, will be considered: (1) internal validity, (2) external validity, and (3) construct validity. A fourth type of validity, statistical conclusion validity, will be discussed in Chapter 5, which focuses on the analysis and interpretation of data generated in social experiments.

The strength of a research design pivots on the quality of the data and the comparisons one is able to make between those exposed to a particular treatment and those not exposed. Such comparisons (typically among groups) allow social experimenters to determine the conditions under which certain changes in social behavior or social structures are effected. Social problems have been explained in many ways, and for each explanation, a number of remedies have been proposed. Each explanation and corresponding remedy suggests a social experiment to test the assumed impact of the proposed solution. For example, what program can provide the most effective relief for the victims of domestic violence? Should battered women have access to shelters, vocational training and/or financial assistance? Or, should educational programs be funded for young women to understand that love and violence do not go hand-in-hand? Social experimentation can help provide answers to these questions and represents a method of testing different solutions to derive valid information about the impact of social innovations (Cook & Campbell, 1979).

Traditionally, social programs have been designed without consideration given the importance of comparison groups. In such instances, the resulting treatments often make valid research designs (such as making comparisons) difficult, if not impossible (Aaron, 1978; Campbell, 1969, 1971; Rivlin, 1971). This occurs because those interested in improving social conditions have, through lobbying or other means, gotten the resources to start a program. Treatments are usually provided to populations that exhibit a need, with no control group; or social programs are administered and no research is conducted at all. Many of the "Great Society" anti-poverty programs of the 1960s were conceived and carried out with little effort given to evaluating their impact (although there are important exceptions). Such unscientific ways of conducting social intervention programs are understandable given the political context in which they operated (Weiss, 1975). But without systematically testing the social innovations—and thus making them more responsive—their continuation may be questionable.

When social programs are instituted without systematic research, those interested in understanding the original social problem and the intervention are often left with confusion. A revealing illustration of this issue is represented by the SAT dilemma. Taken by more than 50 percent of all students in the United States entering college, the SAT has been the most widely used standardized test for college admission during recent years (College Entrance Examination Board, 1977). A great deal of concern about the test has developed as data accumulate. A steady decline in average SAT scores on both the verbal and mathematics sections of the examination has been observed since the early 1960s. As shown in Figure 3.1, scores were relatively stable from 1952 to 1964, but after 1964 the score curve declines steadily. The rate of decline is most pronounced during the period from 1973-1977. Why this has occurred and what programs can be instituted to correct the decline interests many educators and social scientists, as well as parents. As might be imagined, numerous explanations have been offered. The Educational Testing Service (ETS), which designs and administers the test, has initiated its own studies and reviewed the available literature in order to determine the reasons for the decline. Conclusions of these analyses are

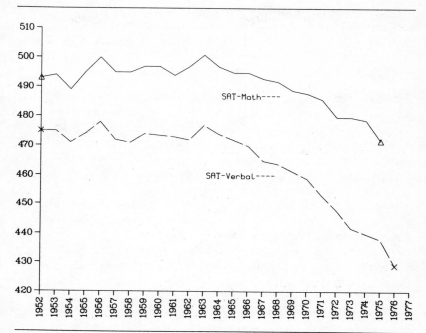

Figure 3.1   Scholastic Aptitude Test Scaled Score Means, 1952-1977

*SOURCE: Adapted with permission from *On Further Examination: Report of the Advisory Panel on the Scholastic Aptitude Test Score Decline.* Copyright © 1977 by College Entrance Examination Board, New York.

complex and sometimes contradictory. Their dilemma illustrates the problem of trying to interpret data derived from research lacking adequate comparison groups.

In order to explain the decline in the SAT data, comparisons are made across nonequivalent groups, groups that are different in many ways. The groups that are compared consist of cohorts of high school seniors during any particular test year since 1952. Comparing one group with another means comparing across time and across different educational, historical, and cultural experiences. Even with large score differences between cohorts, it is difficult to assess why this has occurred. Nonexperimental data that do not include data from adequate comparison groups leave open many factors that may be responsible for the score decline.

A variety of reasons have been proposed to explain the decline in test scores. The list compiled by the Educational Testing Service (College Entrance Examination Board, 1977) offers these possible explanations:

(1) changes in the population of SAT takers,
(2) revised teaching methods,
(3) overreliance by students on television for new information,
(4) a changing and chaotic social environment, and
(5) altered family relationships.

Although each of these reasons makes good intuitive sense, none has been substantiated in any rigorous empirical way as "the cause" of the decline in test scores. The evidence for each of these explanations is merely that the decline in scores seems to be related to changes in the population of SAT takers, revised teaching methods, and so forth. Correlational linkages such as these, however, are not sufficient to infer causality because the comparison groups differ in a number of fundamental ways.

Such data do not appear sufficiently cogent to have major policy changes. If an empirical approach were adopted (based on the experimental model), one could construct a design in which SAT scores are the "effect." Hypothesized causes could then be systematically applied across groups. For example, an experiment might be designed to test the hypothesis that progressive teaching methods produce educational skills which are not measured by SAT. Therefore, progressive education would be more likely to lead to lower SAT scores than traditional teaching methods. Such an experiment might involve randomly assigning classrooms of high school students to one of two conditions: progressive teaching or traditional teaching methods. After one year, the SAT, along with tests of students' ability to abstract, conceptualize, and think creatively, could be administered to assess the impact of the two teaching styles. Although this type of research would not definitively identify the reason for the score decline (it is unlikely there is one reason), if appropriately implemented, comparisons of the scores of various classes exposed to the different teaching methods could help us understand how teaching methods influence student SAT scores. With the present SAT data, such understandings are speculative, at best.

The SAT problem illustrates the interpretative problems that occur when social experiments are not conducted. During the past twenty years, only some of the changes that have been introduced into our educational system were developed and tested as social experiments. One such attempt to develop and systematically test an educational innovation is represented by the "Follow Through" program (Rivlin & Timpane, 1975b; Stebbins et al., 1978). The goal of Follow Through, which began in the late 1960s with support from the federal government, was to determine the effects of different models of compensatory early education. Follow Through represented an effort to continue the Head Start preschool program. It was stimulated by finding that gains made by students in the Head Start program often were not sustained when Head Start students entered first and second grades.

Follow Through, as an experiment, came into being as the fortuitous result of a financial cutback (Elmore, 1975; McDaniel, 1975). Because of a budget limitations, Follow Through could not be implemented as fully as its sponsors in the Office of Economic Opportunity had wanted. It was decided, instead, to implement the program in planned variations across different sites and to conduct Follow Through as an experimental program. More than 20 different models based on various theories of learning, philosophies of education, and community involvement in education were tested. While the development of Follow Through embodies the ethos of an experimenting society, the planned variations were, unfortunately, not implemented as true experiments. That is, at each site, the planned variations did not employ appropriate comparison groups. Partially as a consequence of this design inadequacy, much controversy has surrounded the results of the study and the validity of the research design (Anderson et al., 1978; House et al., 1978).

Validity questions arose concerning the creation of treatment and control groups within each of the planned variations. Because randomization was not used, interpretation of the findings was limited by internal validity problems. It is also unclear that the studies answered the initial questions about the effects of applying different theories of educational development. Construct validity problems may have emerged because the planned variations did not operationalize the theories appropriately. These validity issues diminish our ability to derive valid conclusions about the results of the Follow Through program.

In more general fashion, the following discussion describes the relationship of validity to design decisions. It focuses on the ways validity can be improved and how threats to validity can be avoided in designing social experiments.

Internal Validity

The assurance of internal validity is central to being able to determine the impact of an experimental program (treatment) on participants. With careful design of an experiment, alternative explanations attributing observed impact to factors other than the experimental program can be eliminated. A research design is internally valid when differences in the results of treatment and control conditions can be attributed to the treatment. This is possible only when treatment and control conditions are equivalent, except for the application of the treatment.

Equivalence among conditions of an experiment is typically achieved through randomization. Randomization does not guarantee that groups will be equivalent, but it does increase the probability that this will occur and is usually considered the best method for doing so. Exactly what unit is randomized depends on the circumstances of the experiment. In some cases, participants are randomly selected either to receive the treatment (participate in the program) or to serve as a control (not participate in the program or participate in an alternative form of the treatment). In other cases where participants are not individually exposed to a program (such as in a school), the randomization unit may be a group, such as a classroom, or an entire school. The function of randomization is to insure that no systematic differences exist among the groups (or other units) before the treatment is administered. If systematic differences exist prior to administering the treatment, biases are introduced into the design. These biases could result in different effects being obtained due to factors related to differences among the groups and not due to the effects of the treatment itself.

Although the idea of internal validity seems straightforward and randomization procedures should be a simple way to remediate threats, developing actual research designs that incorporate these principles is difficult. In order to describe some internal validity problems that can develop, a series of threats to internal validity have been identified (Campbell & Stanley, 1966; Cook & Campbell, 1976, 1979). Threats to validity are those aspects of a research design that make interpretation of findings difficult. A threat to internal validity is a design feature that leads to potential alternative explanations for the results. The causes of such threats to establishing internal validity are numerous, and several principal threats that can effect both true and quasi-experimental designs are described.

One central group of threats to internal validity is generated by the inability to compare across treatment and control conditions. These problems are most often found in quasi-experiments. One category of these problems is *selection* threats, which can be illustrated by reexamining the Follow Through planned variations. Follow Through models were tested at almost 200 sites in programs run by 22 different sponsors. For each model that was tested, treatment groups were selected and other groups assumed to be comparable were chosen as controls. It is unclear how children who were included in the programs were similar to or different from those who did not take part. Given the fact that the program was initially developed to eliminate educational deficiencies due to poverty, schools that became involved in the treatment program were the ones most in need; students at these schools perhaps had poorer skills than the students at control group schools. While it may have been an appropriate political decision to construct the program in this fashion, such preexperimental differences could have camouflaged gains made by students in the treatment condition, and possibly made the program seem ineffective (Elmore, 1975).

External conditions that affect the groups under study may also threaten internal validity. These *history* factors generally cannot be controlled, either before the experiment is designed, or later in analysis of results. An historical event might be a snowstorm that closed down the schools or a layoff of a number of teachers. While some history effects can be controlled in a simple comparison group design (if they influenced treatment and control groups in equivalent ways), such effects are especially problematic when the treatment and control groups are affected differently by the event. Because of history effects, every attempt should be made to situate the control and treatment conditions at the same time and in the same place. It is not always feasible, however, to meet this requirement. In such cases, researchers should assure more than one site per condition, with each site having an equal chance of being selected for the treatment or control conditions. In this way, the bias of a unique historical event can be minimized.

The discussion so far has concerned validity problems that emerge when individuals (or other units) in each of the comparison groups are different. A common design for applied research involves the use of pre- and posttreatment observations. In such a before-and-after design, a series of measurements are made at the beginning of a program (pretreatment) and then repeated at the end of a program (posttreatment) with the same individuals. Such a design, usually considered quasi-experimental, is common and readily adaptable to a variety of contexts. Unfortunately, it has a number of internal validity problems.

An obvious problem is *maturation*. People change over time, ideally in the direction of improvement and growth. This is especially true in education programs. No matter what treatment (such as subject matter or method of instruction) is used, students usually develop intellectually and socially between the pre- and posttest. Thus, Follow Through children, if tracked from kindergaren through second grade, would naturally show an increase in their learning even if they had not participated in the program. A properly constituted control group helps develop an estimate of how much of the apparent gains are due to maturation processes (including the education they could normally receive) and how much is due to the intervention.

Another parallel validity threat is referred to as *statistical regression to the mean*. This threat occurs because data are likely to approach a middle value, rather than reflect an extreme value over time. If a group of students who performed very poorly on a standardized test was selected for remedial help, it is likely that the scores of these students would indicate improvement on a second test. This would probably occur, again irrespective of the remedial program, because it is unlikely that they could do much worse on a second testing. So what would appear to be a gain in scores might only be an artifact of the research. This was considered a problem with the Follow Through treatment children who were initially poor performers. It was reasonable to expect that they would improve on a second testing. The same regression principle applies to high scorers, although actual results differ. On a second testing, regardless of the intervention (such as a special classroom for gifted students), average scores would be lower. In this case, regression to the mean results in a score decrement.

Other threats to internal validity deal with the measurement of treatment effects: *testing* and *instrumentation*. In the Follow Through evaluations, several achievement tests were used to measure the cognitive development of children who participated in the program (Stebbins et al., 1978). Repeated testing, as occurs in a pre/post test design, can have its own effects. This problem results when scores improve simply because program participants have used and are practiced in a particular test. It is also possible that instrumentation problems affect validity. If testing procedures are changed from time 1 to time 2, the test is essentially different and change scores may be of questionable value.

The validity threats identified above are likely to occur in what we have described as quasi-experiments—experiments in which subjects (or other randomization units) are not assigned to treatment and control conditions in a completely unbiased (randomized) way. True experiments, in which all participants have an equal chance of being placed in treatment and control conditions, are designed to control against many of the most common internal validity threats. However, implementing a true experiment, despite the randomization requirement, does not eliminate all threats to internal validity. Although random selection avoids some of the most obvious problems, such as selection, it does not insure that one can unequivocally attribute observed effects to the treatment. At least three common internal validity problems threaten true experimental designs, as well as quasi-experimental designs (see Cook & Campbell, 1976, 1979).

Diffusion of the treatment. Experimental designs involve applying a treatment to one group and withholding it from, or providing a different treatment to, at least one other group. Clarity between the treatment and control groups, however, often blurs in implementation. The fact that there is an experimental design does not guarantee that the groups actually receive (or not receive) the treatments as intended. For example, information about the treatment often is diffused from the treatment condition to the control condition. People may discuss their participation in an experiment and, under certain conditions, will contaminate the experiment. In such situations, the conditions are no longer "pure" reflections of the original design. When the design calls for providing different types of educational programs to a group of schools or classrooms, it is possible that teachers and principals talk with one another about the treatment, and share techniques and even materials (Gilbert, Light & Mosteller, 1975). Such communications ultimately could result in the treatment being implemented in both the actual treatment and the control conditions. The intended distinction between treatment and control conditions would, as a result, become blurred.

Such treatment diffusion was the case in the Follow Through program (McDaniel, 1975). Treatment and control classrooms within particular sites ended up using similar materials. Training workshops were generally open to teachers in the treatment and control conditions. McDaniel labels this problem "seepage." While seepage obviously creates internal validity problems and would seem easy to control, one should remember the context in which these programs were developed (that is, to solve particular problems). For this reason, a research design that uses treatment and control conditions within a single school (or even within a school system) may be more difficult to implement than a design which uses cross-school or cross-school system comparison groups.

Compensatory equalization of treatment. A similar threat to internal validity occurs when the individuals in a control group, who are denied the experimental treatment, are compensated in some alternate way. When a treatment group is viewed as relatively advantaged, administrators often feel they must give the control group participants "something" as compensation. For example, in an innovative school program in which treatment condition classrooms may be seen as receiving extra resources (as part of the new program), control group classrooms may be given special grants or other resources. When control groups are compensated for the treatment they are denied, the control groups are no longer "no treatment" groups. They then differ in many ways from the treatment groups and because of the way this occurs, the effects of the treatment cannot easily be deciphered. The treatment is then actually being compared to another unspecified treatment condition.

Compensatory rivalry. Another internal validity problem that arises in both true and quasi-experimental designs involves the degree to which the existence of the treatment is known to participants in all conditions. Depending on how participants interpret the treatment, intercondition rivalry and competition may develop. Members of the control group may realize that they are not expected to do well and, in order to refute the hypothesis, may exert extra effort to prove the researchers wrong. Saretsky (1972) describes this latter problem as the "John Henry" effect. (John Henry is an apocryphal railroad worker whose job is threatened by a steam-driven machine which hammers railroad ties. In order to prove the railroad managers wrong about the utility of the machine, he works so hard that he dies of exhaustion.) The John Henry effect thus occurs when control group subjects try extra hard to outdo their experimental group counterparts.

In an experiment conducted in the early 1970s to test the use of "performance contracting" in schools, such a John Henry effect was obtained, according to Saretsky. Performance contracting is a program where the management of schools is contracted to profit-making companies whose fee is dependent on childrens' achievement test scores. Students in (nonrandomly

selected) traditionally run control group schools performed as well as students in schools managed by outside companies. According to Saretsky, one
reason for the lack of differences between the treatment and control group
schools was that teachers in control group schools exerted extra effort. A la
John Henry, they sought to prove that performance contracting (the treatment in this case) was a poor idea. Although the experiment had other
problems (for example, because of the quasi-experimental design, there may
have been pretreatment differences among the schools), compensatory rivalry was an important threat to developing conclusions about performance
contracting on the basis of this study.

Compensatory rivalry, as a threat to internal validity, is more likely to
occur when jobs or resources are threatened by the results of an experiment.
People are likely to try to out-achieve an innovation if they think they may be
replaced, should the innovation prove to be effective. When participants in
various conditions of an experiment are in proximity to one another and
knowledgeable about the conditions of the experiment, this threat is more
likely to occur.

COMMENTS

The development of social experiments which are internally valid requires
the creation of appropriate comparison groups and the uncontaminated implementation of treatments. The SAT score decline illustrated the importance of the prospective design of social experiments. Without planning the
systematic design, differences between groups are difficult to interpret. The
Follow Through example indicated the importance of achieving equivalent
comparison groups through the use of random assignment procedures. Such
procedures reduce the number of threats to internal validity and therefore
limit the number of plausible alternative explanations. Some readers may be
thinking, "This is all very nice in theory, but how do we actually conduct
these internally valid studies?" We ask you to suspend your disbelief for a
short while. By the end of the chapter, a number of strategies will be offered
for reducing threats to internal validity, with ways for strengthening the other
types of validity as well.

External Validity

External validity is established by designing a social experiment in which
a variety of groups and settings are exposed to the treatment and control
conditions. Whereas internal validity has to do with the comparability of
treatment and control groups, external validity concerns how well the experimental people and settings reflect the people and settings to which the
results of the experiment will be applied.

In essence, any social experiment which has a certain degree of internal validity is also externally valid. If a treatment has a demonstrable relationship to particular effects, then, at least for the particular population and conditions of the experiment, the treatment had impact. These findings can only then be generalized, however, to the particular population studied. To be able to collect data which will permit more broadly generalizable findings, experiments must be externally valid. This essentially involves designing the experiment so that different populations, settings, and time periods are sampled. Threats to external validity occur when the treatment interacts with a feature of the experiment such that the results are generalizable only to the population or setting studied in the experiment.

Some typical problems of establishing external validity can be illustrated again by the Follow Through programs. The goals of the Follow Through planned variations were to develop data about the strategies for enriching the educational experience of disadvantaged children. The results were intended to guide efforts for remediating the educational problems of the poor. However, aspects of the program design (aside from features affecting internal validity) limited the generalizations that could be made from the data.

An important external validity problem with Follow Through involved the assignment of educational models to particular populations. While heterogeneous populations across the country were involved, each model typically was tested with only one type of student. For example, one model, the Florida Parent Education Model, was used solely with children from the South. Other models were applied almost exclusively to black *or* white populations (McDaniel, 1975). While these features of the experiment pose no threat to internal validity, they do make it difficult to compare the educational models across populations and to develop generalizations valid to different groups of children. In effect, these validity problems of Follow Through reflect the two major sources of external validity: *selection* and *setting*. When an unrepresentative sampling of the population was selected for research, external validity became threatened. In the Follow Through situation, potentially important differences between students from different racial groups and geographic settings remained unexplored within the design.

An additional problem for Follow Through planned variations concerns the fact that sites were essentially volunteer schools. Because of unassessed differences between volunteer schools and those which did not volunteer (Bernstein, Bohrnstedt & Borgatta, 1975), unknown biases might readily have been introduced. It is possible, for example, that volunteer schools employ more dedicated administrators or have more active parents. Such differences may interact with the type of educational model being tested. Models that called for parental involvement in the school might have been successful at volunteer sites (that is, internal validity might be established), but quite unsuccessful at sites where parents are not actively involved. Limitations of the findings are unclear when the model is tested at only one site.

A somewhat different external validity problem concerns the time frame within which a study is conducted. Although the ability to generalize to a future time is an impossible external validity criterion to establish, to the extent that the period to which one wants to generalize is similar to the time of the study, external validity will be insured. Unique historical events which affect both treatment and control conditions make generalizability over time somewhat tenuous. In the Follow Through variations, which were begun during a period of educational retrenchment, generalizability to other time periods may be a problem. Comparisons between Follow Through participants and nonparticipants may indicate the effects of the resources at the time of the experiment.

COMMENTS

External validity issues concern the generalizability of the results of a social experiment from the population, setting, and time conditions of the actual experiment. To the degree that one can select experimental participants who are representative of the population, and select representative settings, external validity will be enhanced. Threats to external validity, which arise because of interactions between unique characteristics of these elements and the treatment variable, can be controlled, or at least taken account of, by these procedures. It should be recognized that one can never have perfect external validity in any sense. Although representative, the elements of the original research are never entirely equivalent to new situations.

Construct Validity

The establishment of construct validity has to do with how one conceptualizes the ideas underlying a social experiment. Construct validity is, in part, dependent on the establishment of both internal and external validity. Although construct validity exerts only indirect effects on the approach to designing a social experiment, its role is critical in establishing the utility of a social experiment.

As described in Chapter 2, construct validity involves the correct labeling of treatments. Construct validation is particularly important because it is a necessary condition for being able to translate the findings and implications of one experiment to other problems; and, to use these findings to enrich theory on the particular issue. In essence, construct validity is the degree to which the experiment has effectively tested the theory underlying the social intervention. For example, while Follow Through variation yielded valuable information about the effects of particular programs, the usefulness of the research was that it tested a number of educational theories. The theoretical implications of the research, in terms of the types of educational strategies that could aid disadvantaged children and remediate early school problems, are probably more important than the data generated for the use of particular programs.

To achieve construct validity, a variety of strategies — different than those used with the other validity types — must be employed. Construct validity is achieved primarily through clear conceptualization of the treatment variable and its operationalization. How accurately one operationalizes the concept determines the construct validity of an experiment. If thorough conceptualization is not achieved — and/or the constructs are not accurately represented in the treatment operationalization — construct validity will be threatened.

Underrepresenting the construct. A frequent problem with establishing construct validity is that the actual treatment does not adequately represent the construct. In such cases, the independent variable is too specific and does not fully reflect the ideas underlying the intervention. Thus, if one wanted to experiment with the role of educational innovation as a cause of SAT score decline, educational innovation might be operationalized as the number of elective courses offered. Using a number of schools, one might develop an extensive electives program in the treatment schools and in another group of schools reduce the number of elective courses offered. Our experiment would then compare, perhaps over a period of several years, changes in SAT scores at the various schools as a function of the number of electives offered.

A weakness in this design, although it might produce information about electives, is that it would tell us little about the effects of educational innovation. No matter how clear-cut the differences between schools in the treatment and control conditions (that is, no matter how high the internal validity), the number of elective courses is but one component (perhaps a minor one) of educational innovation (Stebbins, et al., 1978). Since the construct "educational innovation" would not be fully tested in this experiment, it is probably better to relabel the experiment a study of the relationship of elective courses to SAT scores.

Irrelevancies in the operationalization. Just as the operationalized treatment might lack important elements of the construct, so too might it include many irrelevant components. In order to insure that an intervention "works," program designers often offer a package of treatments. If, for example, the innovation study above was labeled an experiment on the role of elective courses, it would be easy to include (inadvertently, perhaps) a number of components to the treatment. For example, offering elective courses may involve an increase in the number of teacher aides, more time for extracurricular activities, or a modified work load in core courses. If such an operationalization was employed, interpreting the results would require a recognition that the construct included all of these other components. One might prefer to label the experiment in such a situation a "resource augmentation" study. Any SAT gains could not be attributed solely to elective courses; rather, the importance of the added resources would have to be noted.

This latter problem is, in fact, one of the difficulties in interpreting Follow Through. The experiment was funded with monies from the Office of Economic Opportunity (OEO) and it required that grantees follow OEO Community Programs guidelines (Elmore, 1975). Certain features of the program consequently had to be included in all models tested. A certain amount of community involvement in the schools was mandated, even though the impact of community actions on education was a test variable (for example, in the Parent Education Model). This tended, in certain of the planned variations, to add irrelevancies to the treatment conditions being tested and to obscure differences between treatment and control conditions.

Reactive effects. Another threat to construct validity has to do with the reaction of participants in an experiment to the knowledge of being studied. Both participants and administrators of an experiment may be affected by the knowledge that research is being conducted. People who are aware of their involvement in an experiment alter their customary behavior in response to the research. This is a problem common to most experimental research because any experiment is obtrusive to some extent.

The well-known Hawthorne study (Roethlisberger & Dickson, 1939) is an example of this validity problem. It was found that plant workers improved their productivity every time a change was made in their work environment, even when the change was negative (such as a reduction in the intensity of lighting). This validity problem is not that productivity is unrelated to the intervention (internal validity), or that the results are not generalizable (external validity). Rather, the construct problem arises because the work changes reacted with the fact that an experiment was conducted.

Reactivity affects participants as well as researchers and program administrators. Some evidence exists that researchers and administrators convert their *expectancies* about what will occur into actual effects. If a program administrator or researcher gives special information to individuals in a treatment group, or merely treats them "special," a new dimension is thus added to the treatment so that it deviates from the construct. Rosenthal's research on experimenter effects (Rosenthal & Rubin, 1978) illustrates how an experimenter can influence subjects in the direction of the hypothesis being tested. Even when the actual researcher is not present during an experiment (as is typical in social experimentation), those responsible for delivering the treatment can contribute unknown biases to the treatment. For this reason, researchers who are "blind" to the condition (that is, unaware of the specific treatment and hypotheses) are often used when expectancies can easily be transmitted (such as in the case of testing a drug).

COMMENTS

Threats to construct validity occur when there is a lack of clarity about what has been done in a social experiment, and when this lack of clarity results in a treatment which conceptually misrepresents the idea being tested. These threats may be avoided by careful prior conceptual work and, if possible, by having multiple operationalizations of the treatment. The more ways that the construct has been tried, the better the ability to generalize. To the extent that one is clear about exactly what has been accomplished during the experiment, one's ability increases in understanding conceptually what has occurred.

From Design Theory to Practice

Central to the design of social experiments is the translation of abstract ideas into practice. In terms of design considerations, it should be obvious that there is no such thing as a design that insures internal, external, and construct validity. A design which controls for most threats to internal validity may be relatively easy if randomization is possible, but external validity and construct validity are established only with some effort. In most cases, a series of experiments are required to insure validity. This should not be regarded as a serious problem, for it only implies that research is an ongoing process and scientific "facts" are established only through multiple investigations.

The present discussion is concerned with ways in which threats to validity can be controlled. Emphasis now shifts from negative examples of studies with design problems to a discussion of conditions under which it is possible to design experiments that optimize validity. The discussion focuses, for the most part, on ways to construct true experiments and employ randomization. It has been assumed that true experiments are difficult to arrange, although they are probably less difficult than their reputation suggests (see Boruch, 1975). Along with discussing ways of conducting straight-forward true experiments, we will also consider the conditions under which true experimental designs can be incorporated within other designs. Because it is not always possible to randomize fully the selection of program participants to treatment conditions, adequate tests of the efficacy of the program can sometimes be made by combining different methodological approaches (see also Saxe & Fine, 1979, 1980).

TRUE EXPERIMENTS

True experiments (those in which participants are randomly assigned to conditions) are designed to maximize validity but require perhaps more planning and monitoring than do quasi-experiments or social programs that are not subjected to careful evaluation. The conduct of true experiments imposes a variety of constraints on social programs concerning the implementation and maintenance of a specific procedure for assigning participants to conditions. Within practical, as well as ethical, limits, it is the optimal strategy for social experimentation (see Campbell, 1969, 1971; Riecken & Boruch, 1974; Rivlin, 1971), although there are clearly situations in which randomization is not feasible (Cook & Campbell, 1979) or is ethically problematic (Bermant, Kelman & Warwick, 1978; Rivlin & Timpane, 1975a). Below some of the practical and ethical issues are considered in implementing randomized social experiments (see also Chapter 7).

Unfortunately, randomization has a poor reputation in discussions of applied social research and because of this, its use must first be defended. Randomization has long been associated with laboratory research and has been equated with the control and manipulation of passive "subjects" (see Lachenmeyer, 1970). The language used to describe randomized designs often reinforces this image (for example, "manipulating subjects in a treatment condition"). In the context of social experimentation, it is rare that a treatment is used that would not have been applied on a nonexperimental basis anyway (that is, to individuals not part of an actual social experiment). Social experiments generally introduce programs that would be implemented unsystematically were it not for the research design. Because new programs and innovations are rarely made available on a universal basis where everyone has access immediately, randomization is sometimes the fairest way to determine who can participate in a program. Access is traditionally determined by a host of factors including wealth, nepotism, motivation, or need. Whatever access factors are operative, selection biases are introduced which make it difficult to measure and generalize about the impact of a social intervention. The use of randomization obviates these problems, making it possible to develop more reliable and generalizable effects of the program.

Although implemention of randomization requires luck and varies in difficulty across types of social programs (Conner, 1977), a number of steps can be taken to ensure its success. The development of a randomized design invariably requires planning and collaboration between researchers and administrators. True experiments require that those knowledgeable about the actual treatment, as well as the research design, work together to plan the experimental program. Such collaboration is necessary because to be successfully utilized, randomization must be seen as an acceptable procedure for selecting those who should receive a treatment. Randomization under certain circumstances is as fair a selection criterion as any other. Especially for social interventions about which there are divergent views about what programs should be supported (and which are working), randomization should be feasible to implement. Some illustrations of circumstances conducive to randomization follow.

When randomization is expected. Sometimes randomization is built into a program as a necessary feature. If, for example, a particular treatment is in short supply, a lottery system may be instituted to select randomly who should receive the treatment. With a lottery, participants expect a random selection procedure. Public housing projects have employed this technique. When a lottery for housing is used, everyone who applies has an equal chance of being selected. According to the assumptions of random selection, those who receive housing should be similar to those who have applied but do not receive housing. Using such a procedure, valuable information can be gathered when it is necessary to assess the impact of a housing program. Those who benefit from the lottery comprise the treatment group while those not selected serve as controls. Comparisons of lifestyles, family, racial and community relationships, as well as economics can inform planners about the impact of a housing program. In such experiments, the design of a social experiment would require no more than what is routinely done to determine who should have access to the housing units. The design is accomplished in part by the routine allocation of the housing units.

Day-care programs provide another illustration of a lottery suitable situation. Demand for these services almost always outweighs supply and a lottery for openings might be feasible at many sites (Travers & Goodson, 1981). Such a lottery would enable researchers to study the effects of day-care programs on children without the interference of factors such as parents' motivation. If a lottery was not used and the services were organized on a first-come, first-serve basis, parents first in line would get their children enrolled. It might be that these children differed from those who were not enrolled, since their parents made an extra effort to being first in line, or did not have to go to work and so were able to be first in line. They might be the children of the most concerned parents or the children of parents most anxious to get them out of the house. Such differences in parents' motivation could be reflected in different parent-child interactions, creating differences in childrens' performance on measures ostensibly used to assess the effects of day care. If access to a program is determined in this type of arbitrary manner, data on the program will be vulnerable to alternative explanations.

Given the social significance of day care (see Kagan et al., 1979), it would seem prudent to assemble the most valid information.

When implementation problems exist. Under certain conditions, it may be impossible to make a new program available to everyone at the same time, although all must be served. In such circumstances, randomization could be used to determine the order in which recipients are enrolled. A program to deinstitutionalize mental patients, for example, might only be possible if introduced gradually. For good reasons, it should probably be phased in to allow time for community-based facilities to be developed (Fairweather & Tornatzky, 1978). If this is not done, it is likely that hospital administrators will first release those patients whom they consider the best "candidates" for deinstitutionalization or the most disruptive. Although this procedure might give deinstitutionalization the best chance to work effectively, it would not be useful in generating information about the effects of deinstitutionalization for various types of patients.

Hospital administrators could randomly select a group of patients to be discharged each month from the pool of those considered able to live outside the hospital. With this procedure, it would be possible to use the not-yet-discharged patients as control subjects and the discharged patients as experimental subjects. Serving in a control group in this situation does not mean no treatment, only that the individuals would be released on a delayed schedule. Deinstitutionalization of mental patients has been taking place over the past 15 years, yet this type of control group has not been available to provide data about our mental health system (Saxe, 1980).

A delay in access to treatment may be quite trivial to the intervention while critical to the social experiment. In a study conducted to evaluate the effectiveness of counseling programs for individuals with the sickle cell trait and disease, a knowledge test about sickle cell anemia was administered immediately after counseling (Saxe, 1979). The purpose of the test, in part, was to demonstrate that individuals can be taught enough about genetics to make informed decisions about having children and dealing with health problems. For control subjects, who received identical counseling, the order of events was reversed. The test was given prior to receiving counseling. The delayed-treatment control group became a treatment group once the data had been collected. One problem with this design is the difficulty in assessing the long-term effects of counseling, because it is not possible to withhold treatment for a full six-month period. Although the research design represents a compromise of sorts, it nevertheless allows for the development of knowledge with little program interference.

When solutions are unknown. An assumption underlying many social interventions—and fueling the traditional rejection of randomization—is that new treatments are better than no treatment. It is often assumed that receiving a new treatment is beneficial, while withholding a new treatment is unethical. If this were the case, social experiments would not be needed. Illusions about the effectiveness of new treatments in many instances are unjustified. This was certainly the case in the oxygen incubator retrolental fibroplasia problem described earlier. In many instances, no known solutions to problems are available (Mosteller, 1981) and new treatments are at best educated hunches. Given the very equivocal and sometimes negative effects of new treatments, random assignment is easier to justify than providing untested treatments.

When rotation is employed. The use of random assignment is relatively easy to implement in situations where participants naturally rotate assignments. For example, consider a social experiment testing the best placement for orienting high school students to the complexities of working in a social agency. Students are given two-week placements in agency units, such as counseling, family planning, food stamps, family welfare, and administration. If students were enrolled into each subprogram on a random basis and rotated after two weeks, data could be collected systematically on the educational value of each subprogram. If, on the other hand, students were allowed to select their placements, the data would be unsystematic and reflect biased perceptions of the subprograms. Since rotation and choice are often fixed before students become involved in a program, it would be relatively easy to implement randomization.

QUASI-EXPERIMENTS

In cases where full randomization is not possible, variations of the randomized true experiment can be implemented (Cook & Campbell, 1979). In such quasi-experiments, some, but not all, of the features of true experiments are present. Usually, in a good quasi-experiment some form of a comparison group is available for assessing the impact of the treatment. However, these comparison groups are not developed through random assignment procedures. While it may be enticing to think of quasi-experiments as poor substitutes for true experiments, that is not really the case. Under appropriate conditions, quasi-experiments can yield very useful information; hence, they are justified, depending on information needs or when it is too costly or otherwise difficult to conduct true experiments.

Quasi-experimental designs are useful and produce meaningful information because they are structured to reduce the number of alternative explanations for the results. They typically accomplish this by collecting a great deal of data about the program participants and by utilizing fairly sophisticated statistical techniques to compare participants before and after exposure to treatment. Quasi-experimental designs are often much more complex than true experimental designs; and, in fact, may be more costly to conduct. Below are some examples of quasi-experimental designs.

Time series designs. One of the most frequently employed quasi-experimental designs utilizes a variant of a time series approach. The examples of true experiments cited earlier were relatively simple cases because data were collected at only one point, or at most two points in time. For example, the Kansas City Patrol Experiment (see Chapter 1) assessed the effects of different patrolling strategies on crime rates over several months (Kelling et al., 1976). If, instead of random assignment of patrol beats to conditions of the experiment, the police had *chosen* which areas would be patrolled reactively or nonreactively, a bias could have been built into the experiment. One would not be sure if differential crime rates resulted from the patrolling practices or from preexisting differences in the beats.

This is a situation where the collection of additional data on the characteristics of these beats (including crime rates) *before* the experiment began, as well as afterward, could help determine the impact of the patrolling practices without the use of random assignment procedures. The collection of these data would involve a nonrandomized quasi-experimental design and could help rule out a number of alternative explanations of possible effects. For example, if crime rates before the experiment were equivalent in the beats chosen to be reactive and nonreactive, then it would be more difficult to infer a beat-selection bias.

The use of a pretest and posttest is the simplest form of a time series design. One complex variation, the single interrupted time series design, has wide applicability. In this design, extensive pretest data are collected on a target group. The treatment is then implemented and multiple posttests conducted on this group of participants. An example is a recently conducted study of the Massachusetts handgun law which went into effect in 1975, specifying a mandatory one-year jail sentence for anyone convicted of possessing an unlicensed firearm. The law was expected to deter significantly the criminal use of handguns and result in a reduction in the number of homicides. Although the law was not conceived as a "treatment," it is not difficult to think of it in this way.

To examine the impact of the law on criminal use of handguns, reliable data are available on crimes committed with guns in Massachusetts, with estimates of the rate of illegal handgun usage across time. Although alternative explanations can be offered for these data (such as some events occurring concurrently with passage of the legislation), to the extent that one can rule out such factors, the time series design may answer some important questions about the effects of this treatment. In essence, the treatment involves a law applied on a nonrandom basis. A time series analysis allows for a test of the effects of the law by assessing data on criminal use of handguns in Massachusetts pre- and postimplementation of the law. Such an analysis was conducted by Deutsch and Alt (1977) on Boston crime statistics. They found that the law effectively reduced assaults with handguns; it did not appear to affect homicide rates.

Deutsch and Alt's design is represented in Figure 3.2, which displays some of their data. The multiple data points are derived from Boston crime statistics (monthly rates of assaults with a gun) and the figure shows the point at which the "series" is interrupted by the introduction of the law. A comparison is made of rates of crime before and after the interruption to determine the effect of the law. In essence, comparison procedures must separate the noise (routine variation from year to year in rates) from actual treatment effects. The statistics for doing this type of analysis are quite complex (McCain & McCleary, 1979) and, in fact, Deutsch and Alt's statistical analysis of their data has been subjected to criticism (see Hay & McCleary, 1979).

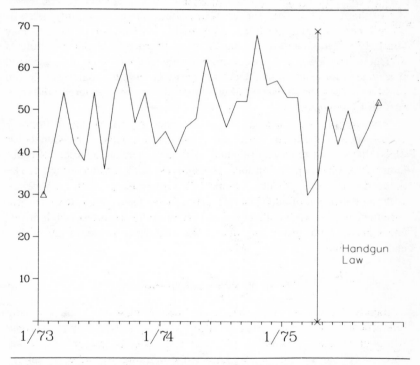

Figure 3.2   Boston's Monthly Occurrences of Assault with a Gun
*SOURCE: Adapted from Deutsch and Alt (1977)

Utilizing multiple outcomes measures represents another way to use additional data in order to rule out alternative explanations of hypotheses in quasi-experiments. That is, instead of using only one measure of test of a program, several are employed. Threats to validity and alternate explanations often can be eliminated when one has more information about a program. To the extent that more than one indicator points in the same direction, one is more confident about conclusions. This is a technique used for improving the design of true experiments as well as quasi-experiments.

In educational programs where a tendency may exist to collect data on a single dimension (such as achievement scores), other information can be crucial in order to rule out threats to validity. If one were studying an experimental mathematics program, for example, the design could be improved by collecting data not only on mathematical ability, but on other dimensions as well. Information from students about their perception of the program might be useful for ruling out alternative explanations. Data on verbal skills, for example, might indicate the normal rate of maturation for the students. History and, perhaps, instrumentation effects might be teased out of the data about student reactions. Other threats to validity, such as those related to generalizability and possibly even construct validity may similarly be eliminated if one has detailed information about the students and their experience in the program. Notwithstanding, it should be stressed that none of these additional data strategies can serve to repair basic design problems. They can, however, often reduce the number of alternative explanations for the data.

Nonequivalent comparison groups. Another important way to improve quasi-experimental designs is to use comparison groups of individuals (or units) that are not randomly selected. Although there are a variety of problems with such groups, often some problems associated with their use can be reduced when nonequivalent comparison groups are used in conjunction with the collection of additional data (in time series or multiple dependent variable designs). One is then able to determine the extent to which differences between the groups are due to the treatment, to preexisting differences, or to both.

From Problem to Experiment

Social experiments have the dual goal of delivering services and providing scientifically based knowledge about the efficacy of social interventions. Although separate treatment and research designs are required, they are necessarily interdependent. The knowledge-building aspects of social experiments and the need to design these elements into social programs have been emphasized (rather than the substance of treatment designs). Social experiments, however, cannot exist without attention to the pragmatic needs of social environments. Without engaging the social environment in the scientific process, carrying out an experiment may not be possible.

It is partially for this reason that converting ideas for social experiments into operation is not exact. There will always be some slippage between how one would choose to conduct a research endeavor and what actually can be accomplished (see Chapter 7). One is never able to satisfy all validity criteria, nor to counteract every validity threat. It is impossible, as noted, to assume that you can demonstrate external validity for all populations. Decisions therefore must be made concerning what information is most important to collect. The most relevant threats to validity must then be considered. In some situations, certain alternative explanations are unlikely or unimportant. In other situations, one may be satisfied if the program under study is effective with a limited and circumscribed population or if the program results generalize only to a specific setting.

The logical approach to social research represented by validity analyses does not require that all interventions be conducted experimentally. Even when nonexperiments are designed (as will be inevitable), the validity framework can help to ascertain the use for and confidence level in research results. In many problem areas (such as health care), there is a long tradition of reliance on case study designs (that is, a single group without control). At the very least, a validity analysis of such research should enable one to determine what factors and problems need to be considered before utilizing the results of such work (see Wortman & Saxe, 1981).

Evaluation of existing research aside, validity concerns are central to the prospective design of social interventions. It should be possible to utilize the validity framework to aid in decision-making about how to organize an intervention or program. Given that trade-offs are an inevitable design feature, the need for collaboration becomes critical. Researchers cannot make a determination about which information to sacrifice without the help of policy makers and administrators. Similarly, administrators cannot in isolation generate the information they need, but must consult with those with expertise in research design.

As part of the negotiating process, researchers and those responsible for the program must determine how to measure the impact of the intervention. What types of impact will be assessed, as well as the means by which data will be gathered, must be determined. Chapter 4 will describe the array of dependent measures available to social experimenters and assess some advantages and disadvantages of different strategies.

CHAPTER 4

THE MEASUREMENT OF SOCIAL BEHAVIOR AND STRUCTURAL CHANGE

"You must know better than I do Inspector, how very rarely two people's account of the very same thing agrees. In fact, if three people were to agree exactly, I should regard it as suspicious. Very suspicious, indeed."

Agatha Christie, *Spider's Web*.

To promote social change, the implications of any social innovation must be understood and measured, and the yardsticks of measurement must be more rigorous than any individual's account. Did it work? For whom? What are the effects? These represent the kind of questions to which social experiments are designed to respond. Although the central issue revolves around the effectiveness of an intervention, such characteristics can be overly simplistic. Typically, there can be several effectiveness criteria; other information also has to be assessed in order to understand the reasons for particular effectiveness outcomes.

Research efforts are aimed at documenting the impact of social intervention in an objective way. Although measurement is intended to be unbiased, the methods for collecting information often have an impact of their own. The intrusive effects of data collection should be recognized so that any resulting biases can be controlled. The objective collection of information about social experiments is the focus of this chapter. Measuring such social program outcomes is a complex, but rational, process which has a logic distinct from the design issues of social experiments.

The previous chapter, with its emphasis on design issues, may have given the mistaken impression that a clever design will insure the conduct of "sound" social research. Additional components must be included. Besides developing a workable design, one must be able to measure, in a meaningful way, the effects of the treatment on its intended recipients. This can be more difficult than is readily apparent. Changes in social behavior and structures—the intended outcomes of social interventions—are basically unstable and subject to a variety of influences. They present unique measurement problems. In the present chapter, the most important issues of measurement (as they relate to social experimentation) will be reviewed. One focus will be the variety of techniques and instruments available to social experimenters. A few basic types of measuring tools are identified and the conditions under which they can be used are described. Some strategies for identifying relevant indicators of program effects will be suggested. In addition, the chapter describes some principles of measurement that aid in understanding the usefulness of particular measurement instruments and techniques.

Of necessity, the discussion of outcome measures will introduce issues which will be more fully discussed in later chapters. This will be the case in terms of the treatment of how outcome measures are selected. Although choosing the conceptual variables to be assessed experimentally is a crucial aspect of the measurement process, a discussion of this issue will have to await further description of how social planners and social researchers collaborate. At this stage, the goal is to identify some basic concerns and develop a conceptual base that can be used to understand measurement problems.

Context of Measurement

Measuring program outcomes requires an understanding of the theory that underlies social intervention, the significance of precise and defined outcome measures, and recognition of potential measurement problems. Perhaps the first question that should be addressed is, "What are outcome measures?" Simply stated, outcome measures are tools or instruments that can be used to observe the impact of a social intervention. In more technical terms, outcome measures are systematic procedures for gathering information about the dependent variables. They are, if you will, the rulers and barometers of social experiments.

If one designs a program to improve police practices, an appropriate outcome measure might be the incidence of certain crimes. A program designed to provide supplemental instruction to educationally disadvantaged children might use a standardized achievement test as an outcome measure. The study evaluating a retraining program for unemployed minority youth might employ corporate records on the number of such individuals hired or rejected for jobs. A program to improve union loyalties would develop a member commitment/satisfaction questionnaire to test program effectiveness. In each of these examples, the outcome measure involves a specific procedure or instrument for measuring program outcomes. No procedure is, however, without its problems. A series of concerns central to measuring the impact of social programs are analyzed.

BEST INDICATORS

However convenient it might seem to conclude that an intervention is either effective or ineffective, social science rarely yields such simple answers. Because of the complexity of human interaction and social interventions, multiple outcome measures are almost always necessary. Frederick Mosteller (1981), recently retired President of the American Association for the Advancement of Science, described an experiment which illustrates this issue. Patients with cancer of the bronchus were assigned to one of two treatments: surgery or radiation therapy. Mosteller reviews the data and questions the conventional wisdom that survival rates should be the sole indicator of treatment effectiveness. According to Mosteller, the results of the study indicated that patients who received radiation therapy lived almost 50 percent longer—their average life span following therapy was 300 days as compared to 200 days for those who underwent surgery. Using survival as the sole or best indicator suggested that radiation therapy is the better treatment. Mosteller challenged the simplicity of this logic. He argued that the quality of life endured for those 100 extra days—the emotional, financial and physical costs absorbed during the "grace period"—has to be assessed before either treatment can be labeled unequivocal in effectiveness.

This example should dispel the illusion that there is a "best indicator" of any intervention's effectiveness. In almost all cases, multiple indicators will be necessary both to know if effectiveness is obtained and to understand why. In our view, no one technique or indicator can provide a complete picture of a program's impact (Campbell, 1972) and the single measure may, in fact, provide erroneous information. Just as survival rates may be an inadequate measure for testing radiation therapy, consider how a program designed to improve police practices might be assessed. The crime rate (that is, the number of crimes reported) is a natural "best" outcome measure for any such program. A lowering of the crime rate should be a straightforward indicator of program effectiveness. The degree to which crimes are reported, however, is unstable and influenced dramatically by the public's perception of the police. The greater the public trust in the police, the higher the levels in reporting. In the discussion of the Kansas City Police Patrol Experiment, the investigators concluded that the number of crimes reported might be affected by police visibility. Assuming that in the Reactive Patrol condition police visibility was reduced and fewer crimes were reported, the reduced crime rate may be interpreted in at least three ways: as improved policing, as a downward trend in criminal activity, or as public reluctance to report crimes. Can one assume that the new patrolling pattern was responsible for the lowered crime rate? Knowing that the crime rate has fallen does not tell us why.

The team of program developers and researchers who designed a union-based program to reduce occupational drinking also confronted the problem of the "best" indicator (Fine, Akabas & Bellinger, in press). The theory behind the program was that "cultures of drinking" pervade some worksites, thus promoting occupational drinking patterns among workers as normative. The intervention involves a program to train shop stewards to establish a peer-support system for problem drinkers that might help to disrupt such cultures and to reduce the norms for drinking and the incidence of problem drinking among union members.

During the planning phase, discussions focused on how to specify outcomes for measuring program effectiveness. A debate has developed about the meaning of referral rates, that is, the number of times a shop steward/supervisor refers individuals for treatment, as the primary outcome measure. The debate focuses on the ambiguous meaning of a high or a low referral rate. Does a posttraining increase in referrals mean that after training:

(1) Shop stewards are better trained to identify problem drinkers?
(2) Union members better understand the problems of drinking and are more likely to seek help?
(3) More people are drinking (for example, because of an increase in job insecurity)?

Conversely, does a drop in referrals mean that since training there is:

(1) Greater co-worker cover-up of drinking?
(2) An actual decrement in rates of drinking?
(3) An actual drop in on-the-job drinking with an increase in after hours drinking?

Using referral rates as the sole indicator in this case could provide ambiguous, if not misleading, program information. Data from a single indicator could falsely suggest program success (or failure).

At best, single indicators can describe one aspect of impact. To supplement single indicator data, that is, to collect information that can explain the single indicator finding, additional information needs to be generated. In the case of the occupational drinking program, additional data may include information about workers' and shop stewards' perceptions of occupational drinking, the training program, and the alcoholism service; in addition, records of workers' rates of tardiness, absenteeism, sick days and/or gastrointestinal disabilities (the diagnostic disability category which includes individuals suffering from alcohol-related illness) may also be used.

Using multiple indicators enables researchers to develop better qualitative understandings of social interventions. Multiple indicators also help to control for the unavoidable bias inherent in almost all measuring processes.

DATA COLLECTION AS AN INTERVENTION

Marciano (1974) conducted a participant observation study of a community of suburban couples, originally "blue collar" but at the time of her study regarded as middle class in terms of residential and income characteristics. The study was an attempt to investigate "marital behavior as it reflects the transitional stage in generational mobility" (p. 490). Marciano moved into the community to collect qualitative information on the couples' relationships, and on the extent to which blue-collar values are sustained during the upward mobility process. After months of data collection, Marciano prepared to leave the community. At her departure, one of her key informants remarked: "I was happy in my life, until I met you." (p. 501).

This example illustrates that the process of data collection can have enormous impact on respondents. While Marciano's respondents did not undergo any "intervention," they changed because they were part of a research effort. In social experiments in which an intervention is tested, every measurement technique elicits its own special effects on respondents; that is, being studied produces changes, independent of the treatment effects being measured. The social science concept of *reactivity* includes all such changes that occur in participants' responses because of the measuring process. Measuring tools have the effect of an intervention, producing data that are biased and which may distort the picture of the program (Cochran, 1978).

The self-awareness of respondents can affect outcome measures in several ways. Weber and Cook (1972) have discussed this problem as it relates to traditional psychological research and have noted that research participants adopt various roles. They may try to act like "good" respondents and behave in ways to please the researchers (and/or program staff); they can be "negativistic" and purposely behave in ways contrary to their actual reactions and views; or they may be apprehensive about being watched and measured and thus likely to exhibit anxiety. Institutions, similarly, may be "paranoid" and "shape up" or "cover-up" in the presence of a researcher. Because reactivity is hard to account for when interpreting data, investigators should design social experiments that minimize obtrusiveness (the extent to which measurement procedures are visible, obvious or disruptive), and/or build in measures of reactivity. There may, however, be a tradeoff between the need to limit visibility of the measurement process and the need to safeguard the privacy and rights of respondents. Often, participants in social experiments must be informed of the nature of the experiment (see Chapter 7) and the uses of the data generated. Such information alters their responses in both obvious and nonobvious ways.

In some cases, reactivity effects are apparent and can be anticipated. Rivlin (1971), for example, has pointed out that most individuals, when interviewed or surveyed, underreport their income. Tax or legal implications may be connected with providing a researcher with facts concerning personal income. A respondent may hope that financial resources will be provided if reported income is low. In still other cases, there may be status reasons for overreporting one's income. Determining which of these reactivity problems will occur (for example, through a pilot study of your mesurement tools), estimating how the data may be affected, and developing procedures to control this bias, are part of implementing a social experiment.

Reactivity is particularly likely to influence the results of a social experiment when pretests are employed. Subjects who complete a survey before an intervention is administered may alter their responses in a posttest survey or go so far as to change their behavior just to prove that there has been a change, or to justify their involvement in the intervention (Festinger, 1957).

Imagine a program designed to study and change the eating patterns of overweight individuals. Participants are weighed-in just before lunch and surveyed about their food preferences. Half of the subjects are hypnotized (the intervention) and induced to curb their appetites for sweets. Results indicate higher levels of rejection of desserts by the hypnotized subjects than the controls. In interpreting these data, one has to consider the possibility that the preintervention "weigh-in" and survey made the participants self-conscious and more susceptible to the hypnotic suggestion. Somewhat self-conscious, they may have cut down intake at lunch. Pretests can sensitize participants to research-relevant issues and produce misleading data. A potentially spurious finding — one that may be due to pretesting — needs to be designed around.

Reactivity is a particular problem in measuring socially sensitive attitudes. In the context of racial attitudes, Crosby, Bromley, and Saxe (1980) documented a discrepancy between results obtained in surveys of racial attitudes and results obtained in unobtrusive behavior studies. As one might expect, a great deal less racism will be expressed in surveys where the intent of the research is obvious than in behavioral studies where the intent is not at all obvious. How and when behaviors are measured influence what data are obtained.

Measurement problems are created not only by the respondents' reaction to the measurement process, but also by researchers' involvement in the measurement process. Intentionally, or unintentionally, a researcher soliciting information may bias the information (Rosenthal, 1966). When committed to particular outcomes, researchers may induce program participants to respond in ways that conform to their expectations.

This can be accomplished in a variety of ways, not the least of which is asking "loaded" questions. There have recently been a number of Federal

Trade Commission decisions mandating corrective advertising (Brock, 1978). Companies whose advertising has been judged false or deceptive are required to correct publicly the original, inaccurate ads. Beyond this, such companies must provide evidence that the corrective campaign has eliminated the erroneous information from public opinion. While this may be a difficult task because first impressions are often hard to "correct" (Hastorf, Polefka & Schneider, 1978), researchers have the even tougher job of measuring the new opinions. It can be tempting in such situations to ask loaded questions such as, "Do you now realize that brand X apricot juice cocktail is not actually a juice; rather, it is largely water?" Because of the way the question is phrased, it is likely to produce a majority of "yes" answers. This result proves only the "effectiveness" of instruments designed to produce desired results, but not the effectiveness of the corrective advertising.

Researchers can mold the nature of the information generated. Outcome measures need to be selected with a variety of concerns in mind. As scientists interested in collecting accurate, valid, and reliable information about social interventions, the potential for intentional and unintentional biases in outcome measurement must be recognized and prevented as possible.

Types of Measurement Tools

For present purposes, data will be considered the product of outcome measurement, including all information gathered for the purposes of understanding the consequences—intended and unintended— of a social experiment. These data can be produced by using a variety of measurement procedures. For the sake of simplicity, the following types of measuring tools have been identified: (a) records, (b) objective tests, (c) questionnaires and interviews, and (d) observations of behavior. These categories of outcome measures are relatively broad and indicate that the measures included within each type also share common themes.

RECORDS

Records refer to the plethora of information routinely collected and available as part of any social program. It is entirely possible that new measurement techniques or procedures need not be developed in order to assess a treatment. Already existing information in the form of records may suffice.

Program administrators routinely collect information about the behavior and, often, the attitudes of participants. Schools, for example, have to keep accurate attendance and truancy records as a matter of law; hospitals, for medical as well as legal reasons, collect data about their patients. Almost every social institution maintains some form of records. Such information, if systematically gathered and maintained, can be used to assess a social intervention. Its attractiveness lies in its availability. The information, however, may be inaccurate and/or inappropriate to the substantive questions about the program.

In an experiment which tested a family approach to dentistry, patients at a dental school clinic were randomly assigned to either a family dentistry module or a more traditional individual patient module (Fine, 1980). After verifying that the accuracy of records were accurate, the number of patient appointments kept, cancelled, and missed were used to measure, in part, the program's impact. The analysis indicated that cancellation rates for the family dentistry module were significantly lower than those of the control module.

The variety of records that might be used is staggering in settings as diverse as legal, work, medical, and academic settings. The courts and police keep records on arrests, convictions, and other indicators of crime. These data can readily be used to understand the impact of any innovation on judicial practices, for instance. Worksites maintain records of income, sick time, disability, accidents, health insurance utilization, and absenteeism. These data can be used as symptomatic measures of employee or worksite problems, and are flexible as outcome indicators for social experiments. In fact, examining relationships among different record bases can be illuminating. Linking worker health records to worksite exposure data (exposure to toxins, carcinogens, and so on) can reveal generally camouflaged findings on occupational safety and health hazards. In medical settings, detailed reports are kept on drug administration, procedures conducted, and patient reactions. For obvious reasons, such records tend to be accurate and are maintained for all individuals who interact with the system. In health care programs, measures of the number of hospital days per patient are used as important indicators of health services changes. In schools, attendance rates and grades are regularly computed. Records provide social experimenters with data that are free from the reactivity effects of most other collection methods. Records are not usually biased by the fact that people know they are being "watched."

Records, however, can be, and have been, tampered with. A documented case was the use of "uniform crime statistics" during the early 1970s to validate the effectiveness of anti-crime programs in several U.S. cities. Seidman and Couzens (1974) noted that because such records are used to assess the effectiveness of governmental programs and police departments, they were reactive. Pressures existed either to under- or overreport criminal activity. Despite the fact that crime data are difficult to tamper with, police still have leeway as to pressing formal charges. Both in terms of how crimes actually are classified and how the records are used, large biases may be present.

Researchers who utilize such records need to learn about the origins of the information, and the manner in which it was collected and maintained. Unknown types of inaccuracies may be present, thereby threatening internal validity. While records are accessible, no information can be context-free; and numerical indices which summarize results do not always compensate for experiential knowledge about a program (Campbell, 1972). Records can only provide a quantitative and somewhat reductionist view of what has occurred. Using record data alone to deduce a picture of program impact may threaten construct validity. Record data, though easily available and valuable in certain circumstances, should be used in conjunction with other information.

OBJECTIVE TESTS

Another major category of outcome measures is objective tests. Tests are systematic procedures for assessing abilities, skills, and knowledge of individuals. They are considered procedures for generating "hard" data about the learning changes that occur during a social experiment.

Tests are used to tap information, abilities, and analytic competencies. Objective tests may measure personality traits, sociometric preferences, aptitude, recall, abstract reasoning, personal interests, and physical fitness (Metfessel & Michael, 1967; Nunnally, 1978). Tests may take many forms. Qualitative data can be collected by tests that use open-ended questions, and physical measures (that is, physiological) can also be included in a test. Common to all procedures is a standardized way of scoring responses (written, verbal, or physical).

Tests, in most instances, are obtrusive. Almost by definition, test takers are aware that their behavior is being measured. For all the reactivity reasons cited above, test taking may provoke behaviors that would not occur under other circumstances. Test anxiety, for example, may interfere with test taking. It may confound research designs if anxiety is related to the treatment. Anxiety aside, because good test performance is socially desirable (that is, most people want to do well), there is usually little incentive to perform poorly. This may make tests useful where an objective outcome must be assessed.

Objective tests may have other problems, however. Perhaps the most obvious of these is their questionable degree of construct validity and "objectivity." It has been shown that intelligence tests—supposedly the best illustration of measuring general intelligence—are culture-biased (Gay & Cole, 1967). Many educational researchers question the validity of standardized achievement tests for assessing students' ability or competence. High scores on a fact-based rote examination may be unrelated to the ability to use information creatively or to think abstractly (Stake, 1971). Not only are such measurement errors a constant problem in objective testing, but the "inane practice of using traditional subject matter tests to assess pupil progress with innovative curriculum materials" (Metfessel & Michael, 1967) demonstrates a misfit between educational procedures and assessments of educational progress. More a problem of how tests have been developed and misused rather than a feature of the methodology itself, achievement measures deserve careful scrutiny because of ethical considerations, social and academic implications.

INTERVIEWS AND QUESTIONNAIRES

Perhaps the most obvious, and most frequently used, outcome measure in social experimentation is the interview. Interviews may be administered by a researcher or may be self-administered in the form of a questionnaire. The essential aspect of an interview or questionnaire is that individuals are asked for their own thoughts, opinions, and/or ideas.

Questionnaires and interviews are methods for collecting both hard and soft data. Hard data are pieces of factual information, like birthdate, race, age, address. Soft data include more subjective impressions or opinions. Although interviews and questionnaires can be seen as ways to collect both kinds of data, they are relatively easy ways to gather soft data. Asking individuals to complete a survey of their attitudes or to participate in an individual or group interview provides them with an opportunity to express evaluations, perceptions, and attitudes about a treatment or social issue.

There are problems with soft data. They provide room for unmeasured exaggeration and biases of respondents for giving only socially desirable responses. The internal validity of questionnaires and interviews is particularly vulnerable to these biases because the measures are highly reactive. Participants know they are being studied.

Other response biases may derive from respondents' relationships to the treatment offered in the social experiment. If respondents are financially dependent on a program, they may evaluate the program favorably even if they do not believe it is effective. Respondents who dislike the program, feel cheated by it, or even dislike the administrators, may go out of their way to say negative things even if they believe program goals have been satisfied. While such biases interfere with the internal validity of the data, they paradoxically provide important information. As long as some method is available to detect these biases—such as the use of a scale which measures respondents' tendency to present socially desirable answers—(Crowne & Marlowe, 1964), a great deal of information may be obtained. In sum, interviews and questionnaires are valuable tools for gathering information about respondents' experiences, information that can not usually be ascertained through a review of records or observation.

Although there are many similarities between interviews and questionnaires, there are also some important differences. Interviews involve face-to-face contact or direct telephone contact between a researcher and a participant or participants. Ambiguities may be cleared up on the spot and rapport established.

Unlike record monitoring, test taking, or observation, interviews provide the opportunity to ask respondents for their personal meaning, and to seek clarification or amplification of the data (Cannell & Kahn, 1968; Richardson, Dohrenwend & Klein, 1965).

Research conducted on the impact of the Vietnam War involved face-to-face interviews with more than 1400 age-eligible men of the Vietnam generation (Fine & Laufer 1979). Although the research was undertaken for a variety of reasons, we will just consider one area of concern: the needs of veterans for government services. To assess these needs, one could review veterans' records at the Veterans Administration (VA) and formulate impressions from that source. One might also administer a variety of academic and physical tests to the returning veterans and deduce needs from these data. Observations of veterans "in action" in work settings, a VA clinic, or in their homes might also help to determine their needs. Given the fact that much remains unknown about what happened to these men when they served in Vietnam and when they came home, combined with the fact that none of these data collection techniques would yield a cross-section, random sample of veterans, it seemed appropriate to conduct lengthy face-to-face interviews with a stratified sample. In these interviews, it was possible to talk about these veterans' needs, to explore their adjustment to civilian life, and to determine what problems they were still facing. Interviews, even though highly structured, still allow researchers a great deal of flexibility. In the case of the Vietnam-era veteran, the interview was designed to explore in-depth issues that might not be revealed in a superficial discussion.

Questionnaires come in a variety of forms and, as noted earlier, can be used to obtain quantitative and qualitative information. In most instances, questionnaires are highly structured and are designed to collect quantitative, attitudinal, and/or behavioral data. In a sense, questionnaires are written substitutes for in-person interviews. If properly structured, they allow respondents to describe freely their opinions, beliefs, and experiences. Questionnaires may be distributed to an existing group or mailed to individuals. The former procedure is preferred, when possible, because mailed questionnaires suffer from notoriously low response rates. Low response rates might mean that a different group than intended was providing responses, thus harming internal validity.

Various forms for constructing questionnaire items are used. Frequently, respondents are asked to indicate, on a numeric scale, their agreement with particular statements. Such an item might be presented as follows, on a Likert scale:

"This program benefits younger participants, age 8-12."

1	2	3	4	5
strongly agree	agree	neutral	disagree	strongly disagree

Respondents circle the number which most closely corresponds to their belief about the program, thereby providing quantitative impression data. This procedure is referred to as a close-ended item. A number of items asking for agreement about a central concept are given in a set, and one's score is the sum of the individual item ratings. For the data to be valid, respondents need to share the researcher's understanding of the items. Items must therefore be precise and consensually understood, or construct validity problems will surface.

Whatever procedure is used to construct interviews or questionnaires, the goal is similar: To provide a mechanism for individuals to share their ideas in a way that can be easily summarized. The ideas, as well as the ways of measuring them, may be imperfect, but they yield easily aggregated information about the effects of social interventions.

OBSERVATION

A final category of outcome measurement is observation. Although each of the previously described types of measurement aspects of observation, albeit indirect, formal observation refers to the actual and systematic coding of individual, group, or organizational behavior (Weick, 1968). Such observation can include taking systematic notes about individual behavior, videotaping interactions, and even observing changes in the physical environment.

Observations can be made either obtrusively or unobtrusively. When a person is sent into a classroom to record the behavior of students (as in Lancy, 1978), the responsibilities of this individual are usually made clear to the teacher and students. In other cases, observation is done behind one-way mirrors or under some other guise making detection unlikely. An interesting example of covert observation is Rosenhan's (1973) participant-observation study of psychiatric hospitals. Rosenhan's assistants posed as patients to obtain admittance to psychiatric hospitals and observed activity and decision-making processes on the wards. They documented their treatment, how they were ignored or responded to, how other inmates interacted with them, and how hospital personnel responded to their attempts at conversation, requests for explanation, and other behavior. Had they presented themselves as researchers, they no doubt would have gathered different information than they did as pseudo-patients.

Observational techniques allow the monitoring of many different kinds of behaviors: friendship patterns, social interactions, nonverbal expressions, and communication styles. Using observational techniques, data can be collected on behaviors of which people are unaware, unwilling to discuss, or which might not generally be enacted for an "observer." With observation it is possible to denote who, when, how frequently, and under what conditions certain events occur or behaviors are performed. An intriguing example of the use of observational techniques is described by Charles Hampden-Turner (1976) in his study of the Delancy Street Foundation, a prison rehabilitation program located in San Francisco. Through intensive observation (which was, in part, participant-observation), Hampden-Turner discovered how a group of ex-convicts created and maintained a successful home and set of businesses. Using overt observation (as compared to Rosenhan's covert strategy), he obtained details of the most intimate activities, such as "community games," in which members and directors described their own and others' most personal problems. Observation affords researchers the opportunity to record uncensored and complex interactions.

The range of situations for which observation is appropriate has been greatly increased recently as audiovisual equipment has become widely accessible. In a study of a program to train students from medicine, nursing, social work, and other health care disciplines to collaborate more effectively, videotapes are made of students during team decision-making (Saxe & Lake, 1978). The videotapes are later content analyzed; that is, every comment is reviewed and coded in terms of interaction categories. From these content analyses it is possible to determine whether or not individuals are listening to one another and making effective use of the information available to each discipline. These data indicated the utility of the training program.

The value of observational techniques, however, needs to be considered in light of their ethical, pragmatic, and potential validity problems. There are a number of ethical constraints on observations conducted without the knowledge of the subject. Perhaps as ethical guidelines undergo change over the next few years, unobtrusive observing of people will be less possible. The basic ethical guideline for data collection involves what is called informed consent, the understanding that individuals involved in the research study are aware of and consent to their involvement in the research (American Psychological Association, 1973). Observational techniques, frequently covert, violate this understanding and circumvent the issues of requesting informed consent. The violation of individuals' rights and privacy are thus serious considerations in the conduct of an observational study. Both the public and social scientists are calling for greater constraints on scientific intrusion (Bermant, Kelman & Warwick 1978; Rivlin & Timpane, 1975a).

Observation is also limited by pragmatic difficulties. Observation cannot always be employed because of the resources needed to do it properly. If complex behavior or large numbers of people are involved, it may be impractical to have enough observers to code behaviors accurately. Although videotape and film expand these capabilities, systematic observation remains a cumbersome process.

Observations of behaviors can introduce construct validity problems. If only observational data are used to assess a program, such data could indicate that a particular behavior occurred, but not why. If nurses failed to respond to requests by the psychiatric pseudo-patients, one could conclude that nurses objectify mental patients. Interviews might have suggested that these nurses were uncomfortable talking with the pseudo-patients because they knew they were not mentally ill, and they (the nurses) notified psychiatrists, only to hear, "You are not the ones to diagnose patients." Were this hypothetical explanation true, behavioral observations alone would camouflage the true situation and threaten the construct validity of the findings.

From Whom?

Whether data should be collected from all participants, from nonparticipants, or only from a sample of participants and nonparticipants, must be decided for each social experiment. Sampling decisions (decisions about from whom to collect data) are made with the intention of maximizing the representativeness of the respondent group; that in turn will highten external validity. Below, some of the issues central to sampling decisions are discussed (see Babbie, 1973; Sudman, 1976, for more thorough discussions).

Sampling issues of measurement are closely related to the question of how participants are selected for inclusion in a social experiment or assigned to conditions (see Chapter 3). In the present context, sampling refers only to decisions about collecting data. In social experiments, many individuals are exposed to the treatment or a control condition. Sampling, as contrasted with assignment to condition, refers to selecting some of these individuals to provide data. In some cases it is impossible and unnecessary to collect information from everyone involved in the program; that is, to collect data from the entire population. If sampling is done properly and the sample can be assumed to represent the population to which one would like to generalize, it can be considered an efficient approach to data collection.

Inappropriate sampling, however, can yield quite biased data. A nonrepresentative sample, for example, would involve interviewing only those people in a job training program who volunteered to be interviewed (Rosenthal & Rosnow, 1975). Using only volunteers might attract a disproportionate number of trainees who are extremely positive or extremely negative about the program. More technical sampling errors can be made by involving too few respondents for the statistical tests to be employed, or by excluding a small but substantial group (such as an ethnic minority) from the research sample. As with the design considerations discussed in Chapter 3, random sampling or random stratified sampling makes "from whom" questions simpler to answer.

Researchers and those responsible for the intervention must make a number of joint decisions about the research sample. Who gets sampled and how this sampling is conducted is closely related to what one hopes to learn and accomplish through the experiment. Are you interested in understanding perceptions of nonparticipants as well as participants? Should data be collected both from men and women? Should information be solicited from blacks and whites in the program? If so, should this information come from equal or representative proportions of each group? Should the sample be stratified by age such that half of the sample is over a particular age, and half younger? These are questions the answers to which require joint determination by the social researchers and those responsible for the intervention.

Different sampling procedures may be developed for different aspects of the design, or for collecting data on specific dependent measures. In the family dentistry program described previously, students were sampled differently at three stages of data collection. In the first two months of the experiment, small groups of students participated in focused group interviews (Calder, 1980) to provide preliminary impressions of the program. Each group consisted of a sample of ten students, five seniors and five juniors, randomly selected from each class list. Half of the groups were in family dentistry programs; half were not. The information collected in these open-ended interviews was used to develop a questionnaire administered at about month 4 to the entire population of students in the program. Additional data were collected during month 7 by observing randomly chosen family dentistry students to assess the quality of their interactions with fellow dental students and with patients. At each of three phases of data collection, a different sampling procedure was used to collect fundamentally different kinds of information.

Sampling decisions influenced the resulting data. This is best illustrated by interviews with the dentistry patients. If, for example, only those dentistry patients who kept their appointments regularly were interviewed, the results would be biased in a positive direction. Although it involved more time and money, it was necessary to get information from patients who cancelled their appointments or were no-shows to see if their perceptions of the program differed from those who kept appointments. Sampling both groups allowed the researchers to make a fair, comprehensive statement about patient perceptions of the program. Of course, such a procedure was time-consuming and its benefits must be considered in light of its costs.

Standards for Measurement

There are some general guidelines which help to determine the quality of the measuring instruments. These guidelines, generally referred to as reliability and validity (Nunnally, 1977; Nunnally & Wilson, 1975), are particularly useful for determining, after data have been collected, the extent to which you have succeeded in developing a good measuring instrument. Reliability and validity are the two general ways of analyzing the usefulness of measurement tools. While the conceptual analysis of the scheme described here is parallel to the analysis of validity in the design of experiments, there are some important differences.

RELIABILITY

The concept of reliability is relatively straightforward. It refers to the degree to which a measuring instrument yields consistent and stable results. A reliable test given to the same person at different times is a test that yields similar scores at each interim and has not improved as a result of taking the test the first time, and if the test is reliable, the scores should be equivalent. In general, if an instrument contains items or questions that respondents do not understand, the instrument will be unreliable, because the questions elicit different responses on different testing occasions.

In the case where a measuring instrument is not a test given to individuals but is an observation of some behavior, reliability assumes a slightly different meaning. Still concerned with the stability of outcome measurement, reliability refers in this situation to the degree to which a number of observers code the behavior in the same way. It might also refer to the degree to which a single observer, on multiple occasions, codes behavior in the same way. Establishing this type of reliability is crucial to using effectively any type of observational data.

The basic way in which the reliability of a test is determined is referred to as test-retest reliability. As the term implies, the same person is given a test twice. If the test is reliable, there will be a high degree of correspondence between the scores from the first and second administration (statistically, the two scores will be highly correlated). Although theoretically this is a good way to determine reliability, it is often not practicable. It sometimes leads to erroneous interpretations because individuals invariably learn by virtue of taking a test (practice effects) and so their second score represents not only the ability tapped by the first test, but also their learning since. To eliminate some of these pragmatic problems, at least three other techniques are utilized (either simply, or in conjunction with one another).

Split-half. With this procedure, a test is divided into two subtests, each consisting of randomly selected items. Two scores, one for each half of the test, are computed. These scores are then compared to each other. Assuming that the test has more than 40 items (to avoid sampling problems in the random procedure), this comparison of scores should indicate whether or not individuals are responding consistently.

Parallel forms. Often it is possible to develop two forms of the same test; that is, a second version of the test is constructed that has similar but differently worded questions presented in a different order. Comparison of the two scores provides an index of reliability. For a test such as the SAT, where parallel forms have to be developed because students can take the test more than once (and in some cases they have access to the original test's correct answers) computing such reliability is a standard procedure.

Internal consistency. A third way of determining reliability is to compute a measure of internal consistency, such as Kuder-Richardson 20. KR-20 is a statistical formula that computes the average correlation between every possible combination of randomly selected items. Conceptually, it is similar to split-half reliability, although it involves a different analytic method.

For observational measures, testing for reliability is relatively simple, though somewhat time-consuming (La France & Mayo, 1978). A situation is constructed where a number of observers watch the same set of behaviors. Without communicating, the observers rate or code the behaviors. The degree to which there is agreement between observers on the behaviors that they code represents the degree of reliability. Often reliability will not be achieved spontaneously. Coders must be trained and common understandings developed. In order to do this, coders must be given an opportunity to explain their ratings and collectively develop some agreement upon a scheme for making ratings.

In the earlier example of content analyses of student health team meetings, it took from 3-6 hours to train coders. After coders saw several teams in operation, they adopted the standard definition (for their study) of an interaction sequence. Once this was developed, they learned what criteria to apply to determine directionality of an individual's response, level of affect, and approximately 20 other categories of behavior.

It should be noted that we have emphasized that reliability should be *similar* across parallel forms, test-retest, but not exactly the same. A problem in dealing with reliability is that test scores may change very quickly. Differences between administrations of a test often reflect an authentic change in behavior or acquired knowledge as well as some inherent instability of the measuring instrument. A correlation of .80—indicating 65 percent of the variance (the correlation squared) between ratings—is usually an acceptable level of reliability.

VALIDITY

In social experiments, validity of measuring instruments has a slightly different meaning than validity of design. Validity, in the context of mea-

surement, refers to the degree to which the instrument is an accurate indicator of the attribute that one is attempting to assess. Rather than threats to
validity, one talks about different areas in which validity is established for a
particular measuring measurement. Four principal types of measurement
validity are described: content, face, cross, and construct.

Content validity. Content validity refers to how well a measuring instrument covers the substantive area it is intended to test. For ability tests, it
refers to the degree to which the test includes all areas related to achievement
as well as relevant skills. A questionnaire designed to assess reactions to a
new teaching method which involves much positive reinforcement should
include questions about how the method affected academic and social performance as well as self-image of the students involved. In the case of
objective tests, content validity reflects the comprehensiveness of the measure in terms of the concept being tested. One criticism of intelligence tests
is that while they allegedly measure general intellectual ability, they over-
emphasize verbal and written skills, thus ignoring such skills as creativity
and abstract thinking (Stake, 1971).

Face validity. Face validity is particularly important for social experiments. It has to do with the degree to which respondents believe that a test
measures what it purports to measure. Usually, if participants are to comply
with a request to complete a form or otherwise provide data, they must
believe that the test is a reasonable and relevant assessment and that it gives
them a chance to reflect their concerns. This is important in social experimentation because program participants are not typically "captive" as they
are in other research situations (Kelman, 1972). Participants in social experiments cannot usually be required to provide certain data. Even if they are
made to feel obligated, there is little that can be done to force participants to
provide accurate information. For this reason, a face valid instrument is an
important incentive.

Cross-validity. A third type of instrument validity is cross-validity, or the
relationship of one measure to other similar measures. While you wouldn't
want an instrument to be perfectly correlated with another instrument (in that
case, why develop a new one?), it is usually desirable that there be a fair
degree of relationshp between similar measures. For example, if a new
college entrance examination were developed, one would want to be sure
that it correlated, at least moderately, with the SAT (assuming you have faith
in the content validity of the SAT).

Construct validity. Construct validity has to do with the degree to which
the results of the test fit with the theory from which the test was developed.
Theories are so complex that they can often explain anything, even incorrect
data. It is important to formulate hypotheses which will permit the development of good construct validity. Thus, we would expect an instrument that

assesses problems of poverty to show more health problems for those with access to the fewest financial resources. If use of an instrument does not indicate that the poor suffer an inequitable proportion of problems (perhaps because the instrument uses sophisticated language or is not available in the language of an ethnic group), it cannot be said to have construct validity.

In summary, although the validity of outcome measures differs from design validity, it is not independent. In this case we are talking about the degree to which the outcome measures, or instruments, are sufficiently comprehensive and substantially representative (content validity), are perceived as relevant and meaningful to respondents (face validity), correspond to already existing and validated measures (cross-validity), and adequately reflect the constructs being tested (construct validity). The validity of outcome measures approximates more closely the use of the term validity in everyday language. Here we are interested in how sound or well grounded the instruments appear to be in light of respondent perceptions, existing instruments, and theoretical speculation.

Conclusion

Our focus has been on ways that researchers assess the effects of social interventions. The resulting outcome measures have many facets. Data can be collected in a variety of ways, from different people, at different times. The "most appropriate" or "best" collection procedures, samples, and times need to be determined on an individual basis for each social experiment. No easy rules, prescriptions, or set answers point to the optimal outcome measures or data collection procedures. Although the specifics of data collection depend on the social experiment, it is desirable to maximize the validity of data collection procedures. The instruments should accurately measure expected outcomes, the participants measured should be representative of the program population, and the timing of the measurement procedure should provide data sufficient to demonstrate change over time. The outcome measures should be valid and reliable indicators of program functioning and should be used in conjunction with one another rather than separately.

As we have tried to illustrate, there are a range of concerns relevant to data collection procedures. Although technical concerns have been emphasized, it is also important to consider practical and ethical constraints on measuring social activities. A variety of such constraints were described, indicating the ethical restrictions of asking certain types of questions and the pragmatic difficulties inherent in procedures such as observation.

In theory, the array of data collection techniques available is limitless. In practice, techniques are available to collect almost any type of information, but there are clear limits. We do not have a right to force individuals to comply, to place people in uncomfortable positions, or to ask participants to take unnecessary risks. It is inappropriate and unethical to trick people into giving information or to engage them in a research study without their consent (American Psychological Association, 1973). It should be remembered that information is being collected ostensibly to improve social conditions. If people elect not to be involved in that process, little can be done to force participation and researchers must respect that decision.

It should be noted that data, despite the belief of some, do not speak for themselves (Kaplan, 1964). Once the data have been collected, researchers and others must make sense of them, and integrate the bits of available information to produce a meaningful picture of the effects of the intervention. Skills of analysis and synthesis are required, and these will be discussed in the next chapter. Insofar as the data are valid, the instruments fit the theoretical questions, and the sample is appropriate, the analysis should produce results which are relevant for decision-making, both within and beyond the immediate social program.

CHAPTER 5

ANALYZING SOCIAL EXPERIMENTS

*"There are three kinds of lies: lies,
damned lies and statistics."*

Benjamin Disraeli

This chapter focuses on the analysis procedures used to interpret the results of social experiments. While a principal emphasis will be on the use of statistics (the actual techniques used to summarize and interpret quantified data), the discussion stresses the logic underlying the analysis of social research. Contrary to Disraeli's often quoted views, we do not think statistics are necessarily misleading when the context in which they are applied is understood. In fact, they form a logical set of procedures that can be used to summarize and analyze the impact of social interventions. A critical analysis of the results of a social experiment is a central feature of applying social science methods to develop utilizable knowledge.

The chapter introduces the spectrum of analysis procedures, addressing general issues which underlie the interpretation of research. Making sense of "data" is a largely subjective process aided by the technology of statistics. How one searches for meaning, decides which version of "truth" will be accepted, and how different kinds of information can be used in the analysis process will be described. No attempt is made to provide details such as how to compute statistics. The purposes and limits of the procedures are explained, and the conditions under which particular statistics should be utilized are delineated. The series of analysis problems that emerge specifically in social experiments will be examined, along with some recent approaches to dealing with these difficulties. Many of these problems represent threats to statistical conclusion validity. Our focus will be on strategies for avoiding these validity problems.

Interpretation

Analysis of a social experiment involves the search for meaning in obtained data. One wants to explain the effects, both expected and unexpected, that result from the treatment. From the analysis of the data, hypotheses can be tested and new hypotheses formulated. Out of bits of information collected from varied methods and sources, an understanding of the problem and the intervention begins to develop. Although the strengths of one's interpretations are directly related to the validity of design and measurement procedures, the interpretation process has a distinct logic. A host of issues requires consideration during this process and eventually affects the utilizability of the data.

The interpretive process frequently uses quantified measures to describe relationships between the treatment and respective outcomes. Statistics are the tools of this story-building. The selection of statistical indices is based on the nature of the data and the questions one wants to answer. The process of interpreting an experiment and developing statistical indices to represent the results usually involves multiple cycles of analyzing and reanalyzing the data. The information generated by a social experiment may need to be reviewed by planners, researches, and consumers, and then reanalyzed. The expected product of the interpretation process is an understanding of causal relationships. This understanding typically yields a "pattern" of information that may be consistent with predictions or not; and is usually stated in probabilistic fashion (that is, as likely within a given range of error). As described here, one's predictions play an important role in organizing the analysis process.

HYPOTHESES

In the terminology of research design, hypotheses specify expected relationships between independent variables (treatment) and dependent variables (outcomes), although analyses are not limited to testing the relationships postulated by formal hypotheses. Unanticipated relationships among variables must also be taken into account. Hypotheses are critical guides to the analysis process. They provide an outline of the analysis strategy by clarifying which aspects of the available data need to be used to understand particular relationships. Without hypotheses to guide analysis, it is difficult to determine what tests are necessary to examine the central relationships in the experiment and to disconfirm alternative explanations.

In the Sloane et al. (1975) study of psychotherapy, the investigators' hypotheses were important in suggesting an analysis procedure. They expected differences in the impact of the two therapeutic approaches (behavior and analytically oriented therapy) and no therapy. These differences, especially between the two therapy conditions, were expected to be pronounced over time, thus the study included a comparison of average outcome scores at four months and one year. This latter analysis was probably obvious from the description of the study. In other cases, it is not obvious until one systematically considers the expected results.

Hypotheses guide not only the analysis of an experiment but also the design, selection, and development of outcome measures. To use the Sloane et al. study again as an example, the collection of social adjustment data at two points in time was logical given the hypotheses. The hypotheses required that these data be compared across treatments as part of the analyses. Just as hypotheses integrate the elements of a social experiment, analysis procedures allow one to interpret these interrelationships.

An additional illustration of the relationship between hypotheses and analysis comes from a similar type of mental health study conducted in Ireland, which concerned the use of megavitamin treatment for schizophrenia. To assess the efficacy of vitamins, McGrath et al. (1972) designed a simple study in which schizophrenic patients admitted to a particular mental institution were given either nicotinamide (a megavitamin), or an inert substance (placebo) three times a day. The treatment was continued either for an entire year or for the length of the patient's stay at the hospital. The assignments to megavitamin or placebo condition were random, and the medicine was coded so that the staff was "blind" to a patient's treatment condition. The hypothesis was that megavitamin therapy would be more effective in treating hospitalized schizophrenics than placebo therapy.

The hypothesis specified an important comparison, that between megavitamin and placebo patients. In addition, it indicated the relevant outcome measure: psychiatric indicators of schizophrenic symptomatology. The analysis, as summarized in Table 5.1, involved a comparison of the number of individuals in each condition classified as "recovered or much improved" vs. "improved or not improved." Because the design included only two randomly selected groups, the analysis was relatively simple. A more specific hypothesis might have required a design that employed multiple levels of the treatment (such as different dosages) and/or the use of megavitamins in conjunction with systematic variations of other therapeutic treatments. It should also be noted that the outcome measure scale—a dichotomous "yes" or "no"—was only one of several that might have been employed. For example, a scale with five or more points might have been formed of "degree of recovery." The use of such a measure depended, in part, on how schizophrenia was conceptualized; that is, was it either present or absent, or did it fall along a continuous dimension?

These examples illustrate some issues central to deducing analysis strategies from hypotheses. Hypotheses should be used only as guides. A great

TABLE 5.1   Assessment of Patients Treated for Schizophrenia With
            Nicotinamide

Assessment	Pts. receiving Nicotinamide		Pts. receiving Placebo		All Pts.	
	#	%	#	%	#	%
Recovered or much improved	58	65	68	72	126	68
Improved or not improved	31	35	27	28	58	32
Totals	89	100	95	100	184	100

deal of judgment still needs to be applied to choosing the most appropriate analysis procedures. An important set of decisions has to do with selecting how one wants to use the data from the various types of information collected. These choices play an important role, not only in analysis, but ultimately in determining the quality of interpretations made about the treatment.

QUALITATIVE AND QUANTITATIVE DATA

As noted earlier, interpretation involves the use of various types of information. Much of the skill of interpretation hinges on the selection of the most important information. The development of useful ways of comparing differing information types is secondary. Often the problem of dealing with different types of information centers around differences between what have been called qualitative and quantitative data (cf. Cook & Reichardt, 1979). Qualitative data are the "raw" reports of an experience. Operationally, they are the open-ended narratives provided by respondents of their perceptions, thoughts, and feelings. Quantitative data are numerical, collected either directly through the use of a numerical item or indirectly by quantifying verbal or written information.

A common error assumes that qualitative and quantitative data represent different approaches to understanding. As Campbell (1974) has noted, qualitative data are often associated with humanism and phenomenology, while quantitative data are often associated with hard science. The implication is that qualitative data yield a "deeper" understanding than quantitative information. Along with Campbell, we reject this view and would prefer to consider qualitative and quantitative data as closely connected and, in fact, interdependent forms of information. Both types of data are directed toward achieving the same end: understanding the effects of a social intervention. Both are probably necessary for adequate "knowing."

One way of thinking about quantitative data is as a shorthand representation of what has occurred. For example, each of us has had the experience of taking examinations. After a test, one sometimes reports to friends and classmates how well or poorly one has done. To do so, one often resorts to some kind of summary, typically in quantified form. One would probably not describe, *ad nauseam,* all of the questions and answers. Instead, one would most likely describe such things as how many questions were on the test and how many we got right or wrong. We would, perhaps, indicate how our score compared with those of others. Even if one were not statistically sophisticated, a straightforward quantitative way of summarizing would be found for what might otherwise be a long and boring qualitative description.

The use of quantitative information as convenient shorthand in analyzing social interventions has limits, of course. Quantitative data do not really replace knowing what actually happened and what individuals experienced. Quantifications merely summarize this knowledge and make it easier to represent for analysis purposes. There are many variations in how quantitative information is collected and analyzed. At the simplest level, one merely assigns numbers as symbols to represent a particular phenomenon. At another level, one counts the frequency of occurrences of certain phenomena. Very often, this is useful for expressing in quantitative form information which has been collected qualitatively. At a more complex level, scales are formed.

To illustrate what is meant by this type of quantification, consider a social experiment which provides a test for the use of shelters for women who have been victims of domestic violence. As part of the experiment, one would certainly want to collect information from the victims. Assume, initially, that the data were collected as responses to open-ended questions. One question, designed to gather background information might ask victims, "How would you describe your relationship with your husband or lover?" The following are, perhaps, typical of the responses that would be obtained:

(a) "We are very compatible. I love my husband and he loves me. But we fight all the time. I hate when we fight in front of the children. I care so much for him. He would do anything for me. He doesn't realize how wrong it is to hit me."

(b) "My marriage is like every other marriage. It's just typical. We have a nice house, good children, and we see our families a lot."

(c) "Our relationship is mixed-up. There are good times and bad times. maybe it's related to work, I don't know. When we're both working things go smoothly. When we're not working, we argue a lot, I get bored and angry a lot. I think we're different from others."

Such information might be interesting in raw or original form, but difficult to use for comparison purposes (for example, to compare those who remain at the shelter with those who return home to their husbands / lovers). It would be especially problematic to synthesize this qualitative information if data were collected from a large sample. One solution to the problem of voluminous open-ended data is to develop codes that can be used to classify the data. Such content analysis procedures can help to organize qualitative data and make them amenable to quantitative analysis (see Holsti, 1969). Codes are derived from the original data, and reflect prominent themes and characteristics of the data. Coders who are blind to the condition of the respondent review the original data and rate the information along a standardized set of dimensions.

For example, the following codes might be developed from these data:

I. Comments on the relationship

   (1) typical, average, like others, ordinary

   (2) different, not like the others

   (3) not applicable

II. Comments on compatibility

   (1) compatible — we get along very well

   (2) not very compatible, we don't get along

   (3) mixed — sometimes compatible, sometimes not compatible

   (4) not applicable

III. Conflict

   (1) we never fight, we always discuss things

   (2) we argue, we have disagreements

   (3) we get into physical fights

   (4) not applicable

IV. External factors which influence the relationship

   (1) children

   (2) in-laws

   (3) community

   (4) employment

   (5) health problems

   (6) money problems

   (7) none

Each individual's response would then be coded according to these categories. When coded into quantitative form, the qualitative information can be analyzed comparatively. Although these transformed data represent a loss of specific information, they increase the ability to deal with large amounts of data. It may not be possible, however, to determine from analyses of codes the nature of these problems.

In contrast, or in combination with a narrative, some of this information might be collected through the use of quantitative items. For example, the following close-ended questions might be used:

I. How good is your relationship with your partner?

1   2   3   4   5   6   7

Very good   Very bad

II. Out of 1,000 U.S. marriages in what percentage do you think violence occurs? _____ %

Such questions are useful for collecting large amounts of information that can be easily summarized and compared with the data of other respondents. However, if close-ended items are used exclusively, many aspects of the phenomenology of domestic violence as viewed by its victim would be obscured. The analyst would lose information on the subjective experience from the words of the victims, themselves. It would make the interpretation of results more difficult or inaccurate.

Regardless of the type of measure employed, the data are interpretable only to the extent that they can be analyzed. Taken together, they provide an understandable "picture" of the effect of the intervention. Our emphasis is on developing analyses that are unbiased but comprehensive assessments of the impact of a social intervention. Although such analyses often involve substantial use of numerical data, such information should not be considered if the context is not clearly understood. It is probably useful to think of numbers in terms of their underlying qualitative meaning and not as quantities, per se.

Types of Statistics

Whatever form of information is collected in a social experiment, it usually becomes quantified at some point in the analysis in order to facilitate analysis and, ultimately, interpretation. This quantification process is not mystical, nor are the subsequent statistical analysis procedures. It may be easy, however, to misuse quantitative and statistical procedures. Both as a consumer and a developer of social experiments, one must be wary. While the situation has probably improved greatly since Huff (1954) wrote his now-classic *How to Lie with Statistics,* it often takes considerable skill to ferret out statistical analysis problems.

Diverse statistics are used to analyze social experiments (Cook & Campbell, 1979; Riecken & Boruch, 1974). Social experiments do not require any "special" statistics, unlike from other forms of social research. Our discussion should be familiar to readers who have been involved in other types of research. Three broad types of statistical procedures, important to experimentation, can be delineated: descriptive, correlational, and inferential.

These procedures represent the principal ways in which quantitative analysis of data is accomplished and are complementary modes of analysis (Kerlinger, 1973). The focus in describing these procedures will be on understanding the characteristics and use of procedures commonplace to social experimentation.

DESCRIPTIVE STATISTICS

Descriptive statistics summarize specific features of a set of data as succinctly as possible. The development of such numerical indices is not at all "fancy" and, fortunately, only a few standard descriptive statistics are used. While summarizing information with descriptive statistics is extremely important, this procedure inevitably results in a loss of information. However good the statistic, it cannot provide all of the information contained in the raw data, regardless of whether the data are quantitative or qualitative. By carefully selecting descriptive statistics, and perhaps by using multiple statistics, one tries to obtain as complete a view of the data as possible.

Frequency measures. Perhaps the simplest descriptive statistic is not really a statistic at all, in that statistical indices are not actually computed. Frequency counts and other ways of organizing and categorizing data are a type of descriptive statistics. The number of juveniles who return to school after involvement in a diversion program, or the percentage of people who get jobs after completing a job training program, represent important pieces of information. The frequency of such activities can either be presented numerically, in the form of a frequency distribution, or graphically, in the form of a histogram. Such descriptions provide a rudimentary understanding of what has occurred as a result of an intervention.

A simple example of the use of frequency statistics is the presentation of results of a health care experiment that tested the impact on patient care of substituting nurse practitioners for physicians (Spitzer et al., 1974). Nurse practitioners are specially trained nurses who provide basic diagnostic and treatment services which have been provided traditionally by physicians. Spitzer et al. worked with a community in Ontario, Canada, to conduct an experiment in the use of nurse practitioners. Patients were randomly assigned to receive care (out-patient primary care) with either a family physician or a nurse practitioner. Figure 5.1 presents the results of the experiment in terms of the percentage of cases in which care was rated as adequate. Two dependent measures are depicted: one, "indicator conditions," in which the care given for specified presenting problems was judged by a peer group of physicians; a second, "drug prescribed," in which a rating was made of the adequacy of drug prescriptions. As can be seen from the small differences shown in Figure 5.1 between the physician (MD) and nursing (NP) conditions, patients who visited nurse practitioners appeared to fare as well as the

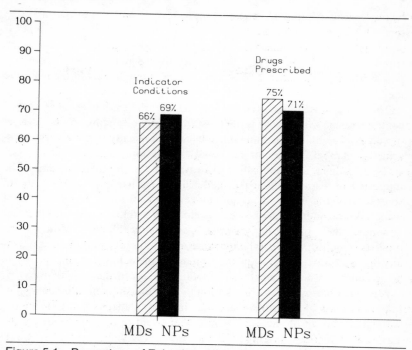

Figure 5.1   Percentage of Episodes of Care Rated as Adequate

*SOURCE: Reprinted by permission from W. O. Spitzer et al.,"The Burlington Random-
ized Trial of the Nurse Practitioner," The New England Journal of Medicine (290;
251-256, 1974), Figure 3.

patients of the physicians. Although further statistical analysis would have
to be done to confirm the lack of a statistically significant difference, the
frequency distribution nicely summarized the results.

Measures of central tendency. In terms of their use both for summarizing
data and for developing other statistical indices, the most important descriptive statistics are those that provide a measure of "central tendency." In
some situations this is the only indicator used to represent the data. Such
statistics include the arithmetic mean (usually called the average), the median or middle value in a set, and the mode (or the most frequently occurring
value).

The mean is an especially important statistic because it can be used as the
basis for computing more sophisticated statistics. It is also very simple to
calculate: the sum of all scores divided by the number of scores. Although
the mean is often the best measure of central tendency, it sometimes distorts
the best estimate of the average. This is especially true when there are a few
values that are very extreme. If, for example, one were interested in assessing the impact of a new jobs program on income in a neighborhood, it might

be misleading to compute mean income. Mean income might be easily distorted by the presence of a few individuals who have very high income. It would take only one grand prize lottery winner to distort significantly what we would consider to be typical income. Consequently, when there is a possibility of a few values being very different than the rest of the data, the median is the preferred statistic.

The mode is used less often than the mean or the median as a measure of central tendency. The mode is the most frequently occurring number in a set of values. The mode has limited use because it usually is not a very representative number. The use of the modal value is applied to describe a "classic type" rather than an indication of an average. One might, for example, be interested in learning about the modal user of a particular service. If resources are being allocated to senior citizens for health care needs, one might want to know both the modal health care costs and the median, to indicate how much the typical elderly person spends on health care. Although the mode is sometimes useful when one has a limited range of numbers, it usually does not provide an adequate summary of the data. Also, the mode has no arithmetic meaning, and thus cannot be used for further calculations.

Measures of dispersion. In addition to measures of central tendency, an important class of descriptive statistics includes statistics that indicate the variability in a set of values. The most important of these measures is the variance. Sometimes presented as the standard deviation (which is computed by taking the square root of the variance), the variance allows one to determine how varied a set of values is. In conjunction with a measure of central tendency such as the mean, one can quickly gain a "picture" of what might otherwise be merely a group of numbers.

To illustrate how the variance can be used to summarize information, along with a measure of central tendency, consider the data shown in Table 5.2. The table has been reproduced from Cook et al.'s (1975) reanalysis of the *Sesame Street* evaluation. The table shows preexperimental achievement levels for two of the original sites. At each site, one group of children was encouraged to view *Sesame Street* and one group was not encouraged. Although one would first have to see a listing of the "raw data" in order to determine how much information is lost by the summary statistics provided in the table (as well as know more about the tests themselves), the table gives a sense of the similarities and differences across sites and groups *before* the intervention. The standard deviation (SD) represents how dispersed the scores are within each group. Since, for most of the tests reported, the SD is fairly large in relation to the mean, one can assume that children within each group were relatively heterogeneous; that is, within each group a wide range of achievement levels was represented. One can interpret these numbers more precisely with the use of inferential statistics, to be described later.

TABLE 5.2 Description of Pretest Learning Measures

Site	Group		Body Parts	Letters	Forms	Numbers	Sorting	Relations	Classification	Puzzles	Grand Total
							Tests				
Boston	Encouraged N=37	M	21.865	17.459	12.297	22.459	2.838	10.676	13.946	2.405	97.892
		SD	6.079	10.381	3.886	9.700	1.424	2.539	4.796	1.518	30.457
	Nonencouraged N=40	M	21.250	14.725	10.600	18.200	2.300	10.025	12.350	1.800	87.275
		SD	5.795	7.355	2.610	7.907	1.324	2.750	3.416	1.344	22.250
Phoenix	Encouraged N=37	M	21.081	14.054	10.000	18.973	2.216	9.459	12.027	1.919	85.243
		SD	5.866	4.515	3.543	7.679	1.250	2.364	3.848	1.299	22.553
	Nonencouraged N=44	M	20.364	13.614	9.364	17.886	1.977	9.432	11.341	1.841	81.386
		SD	5.843	6.066	3.458	7.192	1.338	2.905	3.941	1.293	23.853

*SOURCE: From T. D. Cook et al., "Sesame Street" Revisited, Russell Sage Foundation, 1975, Table 5.1. Reprinted by permission of Basic Books, Inc.

In addition to the variance/SD, the range is also used as a measure of dispersion. The range is the spread between the highest and lowest values. When there is a large difference between the highest and lowest score, or when their values have special meaning, the range may provide a useful index. There are also several dispersion statistics that parallel the median and refer to the position of numbers in a set. However, because such measures (including the range) are difficult to manipulate arithmetically, they are not very widely used.

CORRELATIONAL STATISTICS

The second major category of statistics is correlational statistics. Correlational statistics provide an index of the relationship between variables and indicate the extent to which variations in one variable are associated with variations in another. Although correlations are more difficult to compute than descriptive statistics and their use is subject to many more difficulties, correlations often yield very important information. This information may be used to summarize data and to aid in interpretation.

For present purposes, our discussion of correlational statistics will be limited to the Pearson Product Moment Correlation Coefficient. This statistic, which has values between $+1$ and -1, gives an indication of the linear relationship between one set of numbers and another. The index is linear because it represents the straight line relationship (when graphed) between two sets of values. If there is no relationship between two variables, the correlation coefficient would equal 0; if variables are positively related (both increase or decrease together), the correlation will be positive; if the values go in opposite directions, the correlation will be negative.

A common use of correlations in the analysis of social experiments is to indicate the relationship between an independent variable (treatment) that can be represented as a continuous variable (ranging from 1 to ...) and the outcomes of the experiment. A high correlation indicates that the two covary, not necessarily that one causes the other. For example. Waldo and Chiricos (1977), in conjunction with Florida penal administrators, used correlations to analyze an experimental program of work release for prisoners. Work release programs are designed to help prisoners adjust to life outside of prison and reduce the potential of their continuing criminal behavior (recidivism). Waldo and Chirocos' initial comparisons of the work release and control conditions indicated few differences for many recidivism-related outcomes. In an effort to understand the lack of differences, the investigators computed correlations between prisoners' length of time in the program and various recidivism measures. The original hypothesis, that involvement in a work release program will reduce recidivism, was modified during the analysis, because a refined understanding was developing. A modified hypothe-

TABLE 5.3 Correlations Between Time in Work Release and Recidivism

Recidivism Measure	r	r^2	N
Arrests: number	−.02	.0004	157
Arrests: rate per month	−.07	.0049	157
Charges: number	.03	.0009	157
Charges: rate	−.05	.0025	157
Reincarceration: number	−.07	.0049	157
Reincarceration: felonies	−.08	.0064	157
Severity: total	.02	.0004	111
Severity: average	.01	.0001	111
Severity: most serious	−.07	.0049	111
Severity: sentence received	−.16	.0256	33

*SOURCE: Adapted from Table 5, Waldo & Chiricos (1977).

sis suggested that differences did not appear between treatment and control conditions because many of the prisoners were not given sufficient time in the program. Correlations were computed to test whether there was any relationship between time in the work release program and lowered recidivism.

Table 5.3 shows a selected set of these correlations (a correlation is symbolized by "r"). Unfortunately, the correlations are relatively small (often negative), indicating that levels of recidivism do not seem to be associated with time in the work release experience. One way of interpreting such correlations is to square the correlation coefficient (r^2). This calculation yields the percentage of variability predicted by the independent variable (called the coefficient of determination). The predicted variance is very small in the present example.

In order for a correlation to be considered high, it must be above .7 (Nunnally, 1978). Between .5 and .7, the correlation is considered moderate; below that, it is considered low. The importance of a particular value of a correlation will depend on a number of factors including practical importance and sample size. In some cases, a low interrelationship between variables will be practically, if not statistically, significant. (One wants to avoid a serious disease, no matter how small the probability of its occurrence.) It will also depend on the sample size. In some cases, low correlations generated by a large sample will be meaningful and will indicate a relationship, though small, which may still be important for large numbers of individuals.

One important *misuse* of correlational data is in indicating causal relationships. The fact that two events or characteristics occur simultaneously does not mean that one causes the other; in validity terms, there are a number of internal validity threats in such data. Even when it is clear that the relationship is not spurious (that is, there is a good reason to believe that the variables are related), it is incorrect to assume that a change in one variable has caused a change in another. Even where a causal relationship is suspected, correlational data may be misleading. For example, when the U.S. Congress originally passed legislation in 1939 to control the use of marijuana, it was based on correlational data. These data indicated that the crime rate in New Orleans, Denver, and several other cities had increased at the same time marijuana increased in usage (Whitebread & Bonnie, 1974). It was suggested that the use of marijuana caused the increase in criminal behavior and that, therefore, marijuana should be banned. However, when two variables are correlated, a number of interpretations are possible. The relationship between marijuana usage and crime may be a result of a third variable, such as an increased number of criminals (in turn, due to factors such as economic conditions, demographics) who are more likely to have access to substances such as marijuana. In effect, history may influence two social phenomena so that they are correlated, although they do not represent a causal relationship. Although later evidence did show the relationship between marijuana and crime to be erroneous, the law is still in force.

Correlations are the most frequently employed statistic for demonstrating the relationship between two variables. More complex correlational procedures are available for computing relationships between multiple independent and dependent variables. Multiple regression techniques are used to measure the relationship of multiple predictors (independent variables) to a single outcome measure (dependent variable). To what extent do race, socioeconomic status, and residence predict likelihood of drug abuse? Factor analysis is another widely used related technique that can aid one in determining associations between large numbers of variables. Each of these procedures is an extension of basic correlational methods and, for the most part, relies on linear models.

INFERENTIAL STATISTICS

A third category of statistics, usually more difficult to use than either descriptive or correlational procedures, is inferential statistics. Inferential statistics are used to answer such questions as, "Is the difference between mean X and mean Y large enough to consider it a reliable finding?" In statistical terms, finding a reliable difference is called a "significant effect." It is also a probabilistic statement as to the likelihood that the same effect will be obtained if the experiment is replicated. Such inferential statistics help us to decide how to interpret the obtained data.

Inferential statistics are based on the concept of probability. These statistics do not allow one to "prove" that a difference exists. Through inferential procedures, a given hypothesis is accepted as correct or rejected at a particular level of probability. Typically, we take a conservative position and test the null hypothesis that there is *no* difference between the treatment and control conditions. We hope to reject the null hypothesis and, to insure that we do not make an error in accepting a false finding, we usually choose a relatively low probability for the test. The probability of an error in accepting a null hypothesis is called the alpha level and is usually set at a value less than .05 (5 chances out of 100 that the result occurred by chance).

Two common statistical errors, called Type I and Type II, may be committed. A Type I error occurs when the null hypothesis is accepted when, in fact, there are real differences between the groups. If the megavitamin and placebo groups did result in different levels of schizophrenia symptomatology in the McGrath (1972) study, a conclusion of "no difference" would be a Type I error. A Type II error occurs when the null hypothesis is incorrectly rejected — when the conclusion is that there is a difference between groups and, in fact, no such difference exists. The alpha level specified determines a priori the likelihood that either of these errors will occur. A conservative alpha level (less than .05) is appropriate if the consequences of a Type I error are serious. So, for example, if megavitamins are actually essential to patients' well-being, but statistics indicated "no difference" and megavitamins were withheld as a matter of policy, the consequences could be serious.

Inferential statistics correct for the fact that data have been collected from a small sample of the population instead of the entire population. The assumption is that the sample, a randomly selected group of participants, reflects accurately the composition of the population. However, this is often not the case. In order to determine the extent of the bias (that is, the gap between the sample and the population), we make an estimate of the probability that our sample has provided data that differ from data that we would obtain if we studied a larger population.

A variety of inferential statistics can be used, depending on the nature of the data. Inferences about frequency data can be made through the application of statistics such as chi square (χ^2). To calculate chi square, one compares the obtained frequencies against what would be expected by chance. Using a table which has already calculated the probability of differences from chance for different size populations and categories of responses, a decision whether to accept or reject the null hypothesis can be made.

More common for analyzing social experiments than the use of chi square are statistics which permit comparisons of differences between means. True experiments involving the use of one or more comparison groups can often be analyzed through such comparisons. The simplest of these statistics is the t-test, which provides a way of testing differences between two means. The basis of a t-test is an "analysis of variance." In essence, one compares the variance within groups to the variance between groups. A reliable difference between groups should be substantially larger than the extent of variance

TABLE 5.4   Mean Recidivist Data and T-tests for Experimental and Control Groups*

Recidivism Measure	Experimentals		Controls		t-value	p
	M	N	M	N		
Arrests: number	2.22	188	2.25	93	.08	.93
Arrests: rate	.06	188	.06	93	.57	.57
Charges: number	3.45	188	3.23	93	.43	.67
Charges: rate	.10	188	.08	93	.89	.38
Reincarceration: number	.53	188	.55	93	−.18	.85
Reincarceration: felonies	.32	188	.23	93	1.30	.19
Severity: total	27.76	134	24.46	64	.36	.72
Severity: average	5.73	134	5.73	64	−.03	.98
Severity: most serious	6.28	134	6.28	65	.00	.99
Severity: sentence recieved	61.24	37	30.50	20	1.23	.22

*SOURCE: Adapted from Table 2, Waldo & Chiricos (1977)

within one group. Analysis of variance (ANOVA) procedures (there are a number of models which employ different assumptions) can be adapted to virtually any design where multiple group means must be compared.

Whatever inferential procedure is used, the result is a statement, for a given alpha level (p), that the null hypothesis has been accepted or rejected (p .05). To draw again from Waldo and Chiricos' prison work release experiment, a number of t-tests were conducted on their primary recidivism data. As shown in Table 5.4, all comparisons between the experimental work release and control (no work release) groups were nonsignificant. For each of the comparisons they made, the probability level was above .05. The null hypothesis (no difference) was accepted that treatment and control conditions did not significantly differ on recidivism. It suggests that the program developers should reconsider the treatment.

Multiple Independent and Dependent Variables

In practice, social experiments are not analyzed by computing single statistics or by choosing only one type of statistical procedure. Rather, an analysis strategy is developed which involves a variety of statistics and several analytic approaches. It may be necessary to develop a number of indices to describe the results and to test various hypotheses. In part, complexity is built into the analysis process because of the need to deal with multiple treatments (and multiple levels of each treatment), as well as the need to deal with multiple outcome measures. Although the logic of analysis is not changed when additional independent or dependent variables are

TABLE 5.5 Grand Total Means for *Sesame Street* Pretest and ANOVA Tests*

		Encouragement		
		Encouraged	Not Encouraged	
Site	Boston	97.9	87.3	92.6
	Phoenix	85.2	81.4	83.3
		91.6	84.3	

*Main effect for site: 92.6 vs 83.3; main effect for encouragement: 91.6 vs. 84.3; interaction (site x encouragement) = 89.7 vs 86.3 (diagonal comparison)

*SOURCE: From T. D. Cook et al., "Sesame Street" Revisited, Russell Sage Foundation, 1975, Table 5.1. Reprinted by permission of Basic Books, Inc.

present, the procedures for dealing with such complex experiments are, of course, somewhat different.

COMPLEX TREATMENTS

The prototype experiments cited for illustrative purposes have often been presented as ones in which single treatment and control groups are compared. "Real" experiments are usually not that simple. From the social problems and interventions we have described, it should be clear that most experiments involve the use of several independent variables or, at least, multiple levels of each treatment. Thus, we are often interested in how several variables (that is, components of an intervention) work together to produce effects and/or how different levels of a particular treatment influence recipients' behavior or social structures.

Factorial designs. Typically, multiple independent variable experiments are constructed using factorial designs. A factorial design is one in which all possible combinations of the treatment(s) are represented in the experiment. Thus, in the example from Cook et al.'s (1975) analyses of the *Sesame Street* evaluation presented earlier (see Table 5.2), two treatment variables are shown. The first is the site (either Boston or Phoenix) and the second is the treatment (encouraged-to-view or not-encouraged-to-view). The design is factorial because each combination of levels of each treatment is accounted for in the experiment.

Factorial designs permit the computation of several types of statistical comparisons: main effects and interactions. Main effects are the statistical test differences between groups of each independent variable (Boston vs. Phoenix comparisons test a main effect for site; encouraged vs. not encouraged comparisons test a main effect for treatment). Interaction effects are tests of the differences that result from the joint action of two or more independent variables (to be encouraged in Boston is more effective than to be encouraged in Phoenix). Although both types of effects are important and need to be examined, interaction effects have priority. If an interaction is significant, it makes little sense to discuss the independent action of the component variables (in statistical terminology, the interaction constrains the main effect). In any one analysis, tests of several main effects and interactions may be made. There will be a test for each independent variable and for every combination of independent variables.

In the example of the *Sesame Street* analyses, three effects would be examined for each out outcome measure. Main effects would be tested separately for site and encouragement; in addition, an interaction would be tested for site X encouragement. Main effects for site would indicate whether there were significant differences in the scores between Boston and Phoenix (for example, is the difference in the means large enough to be significant?); and main effects for encouragement would indicate whether there were significant differences between encouraged and not encouraged children. Interaction effects would also be tested to determine whether encouragement affected groups differently in the different cities. Table 5.5, using only the grand totals from Table 5.2, shows the means that would be tested. These are pretreatment means and their analysis says nothing about the effects of the treatment—the table is provided only for illustrative purposes.

If such an analysis were to be done, the actual statistical test would be a variant of the t-test procedure described earlier. Generically referred to as analysis of variance, a series of F statistics would be computed for each effect. F statistics are mathematically equivalent to t-statistics for two groups (they are the square root of t) and are interpreted in the same way. For each value, they are compared to a table (that is, a distribution of F ratios) which yields the probability of error in rejecting the null hypothesis.

Internal analysis. Not all independent variables represent actual "treatments." The different sites where the *Sesame Street* experiment was conducted represent a variable that may be important in the analysis, but is not a treatment in the same sense that encouragement-to-view is a treatment. Very often, however, such independent variables are included in an analysis in order to both examine central features of the hypothesized relationship and to discount alternative explanations for nontreatment influences. Such analyses, referred to as internal analyses, are conducted to tease out the influence of such variables. Internal analysis plays a significant role in analyzing a social experiment and in developing understandings of why particular outcomes were obtained.

An important function of such internal analyses is to uncover "masked" effects. Typically, a treatment interacts with other variables that naturally occur in the setting where the intervention is carried out, and these interactions make it difficult to see clearly the effects of the treatment. In essence, the treatment may affect only a particular subgroup in the program. Thus, for example, a remedial educational program may only be effective with students whose skills are poorest; a prison work-release program may only be effective for those who previously have had stable jobs. A treatment may be quite effective only for a portion of the population. Internal analyses are a tool for testing circumscribed impact.

To conduct an internal analysis, factors beyond those suggested by the hypotheses should be included. These factors may be characteristics of the participants in the program (preprogram achievement scores, age, race) or they may be characteristics of the situation (such as the sites where the experiment takes place). The additional factors may also take shape as variables which reflect how participants respond to the actual treatments. One might want to analyze the data by dividing the sample between those who attended all sessions of the program and those who missed one or more sessions. In each case, a function of the internal analysis would be to refine the analysis and, in effect, delimit the external validity for the experiment. One would be able to determine those populations and settings to which the results of the experiment can be expected to generalize.

While internal analyses permit one to take into account multiple causal factors, they can easily become unwieldy. This represents a problem. An unlimited number of factors could conceivably be used for an internal analysis, but using a factorial approach, one probably cannot analyze more than five factors. If there are more factors, it is almost impossible to interpret the meaning of interactions. Instead, correlational analyses are often performed on such data, either to identify possible variables for conducting a factorial internal analysis or to conduct an analysis that can be used directly in making inferences. An advantage of this use of correlational statistics is that it permits the use of continuous variables. Instead of having to divide subjects into two or more groups, actual scores can be used. Although it sometimes makes sense to divide subjects into groups based on what type of setting they are in (such as Boston or Phoenix), often it is more meaningful to score subjects on a continuous dimension (such as community income) and use this as the variable for examining an interaction with the treatment.

In order to use correlations to identify possible factors for an internal analysis of variance, simple procedures, such as the computation of correlation matrices, may be all that are necessary. Variables, thought to have an effect on the outcome of the experiment, are often correlated with the outcome measures. Where large correlations are obtained, further analyses can be done to understand the particular effects of these variables; variables that interact with outcome measures in nonlinear ways may have a deceptively low correlation value. In this case, one should perform an internal analysis using a correlation matrix.

In the case where one wants to examine the joint effect of additional factors, procedures such as multiple regression can be used to develop predictions of the treatment effects, adjusted by the variability predicted by these additional variables. There are also procedures available for combining correlational analysis with analysis of variance. These procedures, called analysis of covariance, are often used when preprogram factors are thought to be related to the treatment outcome. If one or more of these factors shows a large correlation with an outcome measure, one can statistically adjust outcome scores to take account of (eliminate) such preexisting differences. Such covariates, though not factors of central interest, help to identify the true effects of the treatment.

Summary. Whatever technique(s) are used, the researchers' effort is directed to taking account in the analysis of the multiple independent variables of those affecting the outcome of the experiment. Some of these variables might be central to the design of the program and thus, have been incorporated into the research design; others are important to the outcome and can be controlled for, not by the design, but statistically. Any analytical procedure should help explain the outcomes of the experiment. Rarely are experiments successful or unsuccessful; rather, the experimental treatment will have positive effect in some circumstances and no effect or a negative effect in others. Understanding these circumstances is central to analysis and to the utilization of the results of an experiment.

MULTIPLE DEPENDENT VARIABLES

It is rare that an experiment can be analyzed by examining a single dependent variable. Typically, a fairly wide set of data is collected, with various types of measures and a number of content areas assessed. The analysis problem is twofold; to summarize this information with as little distortion as possible, and to make the information useful for decision-making. This is difficult to achieve because the amount of information collected in a social experiment is often so large. Important outcomes have to be carefully "culled" from the "sea" of data. A variety of analysis procedures are available for dealing with this multiple dependent variable problem.

Scales. Perhaps the most straightforward way of analyzing multiple measures is to form scales based on groups of items. When a set of questions can be conceptualized as measuring a common theme and, in particular, when a common format for questions is utilized, responses can be combined in scale form prior to analysis. If a common format is used, as is frequently the case with quantitative items, the simplest way to form a scale is to sum across items. This is usually reasonable if the items are conceptually related and have similar variances. More sophisticated ways of forming scales involve standardizing each item's score by dividing each score by the SD.

A more complex way of forming scales would be to employ a factor analysis (Kerlinger, 1973). Factor analysis uses correlational techniques to determine which items are associated with other items. It statistically suggests factors (that is, conceptual dimensions) that are common in the data and can aid in organizing the information. There are several ways to conduct factor analyses and several ways to use the results of a factor analysis. One is to select one or more items from each dimension (based on factor loadings) as representative of that dimension. Another method, made possible by the availability of computer programs, involves using all items and summing weighted item scores (called factor scores). The latter method gives a more precise score for each dimension, and thus sacrifices less information.

Analysis of variance. In the earlier description of factorial analyses of variance, the issue of multiple dependent variables was addressed. In the description of the analysis of pretest scores in the *Sesame Street* experiment, we described a *series* of analyses of variance (ANOVA). These are referred to as univariate ANOVAS. Although univariate ANOVAS represent a straightforward way of analyzing data, they yield a tremendous amount of information (a test for each dependent measure). Much of this information, however, is difficult to interpret because different variables are often affected by treatments in slightly different ways.

When a series of dependent variables has been used, ANOVAS can be conducted in several ways. As described above, one can merely sum the items and treat the resulting variable as if it were a univariate response. Two other procedures can also be employed. One procedure, repeated treatments ANOVA, is used to analyze a set of similar items responded to by the same individuals. This approach offers advantages when data are collected in an experiment over time, as respondents answer the same question at several intervals. In essence, a repeated treatments ANOVA considers a set of items as a factor. The analysis yields both a main effect test (Is there a significant difference between the items?), and tests interaction effects with the actual treatment factors. The logic in this case is similar to that of other factorial designs with one exception: a special-error term is employed to test the repeated treatment effect.

Another method of analyzing multiple dependent variables is multivariate analysis of variance. Here, the logic is more complex than repeated treatments. MANOVA (Bock, 1975) takes a set of items, and using correlational techniques combines the unique contribution of each item to form an overall score. This procedure creates a simple significance test which will indicate the reliability of the difference between factors across all items in the set. If significant effects are obtained, it is usually necessary to do subsequent univariate analyses of the item in order to understand specific effects.

SUMMARY

Whichever techniques are used, the objective is always the same: to make data concise and understandable without distorting their meaning. Depending on the nature of data—principally how many conceptual dimensions are represented and whether these dimensions are obvious or not—various statistical procedures are available. Important in a social experiment, one must accept complexity (in terms of a number of variables) and adopt analysis strategies which can elucidate their meaning.

Statistical Conclusion Validity

In this brief description of major types of statistics and analysis problems, the improper use of statistical techniques has been implied. A little knowledge can be dangerous, goes the familiar saying. Misinterpreting analysis of social experiments is very easy. Perhaps the best guard against such a problem is to know which statistics are available and what assumptions underlie the use of each. If you were actually going to conduct a social experiment, you would need to know more about these assumptions and how they affect analyses.

In general, the issue of using statistics correctly in social experiments can again be viewed within a validity framework. The validity question is whether one is justified in interpreting the results of an experiment as indicating a reliable and valid relationship between the treatment and outcomes. Are the specifications of the conditions clear or unclear under which that relationship can be obtained? Is the treatment-outcome relationship vague or sharply delineated? It might seem that the most important issue in social experimentation is to establish that treatments do, in fact, affect outcomes. Equally important is guarding against accepting such relationships when they do not actually exist. These issues, related to the interpretation of social experiments based on the analysis of findings, concern statistical conclusion validity (see Cook & Campbell, 1979).

Statistical conclusion validity involves the sensitivity of statistical tests, the reasonableness of statements about cause and effect, and the strength of cause-effect relationships. Threats to the validity of inferences occur in many ways and a number of strategies are available for improving such validity. Some of these are identified by Cook and Campbell (1979) and described below.

Sensitivity. Each statistical technique brings with it particular characteristics and abilities to detect differences, depending on sample sizes and other features of the data. If a test is used that has low power (that is, poor sensitivity), it may be impossible to detect differences in a given sample. Unless effects are extremely strong (unlikely with many social interventions), actual cause-effect relationships will not be indicated by the analysis. The null hypothesis will be accepted, even though it should have been rejected. This type of error can usually be avoided by increasing the number of participants in the experiment and by increasing alpha level.

In order to know what sample size is adequate and what effect the alpha level will have on inferences, a number of techniques are available to determine the power of a statistical test (see Cohen, 1975). Such analyses allow one to determine (for particular effect sizes) how many respondents and what alpha level will be necessary. The investigator must decide, however, what size effect (difference between treatment and control group) will be required.

Multiple comparisons. One common pitfall in social experimentation is known as the "fishing expedition." With data collected from multiple

items, it can be assumed (by chance) that an analysis will yield some proportion of significant differences (5 out of 100 comparisons). Even when such
differences do not actually exist, they may occur by chance. In social experiments where several hundred different measures are employed, a small
percentage should, by chance, be significantly different, although no actual
difference exists.

There are ways this problem can be avoided. One is to specify a priori,
through hypotheses, which effect is to be explored in the analysis. This will
not deal directly with the validity threat; it does make it less likely that an
error will be made by assuming a difference exists when, in fact, it does not.
A second strategy involves modifying the analysis procedures so that the
alpha level is adjusted to account for the number of comparisons. The alpha
level is lowered as more comparisons are made. This can be done informally
(by decreasing alpha), or more formally by procedures which precisely
adjust alpha by the number of comparisons (known as the Scheffé test). A
third strategy that is usually more practical (because alpha level adjustments
make the analysis conservative) is to form scales. As was described earlier in
the discussion of multiple dependent measures, this results in fewer statistical tests actually being performed.

Reducing variability. One reason that statistical inference seems so difficult is the "noise" in most outcome data collected as part of social experiments. Outcome measures have built-in variability or "noise." Treatments
are implemented in different ways, and both settings and individuals are
usually heterogenous. Such uncontrollable instabilities, which are unrelated
to actual treatment, add to the difficulty of clearly recognizing treatment
effects. Improved statistical conclusion validity can be accomplished by
reducing the variability from these sources. Selecting a more precisely ho-
mogeneous participant group is one way. Such a choice may be inconsistent
with the goals of the experiment. It is then necessary to weigh carefully
improved statistical conclusion validity against tradeoffs with other types of
validity.

In the case of outcome measure variability, it is fortunately possible to
reduce variability without adversely affecting other aspects of validity. As
described in Chapter 4, a great deal is known about assessing the reliability
of measuring instruments. Given the chance to pretest an instrument and use
this information to revise the measuring tool, highly reliable instruments can
be developed. The tradeoff here may be between using an instrument developed and tested for reliability and applying a new test which, though tailored
to the experiment, may be less reliable (and introduce more random variation to the scores). This thinking applies also when interviews and observations are concluded. The consistency with which interviewers/observers
interpret or react to responses can importantly affect the variability in the

data. Standardized measurement reduces variability and therefore facilitates more valid inferences.

A second cause of unreliability results from the different ways in which treatments are implemented (Boruch & Gomez, 1977). Although attempts to standardize treatments may go against the needs of a program, they reduce the chance that the treatment will show no difference. If standardization is not possible, more sites must be used and outcome measures with known reliability should be employed. Manipulation checks, those items which indicate how accurately the treatment was implemented and perceived, should be included, if at all possible, in the experiment and then carefully analyzed.

A final variability problem is related to settings and individuals. This issue is closely related to external validity. In order to establish external validity, one must expose the treatment in various settings and with a heterogeneous group of individuals. The use of such heterogeneity in settings/populations, however, makes it more difficult to develop inferences from the data. Because each setting/population has unique characteristics, it alters scores, usually in a nonsystematic way. On the other hand, if done systematically, some form of an internal analysis would be necessary. There really is no good solution to the problem other than reducing variability in other areas and, if necessary, restricting the experiment to particular settings/populations.

Levels of Analyses

Up to this point, the focus has been on primary analyses, the initial analysis of a set of experimental results. Another category of data analysis is "secondary analysis" (Glass, 1976; Glass, McGaw & Smith, 1981) and refers to analyses conducted subsequent to the initial assessment of results. Secondary analyses provide an opportunity to scrutinize the interpretation of experimental results. A third category of analysis is referred to as meta-analysis. According to Glass, meta-analysis involves the rigorous statistical assessment of a set of individual experiments. It is a procedure for systematically developing inferences across investigations and represents a technically sophisticated procedure for assessing a particular research literature.

SECONDARY ANALYSIS

Secondary analysis provides important protection against the improper use of statistical and analytic techniques (Boruch & Wortman, 1978; Cook & Gruder, 1978). The analysis of data from social experiments by investigators not connected with the initial study guards against particular biases affecting how such data are interpreted. Subsequent analyses may suggest different hypotheses, use different methods, and even detect errors in data collection or statistical computation.

Because social experiments have much greater policy relevance than most social research, the need for secondary analysis and its acceptability will increase. There have been too few examples of this work, owing to difficulties in making data of earlier studies available for analysis by new investigators. The Cook et al. (1975) analysis of the original *Sesame Street* experiment provides an interesting example of secondary analysis. The *Sesame Street* data was originally collected as part of an evaluation study (Ball & Bogatz, 1971). Results indicated very positive learning effects on children who watched the show. Cook et al.'s reanalysis, however, found those conclusions to be not quite as supportable. Although the basic finding of an improvement in certain skills was not refuted, Cook et al. found that it was not the program, per se, but the involvement of parents in watching the show with their children that was responsible for effects, at least among disadvantaged children. This finding was based on careful analysis of experimental groups. Cook et al.'s secondary analysis did not uncover serious statistical problems. Rather, their new analysis generated a reinterpretation of the original data.

Secondary analysis, while an obvious safeguard to the misapplication of analysis procedures, is not a simple undertaking (Boruch & Wortman, 1978). In some cases, a data base may be too poorly maintained to be usable by an outside group or may contain missing or uninterpretable information. In other cases, researchers and program officials may be wary (often justifiably) of the motives of reanalyzers and reluctant to release the data. Fortunately, as standards for analysis become better established (Robbin, 1978), resistance may decrease and more secondary analyses may become possible.

META-ANALYSIS

Meta-analysis actually refers to many procedures. Included are simple frequency counts of the results of several studies and techniques that involve the combining of standardized outcome scores from a few or many different experiments (see Glass, 1976; Glass, McGaw & Smith, 1981; Pillemer & Light, 1980; Rosenthal, 1978). The goal of meta-analysis is to synthesize systematically the results of multiple experiments.

Score-keeping. Score-keeping describes a crude form of meta-analysis. In essence, it organizes a body of literature according to prespecified criteria. Score-keeping usually involves the selection of a particular sample of studies, coding some aspects of their design and/or conceptual framework and classifying the observed outcome(s). Such analyses systematically structure the review of independent sets of data.

The score-keeping method is illustrated by an analysis of controlled studies of psychotherapy conducted by Luborsky, Singer and Luborsky (1975). Each of the studies Luborsky et al. assessed was categorized on a number of dimensions. The central coding variable was research quality, which they determined on the basis of twelve criteria. These included an assessment of each study's method for assigning subjects to comparison groups, procedures for dealing with premature treatment termination, and the adequacy of the sample. Each study was graded on a five-point scale. Reviewers then categorized results as to whether there were significantly better effects for the treatment group (+), the comparison group (−), or no differences between the groups (0). Their sampling procedure identified 33 studies, of which 20 yielded treatment groups which were significantly better than control groups and 13 groups in which no difference was found. The reviewers found no studies in which control groups were significantly better than psychotherapy groups.

Although no statistical tests were employed and the number of studies reviewed was small, the systematic nature of the analysis made it more definitive than other efforts directed toward assessing the same experimental literature. The strength of score-keeping analysis centers on two issues: precise identification of populations of studies to be sampled, and the coding of substantive and methodological aspects of the study according to clearly defined procedures. They are particularly helpful in identifying relationships between methods and outcomes. Score-keeping avoids problems of reviews which only describe research selectively or pay attention to only certain aspects of a study.

Effect sizes. A second meta-analytic technique represents a sophisticated statistical approach to syntheses. Effect size analyses incorporate the actual size of observed effects and permit the determination, across a set of studies, of the magnitude of treatment impact. ANOVAs typically ignore both the size and direction of effects, yielding only a global probability of a significant difference. Effect size analyses are particularly useful for assessing treatments where large numbers of studies exist and where findings across studies appear to have great variability. As used by Glass (1978), it requires available comparison groups and original research reports containing statistical information as to group means and standard deviations.

Effect sizes are determined by the difference between the mean of treatment groups and the mean of comparison groups, divided by the standard deviation of comparison groups. This procedure converts the average effect of each dependent measure into a standard score, which can be compared on the same scale to other scores. If a treatment is effective, this number is positive; if the treatment is inefficacious, the outcome score is negative— assuming that positive outcomes are desired. By making assumptions about the skewness of experimental and control group scores within each study and the distribution of effect sizes across a large number of studies, one can convert effect sizes into percentile ranks and develop inferences about the probable effects of a treatment.

A good example of the use of effect sizes to summarize analyses of social experiments is a particular analysis of psychotherapy experiments (Smith, Glass & Miller, 1980; Smith & Glass, 1977). Smith et al.'s approach provides an interesting contrast to Luborsky et al. The former included within their analysis all available control group studies of the effectiveness of any form of psychotherapy as well as unpublished studies of psychotherapy. By coding an extensive number of variables for each study, including characteristics of therapist and patient, methodological criteria about the nature of patient assignment to condition (such as random vs. matching), experimental mortality, and internal validity, Smith et al. calculated effect size scores for each principal dependent measure. They then coded the validity of the outcome measures.

Smith et al. found that the average difference between scores of the groups receiving psychotherapy and the control groups was .85 standard deviation units. Assuming the normal distribution of effect size scores, this average standard score can be translated to indicate that a typical person who receives psychotherapy is better off than 80 percent of the persons who do not. Smith et al. also conducted a number of analyses to determine whether methodology actually made a difference in outcome and whether different therapies (or other factors) were differentially efficacious. Uncovering few methodological differences, it appeared to Smith et al. that outcomes were not related to the use of randomized control groups (although it should be recognized that all of their sample studies used comparison groups and were generally high in internal validity.)

Some have criticized Smith and Glass, claiming that meta-analysis lumps together too many incomparable elements and obfuscates true findings (such as Eysenck, 1978). The strength of the effect size technique, however, is that it provides a common metric that permits analysis of methodological and substantive differences across studies. Thus, rather than confusing incomparable pieces of evidence, it seems to identify similarities and differences among a group of studies. What is problematic about such meta-analysis, however, is that the findings are heavily dependent upon which subset of literature is sampled. Smith et al. had sampled a well-designed group of studies. It is not possible to ascertain biases included in this sample and whether only certain types of therapies were assessed using control group designs (see Saxe, 1980). A broader analysis of psychotherapy research might yield different conclusions than those of Smith et al.

Other meta-analytic techniques. Other methods exist for statistically combining the results of independent studies (Cook & Leviton, 1980; Leviton & Cook, 1981; Pillemer & Light, 1980; Rosenthal, 1978). The effect size method described above actually incorporates several different procedures. Of these methods, most important are the comparison of treatments and the investigation of interactions between characteristics of a study and outcome. Some of these can be employed even when effect scores are not computed. Other statistical methods involve the combining of probability values from various studies.

Rosenthal (1978) describes a number of procedures for combining probabilities which range from adding observed probability (p) levels across different studies to adding weighted standardized (z) scores. These methods permit the testing of mean probability values and allow one to indicate whether significant effects are obtained across a set of studies. The problem in using probability values is that by not taking into account the magnitude of effects, the number of participants per study influences whether significant overall differences are obtained.

Another synthesis procedure involves aggregation across several studies. This procedure (called blocking by Rosenthal) is feasible only sometimes. Its use requires that means, sample sizes, and mean squares for each study be available. These data can then be combined into an overall analysis of variance in which each study is treated as a blocking variable. In order to minimize data heterogeneity, outcome measures can be standardized to reflect common scale units. Although this procedure provides a useful method of research synthesis, it can easily become unwieldy with large numbers of studies and is probably important only when a small number of studies with low n's have been conducted. It is most useful when only a few similar experiments have been conducted.

Conclusion

The chapter has delineated some of the central analysis issues faced by social experimenters, including those techniques used in integrating results across studies. The reader is strongly cautioned that this review has been a cursory one, touching briefly on selected analysis problems. Our goal has been to make you a better consumer of statistical analyses. We have sought to demystify the procedures involved, although statistical analysis is obviously a complex process. This review of analysis issues does not provide the tools to conduct actual analyses. It should, however, permit readers to understand better the development of inferences from social experiments and the use of statistical tools as part of that process.

It should be obvious that making use of the results of social experiments is not possible without proper analysis. Proper analysis, if definable in an absolute sense, does not come about easily. Social experiments must be designed from the beginning to allow for appropriate analysis, and for scrutiny after the fact to make sure the first interpretation of findings was adequate. Analysis is hence a multistage process that, as will be described in the next section, requires the joint efforts of social researchers and program developers.

SECTION III

SOCIAL EXPERIMENTS: PRACTICE

CHAPTER 6

THE VARIETIES OF PRACTICE

*Experiment[ation] is the marriage of
reason and experience.*

Abraham Kaplan, *The Conduct of Inquiry*

Although many features of the application of social science parallel the way current social policy is formulated, there are some important differences. The most important of these differences is, perhaps, the relationship necessary between social scientists and social planners. The next several chapters focus on a description and an analysis of ways the social scientific community can collaborate with those responsible for social policy in order to understand and develop improved social interventions. The goal will be to demonstrate how the principles and logic of science can be translated into practice. The principles of design, measurement, and analysis described in the earlier chapters will be shown as they are tempered in the study of actual problems.

It is hoped that readers, at this point, have a fairly good idea how social experimentation *should* be conducted, but it is probably still unclear how social experiments actually are carried out. There is a vast difference between proposing an experiment to study an intervention and its actual implementation. The practical application of social science follows directly from the earlier chapters' discussion of principles, but there are a number of additional complicating factors. One underlying difficulty is that social science is represented by principles rather than rules, and these principles can be applied in various ways depending on the problem and the host of factors unique to each situation. In the present chapter, we discuss the different contexts in which social experiments take place, the activities of social scientists, and the levels on which social policy is developed. Readers are provided a framework for the use and application of social science principles to social policy problems. A description of the nature of policy

development and ways that social interventions are organized for research
purposes are also covered. A central element of this analysis is the interaction necessary between social scientists and social policy makers. Such
interaction differentiates social experimentation from other forms of research. Interaction is essential to the effective development of social policy
and the utilization of the social science perspective.

Although some take for granted that social scientists and social policy
makers can work together, this collaboration will not necessarily be effective. There are opportunities for and dilemmas in collaboration which have
implications for the conduct of social experimentation. The discussion here
will emphasize how such collaboration can be improved. In this chapter, a
preview of the next chapters is also included. These later chapters describe in
greater detail the practice of social experimentation and the actual conduct of
intervention research studies.

Contexts of Social Experimentation

In earlier chapters, a variety of examples were used to illustrate the
principles of social experimentation. While the examples highlighted specific technical issues, they also illustrated the applicability of social experimentation to different types of problems and social interventions. Because
of the emphasis on methodology, however, no effort was made to be precise
about the differences among applications of social experimentation. In particular, no distinctions have been made between the various settings in which
social experiments are conducted.

These settings cut across the types of problems and interventions for
which social experiments are conducted and affect both the design and
utilization of the experiment. A basic though crude distinction can be made
between federal and local programs. Many social experiments described so
far have been federal programs, studies of programs initiated by the federal
government *and* / or implemented as a part of an attempt to develop national
policy (such as Head Start, the Negative Income Tax Experiment). In some
cases, federal projects were congressionally mandated, although federal
monies were supplied to states, cities, and other agencies to carry out the
programs. In other cases, federal projects were designed by organizations
wholly outside the government, with federal funds committed to their design, implementation, and analysis. Each of these programs can be considered a federal program because the outcomes have a direct impact on national policy. It is likely that, at least in the early part of the 1980s, fewer of
these programs will be federally sponsored.

Other social experiments may be better characterized as local programs.
Although federal funds may be utilized, the projects are designed to provide

a local agency or community with specific information or to test theoretical ideas relevant to a social problem. They may also influence federal policy, but this is not the reason for which they were originally designed.

There is a great deal of variation in how such studies are implemented and utilized. Both within and across federal and local programs, the distinction between the two is useful in illustrating the varieties of social experimentation practice, and also suggests the complex relationship between social experimentation and social policy.

FEDERAL PROGRAMS

The development of social policy is a complex process in a society as large and multifaceted as that of the United States. Nevertheless, understanding the elements involved in the formulation of social policy is crucial to determining where and how social experimentation "fits." In this cursory review, we will use a somewhat simplified model of how programs are developed.

Federal programs almost always react to accumulated and complicated sets of pressures and processes. Most ideas for social programs begin at some local level, which, from the outset, suggests that our basic distinction between local and national programs may be paradoxical. In order for any new social policy to be implemented, a constituency must exist. This helps the incipient idea to receive some sort of public response, which may be support or dissent, and is likely to be both.

At the federal level, within the United States, three spheres of policy development can be identified. First, of course, the U.S. Congress holds the basic responsibility for representing public interests, for deciding which particular social policies are to be implemented as priorities, and how these policies are to be formulated (Fiorina, 1977; Hammond & Fox, 1977). For example, community mental health centers were instituted in response to a need for local mental health services which could reduce the long-standing reliance on inpatient facilities.

Second, the executive branch of the government plays a critical role in designing, advocating, and implementing particular policies. Each cabinet-level administration department which reports to the President (such as the Department of Health and Human Services) along with numerous independent agencies not attached to a department (for example, Action/Peace Corps) analyzes legislative proposals and often develops legislation on behalf of the administration. After legislation has been enacted (and whether or not the administration's form of the legislation has been accepted), an executive agency is responsible for administering the policy.

The third sphere involves the individuals and groups responsible for carrying out social policy and translating it into program administration.

Although executive agencies typically write guidelines for programs and control funding, local government agencies, along with nongovernmental groups, implement these policies. Those at the local level are given some latitude (exactly how much often becomes a matter of dispute) to tailor the federal programs to their needs.

While the obvious contributors to federal policy development are in Congress, in the executive branch, or affiliated with program implementation, many "behind the scenes" individuals, including lobbyists, advocates, and civic/community based individuals, contribute to the formulation and implementation of public policy. Other branches of government and interest groups may also contribute significantly to the development of national social policy, although their input may not be as direct as those of the congressional and executive agencies. For example, the judicial system represents a coequal branch of government; however, its responsibility in terms of social policy is usually as mediator, not idea-initiator (Saks & Hastie, 1970). While there are some significant examples of how the courts have influenced federal policy, such as school desegregation (Abrams, 1975; Coleman, 1976; Pettigrew & Green, 1976), they only become involved once the issues reach a point of dispute. The general public, as well as special interest groups, generate many ideas for social programs. Often these ideas are neglected, at other times, however, public concerns do play an important role in social policy development. It is difficult to assess the conditions under which the public influences policy, since they may take many forms. Groups ranging from professional lobbying groups to groups of concerned citizens (Ralph Nader's Public Interest Research Group, women's organizations, coalitions of Vietnam Veterans) make frequent contact with their governmental officials. Their impact is difficult to calculate. Local level social experiments are often conducted to legitimate (to the federal government) the need for change and/or program development for particular social problems. Citizen groups, which lack large numbers of supporters or other resources, may influence policy by being able to provide evidence of the validity of their ideas. The documented impact of a social program could strengthen one's position in influencing public policy.

Social research as a vehicle for influencing social policy has impact on all levels. First, at the congressional level, legislation is often based upon findings from social research (including true experiments) and mandates that social programs be researched once implemented (U.S. Senate Committee on Human Resources, 1978). Second, at the administration level, there are distinct roles for social research. The administration needs to be able to demonstrate that its programs are effective, and to assess competing program ideas (Wholey et al., 1970). To do both, various types of social experiments are carried out. Third, at the actual implementation level, information needs to be collected confirming the impact of particular programs.

Systematic social research, while not necessarily true social experimentation, is necessary to serve these information needs.

Perhaps the ways in which social experimentation influences social policy can best be illustrated by describing two prominent programs that have been extensively researched. Community mental health centers and income maintenance programs illustrate two very different approaches to social experimentation. Given the differences in approach, it is particularly interesting to examine their relationship to the development of federal policy.

Community Mental Health Centers. A revolution has taken place during the past 20 years with respect to mental health services and treatment. During the past decade, a large-scale effort has successfully deinstitutionalized thousands of mental patients and provided mental health treatment in community settings. This program has also made mental health services available to a wider range of individuals than previously (President's Committee on Mental Health, 1978). A major impetus for this change was legislation initiated in the early 1960s which allocated federal monies for the development of community mental health centers.

The legislation authorizing community mental health centers (CMHCs) can be directly traced to a five-year study initiated in 1958 under the sponsorship of the Congressional Joint Commission on Mental Health and Illness (Macht, 1976). The Commission's final report, submitted in 1962, was based on the analysis of research studies as well as the expertise of its members. This report described the isolated, overcrowded conditions and antiquated facilities in the country's public psychiatric hospitals. Based on the Commission's report, bills were introduced in 1963 in both the U.S. Senate and House of Representatives. During that year, public hearings were held to examine the legislation, with testimony provided by members of the administration, as well as by representatives of mental health organizations and the public. As a result, in 1963, preliminary authorization for the construction and development of community mental health centers to be run by indigenous organizations was provided. A 1965 amendment to the Community Mental Services Act provided funds for professional and paraprofessional support staffing these centers.

From the time of the initial authorizing legislation until 1977, 60 community mental health centers (CMHCs) were established throughout the United States, providing access to mental health services for approximately 87 million individuals (U.S. Senate, 1977). During this period, the nation's psychiatric hospital population was reduced by 50 percent. It is not clear, however, how these two events—the reduction in psychiatric hospital population and the passage of the community Mental Health Services Act—are related. Various other changes, including the widespread use of psychoactive drugs, may be responsible. Although CMHCs were developed in response to substantial data indicating the failure of the old institutionalization approach—they seemed like the logical extension of some developing ideas in mental health field—the efficacy of the community mental health approach continues to be a source of debate.

Legislators who conceived of CMHCs were not unaware of the need for data about their impact. The initial legislation authorized community mental health centers to conduct evaluative studies of their programs. Later amendments to the Act made the evaluation of funded CMHCs a requirement (Windle & Woy, 1977). CMHCs since 1975 have been required to spend specific portions of their federal funds for evaluative research. Unlike some other federal programs in which evaluation is mandated, for CMHCs the allocations are determined almost entirely at the local level. While federal level administrators in the National Institute of Mental Health earmarked funds for national data collection about program effectiveness, the bulk of these monies is allocated to individual centers which examine their treatment services based on their own impressions of what aspects are important to research.

Although some have complained that this approach has not produced the type of data necessary for making decisions about continued funding of Community Mental Health Centers, others have argued that this outcome is inappropriate. Mental health treatment remains an unsure science, according to this view, and the best use of research is to identify what is being done, not to judge its effectiveness. The best approach to treatment cannot, as yet, be identified from research. Therefore, local level evaluation, which can provide descriptive feedback to the administrators of individual centers and to policy makers, is the most useful type of research.

The case of community mental health centers is an interesting example of the potential use of social research in the determining of social policy. In this case, social research has been utilized both to demonstrate the need for a "new" community-based mental health approach, and to determine the relative efficacy of the resulting community mental health programs. Yet the overall use of social research to understand the impact of CMHCs has, for the most part, been post hoc and nonrigorous. Data are not systematically collected from comparison groups and the research is generally initiated as an appendage to local programs. Although there have been a number of validity problems, much of the descriptive data collected has been useful and influential in developing mental health policy.

Negative Income Tax Experiment. A rigorous application of social experimentation on the federal level is represented by the New Jersey-Pennsylvania Negative Income Tax Experiment (Kershaw, 1972; Rossi & Lyall, 1976). This illustration differs from the CMHC example in several ways: The negative tax experiment was designed as a *test* of a possible national policy, and was carried out as a true experiment, with participants randomly assigned to income conditions. In addition, the program did not last very long in contrast to CMHCs, many of which still operate with diminished federal support or local funds. The true experimental approach used in the negative income tax test provided a more clear-cut assessment of feasibility than the "optional" research of CMHCs.

The Negative Income Tax Experiment (NIT) developed out of the "War on Poverty" programs implemented during the 1960s. Formally called the "New Jersey Graduated Work Incentive Experiment," the study was designed to test an alternative to the current welfare system: a negative income tax (that is, a payment instead of a subsidy program). The program was intended to provide each person/family with a guaranteed income. Should participants earn incomes raising their total earnings above the guarantee, that income would be taxed at progressively higher rates.

A number of potential advantages to the guaranteed income program have been cited (see Rossi & Lyall, 1976). It is offered as a possible solution to the unmanageable and degrading welfare systems in which the poor are placed in positions where they must convince the welfare bureaucracy that they deserve a "dole." The system also provides incentives for recipients to work, assuming jobs are made available. Another basic program assumption is that poverty is neither a disease nor a permanent state; rather, it is an economic condition that could be remedied by appropriate economic adjustments.

The idea for the experiment initially came from the Office of Economic Opportunity (OEO), which was established as the lead agency to develop anti-poverty programs. While some in OEO wanted to propose the program as legislation (like the CMHCs), it was regarded as politically unsupportable. Since the criterion for entry into the program was not inability to work, but rather criteria based on economic variables, it was thought that there would be serious political objections.

While the NIT proposal did not seem to have an adequate enough basis to be put forth as a legislative initiative (of course, it also represents an ideological shift which would be opposed by some regardless of "data"), it was seen as worthy of a test. In 1968, a decision was made to implement the proposal on a limited basis and to use the trial as an opportunity to assess it as a model for a change in welfare legislation. While this too required authorizing legislation, it was accomplished as part of legislation authorizing other research efforts.

OEO contracted with several groups of economists and social scientists, providing money for the test program (for guaranteed incomes for program participants) and for an analysis of the experiment. Several models were proposed. As the study design finally emerged, more than 1000 families were enrolled and randomly assigned to a variety of income maintenance plans. These plans varied in the levels of guaranteed income provided (50 percent to 100 percent of the then-current estimate of the poverty level) and the amount of tax applied to the income earned above the guaranteed level

(30 percent to 70 percent). The experiment, conducted in urban and suburban areas of New Jersey and Pennsylvania, ended in 1972 after three years of implementation and data collection.

While the results of the NIT are complex and not easily summarized, a clear outcome was that guaranteed income did *not* reduce incentives to work. Experimental participants did spend more time seeking jobs than did control participants. More important than the study results was the fact that NIT informed the developing national debate about reforms to the welfare system. The study received widespread congressional attention (Boeckmann, 1973), although its impact on policy was mixed. The study was also widely discussed within the then-existing Department of Health, Education and Welfare (Mahoney & Mahoney, 1975) and led to subsequent experiments. The later studies have attempted to assess the robustness of the conclusions of the NIT experiment and to test its generalizability (see review by Lynn, 1978). NIT is also viewed as the prototype experiment for testing new ideas about federal policy; this was responsible for stimulating much recent interest in social experimentation (Rossi & Lyall, 1976).

LOCAL PROGRAMS

In contrast to federal programs, many social experiments are carried out in purely local contexts. These tend to be conducted on a relatively smaller scale and are probably far more numerous than experimental interventions conducted to test national policy. The involvement of the federal government in social experimentation is a recent phenomenon, and may also have a short-lived history. Social problems, until very recently, were not regarded as the central concern of the federal government. If tests of programs occurred, they were sponsored by other agencies (Suchman, 1967). Many situations occur in which local policy issues are not well understood and methods of social experimentation are used (often unwittingly) to test new solutions to unclear issues. Schools, for example, regularly change their curriculum—back to basics, new math, experimenting with sex education, and so on. School administrators are very concerned about understanding the effects of these changes; consequently, schools have had a long tradition of systematically developing and testing new educational ideas. In much the same way, social service organizations are constantly modifying their procedures and testing the effects of the changes. Local social experiments are characteristically treatments that are more specific to the community than to national policy. Such treatments are usually offered to small groups of program participants.

Local experiments are sometimes easier to conduct than national studies. They do not necessarily involve major shifts in political policy, nor do they require the development of a supporting constituency. They may also not require large numbers of participants and be far less complex and expensive to conduct. Local experiments may be problematic, though, and difficult to implement if samples are small and local conditions are difficult to influence. This may result in a difficulty in obtaining control groups, and/or randomized samples. Implementing local social experiments can be made difficult simply because people are unfamiliar with social experimentation, or lack the resources and available technical expertise to develop an adequate experimental design. Local program administrators are typically not concerned with collecting generalizable data and, accordingly, often see good research design as irrelevant. This occurs when local programs are funded to respond to limited local needs rather than to test theoretical notions or generate information relevant to other sites. Yet local programs are often designed as prototypes to provide generalized data and to test theoretical hypotheses. The following examples illustrate the kinds of social experiments conducted at the local level, but designed to assess broader questions.

Infant day care. Kagan, Kearsley and Zelazo (1977) designed an experiment to test the effects of different forms of out-of-home day care on the psychological development of infants. The researchers studied three samples of infants, aged 3.5 to 29 months, matched on several demographic variables. The infants were not randomly assigned to conditions; in some ways, the study was a national field experiment. One group attended a day-care facility administered by the researchers, a second group of infants was cared for exclusively at home, and the third group attended group care outside their home on a part-time basis. The researchers were interested in the data both for its theoretical implications and to assess the day-care program they had established.

Measures of development were taken every two months, from 3.5 to 13.5 months, and again at 20 months and 29 months. The dependent measures included the infants' reactions to their mothers, strangers, day-care workers, and family friends; their freeplay activities, peer play, and concept familiarity. Results, though difficult to interpret because the children came from two distinct groups, indicated that, overall, infants in day care did not differ psychologically from children raised exclusively in home environments. The day-care experience did not diminish infants' identifications with or attachments to their parents. The researchers suggest that theories about the role of parent may need to focus more on the quality than on the quantity of interaction.

This study provided an interesting illustration of a locally conducted program designed to produce data relevant to the particular setting (the day-care center studied), and insights into the general impact of parent surrogates. The study may have important theoretical implications, but it was not without flaws due to local constraints. Because the researchers could only accept volunteers in the day-care center, they had to adopt a quasi-experimental design using a matched, nonequivalent control group. Despite the fact that control group infants were selected on the basis of comparable sociodemographic characteristics, the treatment and control groups may have differed along with another dimension. Treatment group parents may have been more familiar with the day-care center than control group parents because they were more socially connected, professionally informed, or geographically closer to the center. Nevertheless, the Kagan et al. study has had a major impact on the national debate on outside-the-home care for infants. Although the constraints imposed on local programs should be recognized, this example documents the viability of social experimentation conducted on a local level, with broader implications.

Patrol staffing. A slightly different example of a local program is represented by a field research project carried out in San Diego to examine the use of one versus two police officer patrol cars (Boydstun, Sherry & Moelter, 1978). The staffing of police cars is highly controversial. Police often argue that two officers working together are safer than one. In contrast, city government representatives view one-person patrol cars as a way to achieve personnel reductions and more efficient use of police. Because the circumstances of every city are somewhat different, no clear-cut national policy issues are involved and the federal government has played a passive role in providing research monies to support local studies.

Such was the case in San Diego, where a true experiment was conducted to test differences in the safety and effectiveness of different patrol car staff configurations. Because police needs vary according to the time of day, police function, and area of the city, multiple treatments and control conditions were included in the study design. Although results involved many elements, some trends were clearly evident. One-officer patrol units had higher performance ratings (that is, more arrests) and fewer complaints about officer behavior than two officer units. Furthermore, one-officer units were less likely to be involved in resisting arrest situations (a dangerous condition for police). One- and two-officer cars were found to have equal chances of being assaulted or injured. Some of these differences between one- and two-officer patrols can be explained by the fact that dispatchers did not randomly assign cases to patrol cars, and may have tried to assign two-officer units to handle serious disputes and ordered backups for one-officer units in such situations. These factors, however, do not necessarily modify Boydstun et al.'s conclusion that at least some single officer patrol staffing was justified in San Diego.

Whether or not the findings of the Boydstun et al. study are generalizable remains an open question. There are some differences between San Diego's geography and demographics and those of other municipalities. Also, unlike other cities (such as New York) where police officers are strongly opposed to one-person cars, in San Diego opinions were mixed. To come to clearer conclusions about the conditions under which single officer patrols could be expected to safely and effectively respond, it will be necessary to experiment with police patrol practices in other cities.

Participants in Social Experimentation

A variety of contexts have been described in which social experiments are conducted collaboratively by government officials and human service professionals. Just as the contexts of social experimentation can be distinguished, a variety of roles essential to social experimentation can be described. The roles played by people involved in social experiments are not rigidly defined. They represent the different concerns and perspectives that must be integrated in order for research on social problems to be conducted effectively. A somewhat crude distinction, in this case between social researchers and social policy makers, will be used to organize the discussion.

Accounting for all of the actors involved in social experimentation is not an easy task. The day-care study described earlier may offer the simplest illustration. In this case, the same individuals were responsible for administering the day-care centers (provision of the treatment) and for collecting data applicable to decision-making (design of the research component). Kagan et al. are social scientists who became involved in providing day care as part of an investigation of theoretical questions about childrearing practices. The experimenters were engaged in many activities: theorizing about the effects of day care and home care on infant development; administering the day-care facility; designing the research; collecting the data; and disseminating the information. Other people have used Kagan et al.'s data to lobby for money for day care; others may use these results to design further studies of cognitive and psychological development. (Kagan himself is continuing this line of research). Both policy-oriented and research-oriented individuals have used the information generated in this social experiment.

The Kagan example is unusually simple. Social scientists are only sometimes involved in both policy and research. Typically, different individuals deal with the policy and research components. In fact, we know little about the actual organization of Kagan et al.'s research team and it is likely that among the investigators there was a clear division of responsibility.

Those involved in policy formulation are subject to many, often competing, pressures. With practically any social program, policy makers must listen to those who defend the idea, those who believe they may be cheated, and those who predict failure. To juggle these pressures and formulate an "equitable" policy, researchers often are called upon to provide "evidence" — to collect valid information about the relative effectiveness of one program over another. Policy makers and social researchers bring distinct perspectives to and have distinct objectives about their work. Accordingly, the tasks they perform are usually quite different (Jones, 1980).

SOCIAL RESEARCHERS

Social researchers perform various activities in the conduct of a social experiment, and they themselves represent a diverse and heterogeneous group. Social researchers, in their diverse roles, serve as substantive experts about a particular social problem, as technical consultants about research strategies, as advocates of particular policy positions and, ultimately, as consultants to policy formulators. Activities of social researchers are probably as numerous as the number of individuals involved. Social researchers are also not easy to characterize in terms of their background and adopted perspectives. Researchers involved in social experimentation come from psychology (Campbell, 1969), sociology (Rossi, 1975), economics (Kershaw, 1972), as well as political science, history, philosophy, and other disciplines. It is probably true that those social researchers who are successful social experimenters reflect interdisciplinary perspectives. They are able to assimilate knowledge and expertise in their own discipline with that of other fields in their attempt to solve a particular problem. They are also able to work with others who do not share their backgrounds and perspectives.

Three tasks represent typical "labels" applied to the activities of social researchers: (1) evaluation tasks, (2) methodological tasks, and (3) analysis tasks (Anderson & Ball, 1978; Riecken & Boruch, 1974). However, as will be clear from the following descriptions below, there is a great deal of overlap between these tasks and no clear consensus as to how the tasks should be differentiated.

Evaluation tasks. During the past decade, probably the most prominent policy activity of social researchers has been the evaluation of social programs (Anderson & Ball, 1978; Guttentag & Struening, 1975; Struening & Guttentag, 1976; Weiss, 1972). The federal government, increasingly, has added a requirement that its programs, particularly social welfare and human service programs (Perloff, Perloff & Sussna, 1976), be systematically evaluated (see Congressional Research Service, 1976; Rentz & Rentz, 1978, U.S. Senate Committee on Human Resources, 1978). Many examples of social experimentation utilized in this book were developed as part of evaluation research efforts (for example, Head Start, Community Mental Health Centers, Sesame Street). The task of program evaluation involves assessing social programs in order to provide information for the decision-making process.

Although not always the case, one common problem with evaluations is that many are introduced post hoc, after a program has been developed or implementation has begun. Insofar as social experiments are built into program implementation, evaluations are often added as afterthoughts. In social experimentation, the emphasis is on joint development (by policy makers and researchers) of social interventions that can be researched *in vivo*. In program evaluation, the emphasis is on developing assessments that are independent of the program's operation. Because of these differing orientations, evaluations tend to begin after the program has been designed.

Quasi-experimental or nonexperimental designs are the common consequence when control groups are unavailable and random assignment impossible. Such was the case in the initial evaluation of the Head Start program (Cicirelli et al., 1969; McDill et al., 1972). Such programs should be studiable even after they have been implemented. However, such situations present clear impediments to designing studies with randomized control and treatment groups and generating unequivocal information.

In evaluation studies, social researchers can "evaluate" from inside or outside particular programs (Anderson & Ball, 1978; Bernstein & Freeman, 1975). The internal evaluator constitutes a member of the program staff who is responsible to program developers. Recall the earlier discussion of Community Mental Health Center evaluations. Individual centers directly received funds for evaluation. In most cases, each center hired its own evaluation staff which reported to the center's administration. An external evaluator, in contrast, has no structural connection to a program and is engaged expressly to conduct the evaluation. Members of the Westinghouse team that evaluated Head Start were external evaluators.

Some (such as Scriven, 1976) feel that the potential bias and lack of objectivity introduced by an internal evaluator beholden to the developers (and hence advocates) of the program is too great (see also Satin & Saxe, 1979). Although such problems of the internal evaluation role are well recognized, there are also problems with the role of external evaluators. Because external evaluators may know little about the program and may have no impetus to find positive results, a misleading evaluation is a possible outcome. Such an evaluation might answer questions that are of little importance to those knowledgeable about the program, or answer the important questions poorly. It is important for external evaluators to work closely with program developers while maintaining a relatively objective stance.

Methodological tasks. Campbell (1971), in a provocative discussion of social experimentation and society, referred to social researchers as "methodological servants" of an experimenting society. In Campbell's model, social researchers offer methodological assistance to program developers and policy makers throughout the development of a social experiment. Methodological tasks involve aiding social planners in developing a treatment with a clear intervention, specifying expected outcomes, organizing their programs in terms of valid design, and developing measureable out-comes of program efficacy.

To design a social program that meets the requirements of a social experiment is perhaps the most important function of a social researcher engaged in social experimentation. The social researcher in this role acts as technical consultant to the program staff in facilitating a rigorous research design.

Organizing treatment and control groups appropriate to the goals of the study is a complex and, as we have seen, important activity. Researcher involvement at an early stage is a feature of successful designs. The earlier a researcher becomes involved, the more likely that the program can be designed to fulfill research, as well as program, concerns. Involvement of a social researcher in program design is often indistinguishable from involvement in research design. It should be obvious that in order to design a true experiment, the social researcher must be involved in a program and understand its content. Without this inside information, the researcher cannot know which variables to randomize and how to "fit" randomization requirements within program needs. However, while they are making methodological suggestions, researchers often make valuable contributions to program content.

The second methodological task involves the development of appropriate indicators of program efficacy. We refer here to various ways researchers have measured social behavior (see Chapter 4). In some cases, instruments developed by social researchers are merely "taken off the shelf" and adopted for a particular study. Kagan et al. (1977), for example, used standardized measures of cognitive development to assess the impact of day care on young children. In other cases, a social policy researcher was responsible for developing appropriate mesures of program efficacy. One such illustration is Schofield's (1978) development of a measure of friendship and interaction between students in a school designed to promote racial integration.

As we learn more about the practice of social experimentation, it is clear that the potential for providing methodological consultation to programs will greatly increase. The interest in this type of applied research by those sub-stantively involved in programs will result in the need for consultants on experimental approaches. Not only are there myriad possibilities for providing such methodological assistance, but social researchers can adopt multiple roles for providing this help. Social researchers will be involved both as internal and external methodologists, and other patterns for collaboration will develop as well.

Analysis tasks. An important activity performed by social researchers is the analysis of social research. Social researchers are often called upon to make sense of available information and ideas about a particular social problem. Very often a variety of data are available, some collected for the purposes of research and some collected as part of normal record keeping. Reducing this information and utilizing its most appropriate components are common tasks for researchers. The resulting judgments about the nature of problems are often utilized by program decision makers and policy makers.

Analysis consists of integrating available information and interpreting findings. Social researchers are called upon both to analyze the results of particular social experiments *and* to make policy recommendations by synthesizing the new data with other available information. The two tasks are slightly different. Interpretation, for the most part, involves the results of a single social experiment. Integration, however, considers the new data in light of existing information by looking at various social programs, a number of social theories, and earlier policy decisions (e.g., Wortman & Saxe, 1981).

Aaron (1978) has noted in a monograph critical of the role that the social science community played in the development of President Johnson's "Great Society" programs that the integration function has had a clear, though not always beneficial, impact on social policy. In the case of the Great Society, it was social researchers who, in integrating available information, concluded that poverty was a cyclical process that could be "broken" by carefully placed economic and educational interventions. Although Aaron believes this position was incorrect, his analysis played an important role in how the Great Society programs were developed.

Although some of the analytical work of social researchers involves integrating research findings, they are often called upon to synthesize theoretical ideas and reports of experiences. The social researcher must develop and critically examine different views of social problems and programs. No data offer self-evident interpretations, although that is a popular misconception of science. The social scientist must utilize available conceptual tools to analyze the problem and fit the data to relevant ideas and information.

Social scientists who assume these responsibilities function as translators. Integrating data and theory into concepts and policy involves collaboration with participants, program administrators, policy formulators, and diverse constituencies. The sometimes complex and contradictory results of social research need to be made understandable not only to other members of the scientific community, but also to social policy formulators and the public. Social science is replete with cases where inconsistent and conflictual analyses of problems are reported (see, for example, aspects of the controversy over the use of social science data in desegregation court cases in Coleman, 1976; Pettigrew & Green, 1976). Analysis requires picking a path or paths that can be supported by data about socially important problems.

POLICY MAKERS

Just as social researchers performing various activities come from a diverse set of backgrounds, policy makers also cannot be easily categorized. In part, this is because social policy, as we have noted earlier, is formulated at every level of society and requires diverse skills for implementation. On the national level, policy is developed through the collaboration of the legislative and executive branches. On the local level, many individuals and organizations are involved in carrying out and supervising programs.

Of course, social policy makers also come from a variety of backgrounds. Individuals involved in the development of social policy sometimes are trained in law, social work, and public administration, as well as each of the substantive areas of social policy (such as health, education, welfare, criminal justice). In addition to their professional reference groups, policy makers often represent different political constituencies. Thus, they usually attempt to adopt positions that are both intellectually sound and politically tenable.

As difficult as it was to categorize the various activities performed by social researchers, it is even more difficult to categorize activities of policy developers. However complex, three parallel levels of policy-making can be identified: (1) legislative level, (2) executive level, and (3) program implementation level. While these categories are useful for distinguishing broad responsibility differences, as we will demonstrate, a wide range of skills and knowledge is included within each category.

Legislative. On the legislative level, policy rules are formalized as broad decisions about how social interventions are made, that is, as laws. Although legislators often focus on small-scale problems, this is often only a device for enabling understanding of larger problems. Most individuals involved in legislating policy view problems vary broadly. By virtue of the pressures imposed on the legislators, they must consider multiple facets of problems and process enormous amounts of information in order to develop policy decisions.

Executive. This level, associated with the federal executive branch, is responsible for developing specific social policies and monitoring their implementation. Individuals involved in this type of social policy formation specify guidelines for social programs and oversee their administration.

Although executive branch social policy makers have a task more circumscribed than that of legislators, they still must be concerned about whether specific programs work, cost effectiveness of programs, and positive and negative effects of other social programs. Because this actual overseeing is often removed from level of program implementation, the tasks involved are often quite difficult. How they function is currently a source of debate, and it is likely that the role of the executive branch will be reshaped in coming years, with more responsibility given to local agencies.

Implementer. A third social policy level is that of program implementation, which is represented in various ways. In one situation, an individual on this level may be a social agency administrator (such as a local government official) responsible for a class of programs. In another instance, the individual may be the actual treatment implementer directly responsible for the program. What should be clear is that depending upon one's position, information needs will differ along with the types of relationships with social scientists.

INTERACTION

The extent to which social researchers and policy makers interact is central to the principles and practice of social experiments. Social experiments are rooted in the assumption that collaboration is good, and necessary for valid, progressive research and for effective, responsive policy-making. The nature of this collaboration can vary.

Technical reports are a formal mechanism for collaboration. While valuable, they are not sufficient because they do not require interaction. Research findings and program decisions require input from many sources. For example, the Vietnam Era Project presented its results to a conference of veterans groups for feedback and interpretation. The multiconstituency analysis of findings helped program implementers and researchers define their next steps. Open forums in which participants, researchers, and program developers can exchange ideas and views about social experiments are central to the philosophy of social experimentation. Such structures need to be built into early planning in order for such communication to be facilitated. Conflicts can emerge, but they should be viewed as heightening rather than threatening the validity of the data and the program.

Conclusion

Activities of social researchers and levels of social policy may be described and delineated in the abstract; in reality, distinctions are hard to apply. Sometimes the same person conducts research and makes policy; social researchers can simultaneously provide methodological assistance, integrate available information, and make policy decisions. Policy makers similarly perform social research. In order to develop or promote a particular program, they may collect and integrate information about the social intervention. Researchers may enter the political arena in order to gain support for their experimentation. Research and policy are then interdependent. Although researchers and policy makers sometimes see one another as adversaries, they in fact can further the objectives of the other through meaningful collaboration. Implementing social experimentation facilitates and requires collaboration between researchers and policy makers. The situation is complex. Participants and tasks involved in social experimentation represent complicated relationships.

The thrust of the next three chapters will be to describe how this complexity can be managed and rigorous experiments carried out. The following chapters will examine, in turn, the principles described in Section II and how they can be realized in practice. Chapter 7 focuses on independent variables and the arrangement of programs to meet research design requirements. Chapter 8 discusses dependent variable problems and how questions about programs can be operationalized as measures of social behavior. In Chapter 9, the utilization of data from social experiments is examined. These chapters, taken together, should provide a more realistic assessment of the conduct of experiments than the earlier material.

CHAPTER 7

COLLABORATION IN THE DESIGN OF SOCIAL EXPERIMENTS

Between the idea
And the reality
Between the motion
And the act
Falls the shadow

T. S. Eliot, "The Hollow Men"

T. S. Eliot's poetry captures a central problem in realizing an experimenting society: How to move from ideas about the applicability of social science methodology to their implementation. As should be clear from previous chapters, the logic of experimentation is relatively well developed, although this does not guarantee its comprehension and utilization. Concepts underlying utilization are, in general, better developed than the understandings of the social scientists. Each group possesses important components of the requisite information and skills, yet unless joint problem-solving and action occur, the potential for designing "researchable" interventions is limited. The larger sociopolitical context within which social science experimentation exists must also be considered (Campbell, 1971). Social scientists and planners cannot work in isolation, nor should program participants and others interested be separated from planning and implementing experiments. Their cooperation is often essential to an effective social experiment.

In designing social experiments, the resolution of problems is often represented as developing a compromise between scientific criteria of validity and sociopolitical limitations. It is often assumed that scientific criteria will conflict with the needs of recipients. It is true that a program that is poorly designed in terms of validity criteria, no matter how necessary the compromises, will yield data that have low utility for developing policy. Also, implementing certain experimental designs may not mean reducing service to any group. Scientific criteria are not absolute guidelines, which should be made clear to nonscientists. Also, validity requirements should be translated into language understandable to them. It may be useful, as shorthand, to conceive of such designs as representing a tension between the principles of science and practical limitations. Social scientists generally adhere to validity criteria, while social planners usually represent the side of practical constraints. The resulting tension appears as a divergence of perspectives between social researchers and those responsible for social planning and administration (Jones, 1980; Weiss, 1972, 1975). These perspectives, it is hoped, can be meshed, as the remainder of this chapter will illustrate.

Designing a social experiment involves a series of steps. Although not fixed, these steps occur in some form in order to accommodate the development and study of a social intervention. Initially, there are processes of problem definition and idea generation. At the most basic and perhaps most important level, these processes require that a set of questions be proposed. The development of tentative hypotheses about the relationships among variables is a usual next step. Although this step should evolve into the actual construction of an experiment, that is not always the case. A second major step is the selection of an appropriate design for dealing with the problem, one that can generate data about the effects of the intervention, and is able to be implemented within the constraints of the program. Our particular bias favors the use of true experimental designs, which we believe are often needed to generate appropriate data. Nevertheless, the basic principle remains that whichever design is employed must yield the information needed within whatever limits of validity are acceptable. One must be willing to permit flexibility and consider various designs. In practice, no design is a "pure" representation of an experimental type, so that even when a true experiment is conducted, not all variables will be randomized. The same holds true for quasi-experiments and other designs that do not rely on randomization.

A critical aspect of the process of developing an experiment is to consider the ethical implications of the procedures. Procedures must be developed to improve the experiment's benefits to participants, while at the same time minimizing any negative effects. This is usually accomplished through a set of complex tradeoffs and requires sensitivity. Both short- and long-term effects on participants must be monitored and the study altered or terminated if problems develop. Design development does not end the process. Maintaining the integrity of the design and knowing how and when to alter the experiment once it is underway are also important. At each stage in developing an experiment, there are opportunities for creative resolution of competing goals, as well as dilemmas with potential to harm the program, the research, and /or the participants. These opportunities and dilemmas are described next.

Problem Definition

As noted, the first stage in developing a design for a social experiment involves problem definition. Through discussion between planners and researchers, an understanding emerges about the problem and potential intervention strategies. This preliminary understanding of a problem usually develops over a long period of time and typically involves input from a number of groups. Researchers, government officials, program administrators, community groups, and private citizens may provide ideas at different points in the process. The process does not really stop by the time an action program is initiated. Continued redefinition of the problems and skepticism about the best intervention strategy are normally an ongoing feature of social experimentation.

The process of problem definition is necessarily complex and does not always result in a useful conceptual model. It is not that efforts are not made to understand the causes of particular problems and possible interventions, it is just that our ability to do so is often limited. Aaron (1978), as noted, has analyzed the origins and the effects of the Great Society programs. Subsequent evaluations of the programs have served as the basis for debate about the value both of the programs and social research. Much of the evidence was inconclusive and has been interpreted by some (like Aaron) to indicate that the programs were unsuccessful. Aaron's contention is that the Great Society programs were developed from incorrect assumptions about the causes of poverty in the United States. According to this view, the Great Society programs were based on the inaccurate belief that poverty is a closed cycle. This assumption holds that the adult poor are individuals without the skills or education to improve themselves or their children. The cycle of poverty is perpetuated because poor children do not receive the help they require to avoid the conditions faced by their parents. Aaron claims that this "poverty class" view was an erroneous understanding promoted by the academic community and that it greatly influenced the nature of the Great Society interventions.

Aaron's view is that the poor are a changing group, and that poverty is not really a permanent state. The poor, according to Aaron, were able to get jobs and education and to leave economic ghettos even before the Great Society programs. The implication is that job training and compensatory education programs, which formed the core of the War on Poverty, did not alter this process. They were merely stimulating changes that would have occurred naturally. In Aaron's view, the Great Society programs did nothing to change the basic economic structures that create poverty.

Aaron's analysis is limited, of course, to one set of federal programs and one point in time. Whether it is a valid point of view is not yet clear. However, the dictum implicit in Aaron's commentary that social experimentation should develop from an understanding of social problems as well as from an understanding of the intervention itself is probably good advice. We need to examine the untested assumptions which invariably influence our design of social interventions.

An example of an important assumption beginning to come under more scrutiny, is "Who/what is the target of change?" Many social programs define the individual as the target of change and do not try to change the social conditions that contribute to the problem. For example, assertiveness training programs for women seeking employment or promotions generally neglect the realities of labor force discrimination. Training women to be assertive may be based on the assumption that other factors, such as discrimination against women in the workplace, do not have a central impact. Such a program may ignore structural contributions to the problem (that is, labor force discrimination in hiring and wages) and make it more difficult to change these conditions. Assumptions about who/what should be the target of change need to be clarified a priori.

The importance of goal setting in the problem definition process is usually difficult to define, and it is a matter of debate (see Deutscher, 1976; Scriven, 1975; Weiss, 1972). There are some who feel that it is crucial because experiments can only be designed and interpreted in terms of what goals were initially sought. Others, however, feel that extensive knowledge of the program's goals biases the researcher's objectivity. Some, such as Scriven, have suggested that the best procedure is to have those who evaluate programs be unaware of program goals. In this way, knowledge of what was supposed to happen can not bias a researcher to see effects of an intervention just because they should be there. Scriven's assumption that knowledge about program goals will yield biased interpretations is hard to demonstrate. It would appear that in most cases situations are too complex and too many actors are involved for researcher bias to unduly influence the experiment.

Another difficulty with goal definition is that researchers and program planners reflect distinct and often divergent perspectives. The researcher requires information about goals to construct an appropriate design and to develop relevant instruments and measures. If the goals are unclear to the researcher, the design may not test the most useful hypotheses and the data may be meaningless. The planner, in contrast, is principally concerned with the operations of the program. Although planners may value the study's contribution to knowledge about the problem, their primary concern is the concrete problem of how to organize and deliver the treatment. The planner's constituency may be broader than the scientific community, which typically is the focus of researcher's interest. The nonresearch constituency is usually more interested in the operation of the particular program than in the knowledge to be gained from it.

A partial solution to these problems lies in both parties communicating to each other their assumptions and understandings of the goals of the programs. While there are undoubtedly unresolvable conflicts that result from divergent perspectives, many problems can be avoided through communication. A commitment to working toward an understanding that satisfies both parties, as well as agreement on the primary goals of the program, should aid in developing a research design that satisfies the various constituencies.

A recent study of genetic counseling programs, in which one of the authors was involved, provides a good illustration of this process of problem definition. The National Institute of Health (NIH) which, along with other governmental agencies, sponsors sickle cell disease screening and counseling centers, wanted to determine the impact of its counseling programs on individuals identified as possessing the sickle cell trait. The trait, which occurs in individuals who have ancestors from Africa and certain Mediterranean countries (about 1 in 8 black Americans) can be passed on to offspring. If both parents have the trait, a child has a twenty five prcent chance of acquiring the trait, thus developing a serious form of anemia. Counseling programs are designed to provide individuals with information about genetics and the natural history of sickle cell disease, as well as to help individuals deal with the implications of having the trait (such as deciding whether to bear children). Counseling is assumed to be an important component of screening, although there is no systematic evidence about the impact of counseling on those who are screened.

With the support of those involved in the sickle cell programs, NIH decided to conduct a study to assess the effects of counseling. A research team was assembled, including two physicians, a social worker, a statistician, and a psychologist. This group's mission was to develop a design and instruments to assess the impact of counseling. A lengthy design process was involved in clarifying the nature of the problem and determining which counseling goals would be examined.

Several goals, and consequent information needs, quickly emerged. The most pressing need seemed to be determining the amount of information that was learned about sickle cell trait and disease during the counseling process. The underlying hypothesis was that increased knowledge about the genetic problems could significantly improve clients' health and life satisfaction.

Evaluating individual counseling centers and assessing the psychological impact of counseling, while of interest, were lower priorities.

Other considerations emerged. It was realized that "counseling" was too simple a term to describe what most counseling centers actually did. In almost all instances, counseling was preceded by an educational session in which pamphlets, slides, and lecture material were provided. The research team did not want to alter drastically the procedures or the types of services being provided, but they realized it was important to remain aware of the practices of different sites. Because the program was a national one involving 30 sites, it was important to collect information from as many sites as possible. It also became apparent that although this was a study specific to sickle cell, it would be beneficial to collect information that might have relevance for other types of genetic problems. A final consideration was that in order to make the study cost efficient, on-site personnel should be used to conduct the study.

These understandings had a profound effect on the design of the study. First, a small study was initiated to test a version of the knowledge test of sickle cell (Saxe, 1979). Over 400 clients in 12 centers took the test, half before they had received counseling, half after they had received counseling. On the basis of this pilot study and a careful examination of the responses to each item, a short 25-item multiple choice and true-false test was constructed. Second, it was decided that in order to develop data that would convince skeptical observers, a true experiment of counseling would be conducted. Although the experiment involved random assignment, it did not require a major change in center procedures. The specifics will be discussed in the next section on selecting a design.

Up to this point, the process of problem definition has been presented as a relatively informal set of procedures. A problem definition can often be more formal. Thus, for example, an experiment is usually not undertaken without a thorough literature review to determine what is already known about the problem and what intervention strategies have already been tried. In some cases, preliminary studies called "need assessments" are conducted to determine what those affected by the problem think about it (see Warheit, Bell & Schwab, 1974). In other cases, formal decision-making techniques such as the Delphi procedure (see Dalkey & Helmer, 1963) are used to insure a consensus about the problem definition. The next section describes how these problem understandings are used to develop an actual experimental design.

Selecting a Design

Despite the importance of a clear problem statement, a design for an experiment will not naturally suggest itself from the conceptualization of the problem. The nature of the problem and available interventions for dealing with it, as well as a host of scientific, political, and ethical issues, must be considered in selecting a design. The weight of each of these factors depends on the situation and changes as the nature of social problems and concerns shift.

ILLUSTRATIONS

The experiments described below illustrate a number of problems involved in the design of "true" social experiments. Because of the utility of true experiments in providing unambiguous assessments of relationships between variables, and because such designs include most of the pragmatic problems of other types of studies, they seem most important to illustrate. The special feature of true experiment designs, random assignment of units to conditions, is an aspect of each of the experiments described below. As you will note, each study deals with random assignment in a different way, particular to the situation in which the experiment is conducted.

Sickle cell counseling. As described above, an experiment was conducted to assess the effectiveness of sickle cell counseling programs. Initially the goal was to determine how much knowledge is retained by counselees about the etiology, effects, and management of sickle cell trait and disease. A knowledge test about sickle cell was administered to counselees. It was hoped that this design would only minimally interfere with patient treatment and at the same time provide a direct way of assessing the impact of counseling. However, there were internal validity problems. The principal threat to validity was a testing problem: improvements in scores from pre- to posttest might only reflect learning from the test itself. To resolve this validity threat, a randomly selected comparison condition might be added in which only a posttest is given:

	Time 1		Time 2
Test-Retest Condition:	Test	Counseling	Retest
Comparison Condition:	No test	Counseling	Test

Thus, testing effects could be mesured and it could be determined whether (and to what extent) learning from the pretest distorts findings of the effects of counseling.

Although a two-condition experiment would certainly improve the quality of the data, the treatment involves more than counseling alone. In addition, a good design would identify separately the effects due to the educational materials and those due to counseling. For ethical reasons, blood test screening could not be performed without giving clients basic information about sickle cell trait and disease. Testing after education but prior to counseling was used to determine how much information was gained from the educational component alone. Otherwise, it would not be possible to know how much of the learning about sickle cell was due to counseling and how much was due to the educational materials. The two-condition design suggested above requires other conditions:

	Time 1	Time 2	Time 3
Condition 1:	Test - Education (screening) - Test - Counseling		
Condition 2:	Test - Education (screening) -	Counseling - Test	
Condition 3:	Education (screening) - Test - Counseling		
Condition 4:	Education (screening) -	Counseling - Test	

Comparing the results of conditions 1 and 2 indicates the difference between learning after education only and learning after education and counseling. Conditions 3 and 4 are needed to rule out (or estimate the effects of) testing and, perhaps, maturation threats to validity.

This design, as it developed, incorporated a selected set of comparison conditions, rather than all possible factorial combinations. The reason was that the design had to be superimposed on an already existing service delivery system. Although it is not possible to withhold some components of the treatment from some participants (such as education and counseling), it was possible, through scheduling changes, to have the treatment provided at different times depending upon a client's randomly assigned condition. Experimental variations of the treatment, such as counseling without education, were not utilized because of ethical constraints (such as the need to obtain *informed consent* prior to blood test) and because such interventions lack validity, as they would never be used in practice.

Another pragmatic design consideration was how to assign patients to conditions. If patients were permitted to select themselves into conditions, a bias might result. For example, the postcounseling test condition (2 and 4, above) might be disproportionately composed of individuals who felt most confident about their knowledge. Randomization was not conceptually difficult in this situation because scheduling flexibility was possible, but as a practical matter it was complex. Over 30 different sites, each with its own procedures, had to be accommodated. Individuals from each site were brought together to agree upon standardized procedures for conducting the study. This problem-solving group was briefed on the purpose of the study, the considerations that went into development of the design, and the potential use of the data. From these meetings, a flexible set of procedures was agreed upon which insured unbiased selection of clients for conditions without constraining any of the counseling centers in their services or ways of operation. Additional agreement was reached on how to use the data and development of internal analyses which would meet the needs of the centers for information on program effectiveness.

Health insurance study. A very different type of design is represented by the Health Insurance Study, initiated in 1973 (Newhouse, 1974a, 1974b).

The study was a massive social experiment funded by the Department of Health and Human Services and conducted by the Rand Corporation (at a projected cost, in 1973 dollars, of $32 million). The goal of the study was to test the effects of various health insurance plans on demand for medical services and on health status. In essence, the question tested was how various health insurance plans would affect the use of medical services and whether universal availability of health care services would result in improved health status. It should be noted that the U.S. Congress has considered national health insurance plans in almost every session since the 1940s, but the idea has gained substantial acceptance only recently. Discussions centered around whether the resources are available to fund such a program and whether it represents the best way to spend health monies. Unfortunately, data based on current health care utilization patterns, surveys, and other data sources do not directly help us estimate the impact of a national health insurance plan.

The study's design was complex, reflecting the complexity of the rules of operation regarding how randomization is to be achieved and how to deal with study participants. Initially included in the design were sixteen variations of insurance plans, along with a variety of control conditions. The control conditions were incorporated in the design of the study to rule out possible alternative explanations for the results. The experimental conditions differed in terms of the percentage of inpatient and outpatient charges participants were required to pay, ranging from 0 percent to 100 percent. The conditions also varied in terms of their deductible limits (minimum amounts to be paid by participants before receiving insurance benefits). The rules of operation included guarantees that no family would be worse off by virtue of its participation in the experiment than it was with its preexperiment health insurance plan. Another provision of the experiment was that families would be paid for record keeping.

An important aspect of the study was the inclusion of multiple control conditions to deal with potential validity problems. One set of control conditions attempted to rule out "Hawthorne effects," which result because participants are aware they are in an experimental program. This was made salient by the fact that participants were required to keep careful records of their health care system contacts, their health expenditures, and their health status. To determine the impact of this aspect of the design, a number of control conditions were developed in which the frequency of record keeping (and interviewing by the research staff) was systematically varied.

Another set of control conditions was established to estimate the effect on health care costs of participants' temporary involvement in the experiment. With temporary participation, individuals might use the experiment (assuming that they are in a generous insurance condition) as an opportunity to receive treatments they had either delayed (such as eyeglasses) or would normally not obtain (such as cosmetic surgery). Although the period of the experiment was to be either 3 or 5 years (length of participation was another control variable), the results might show greater costs for the experimental insurance plan than would be the case if a permanent insurance plan were established. A control condition of individuals who maintained their current insurance was used to estimate the effects of this feature of the experiment. Finally, other control conditions were included to estimate the effects of offering different types of health care services (such as psychiatry) in the various insurance plans. The impact of these optional services was examined by adding control conditions in which variations of the basic insurance were allowed.

This study was very sophisticated and incorporated multiple treatment and control groups as well as procedures for insuring unbiased selection of families to conditions. The study's complexity, however, entails risks. Even before randomization to conditions was accomplished, locations where the study was to be carried out and families needed to be recruited (three sites were used, with approximately 500 families at each site). There is some evidence that despite the free benefits, many individuals declined participation (Ferber & Hirsch, 1978), introducing a selection bias. This reduces the study's external validity, but reflects only one aspect of the validity problem. Actual implementation of a national health insurance program might fundamentally affect the nature of the health care system. Although this impact cannot now be measured, the health insurance study can provide one type of information about the problem. Given that development of a national health insurance program has resisted solution through traditional channels, it may be an important set of results.

Interactive telecommunications. A somewhat different example of practical design issues is provided by an effort to develop an interactive telecommunications system (ITS) and to measure its impact. The system, which consisted of two-way television connected by microwave, was designed to facilitate communication among health professionals practicing in rural areas where they are isolated from their peers (see Saxe & Fine, 1979). With base stations located in five rural hospitals within the same area, it was hoped that an ITS would enable frequent, effective communication equivalent to face-to-face encounters. Case conferences and continuing education seminars, as well as patient care, were to be expedited by the system.

Because of the potential importance of such systems to improving the delivery of health care in rural settings (and the potential expense), data were requested about the utilization and impact of the intervention from a number of sources. While ideally these data should be free from validity threats (particularly internal), it was impossible to use a fully randomized control group design. Neither hospitals nor users could be randomly assigned. The participating hospitals had already been selected (on the basis of location and internal resources) and all hospital staff were encouraged to use the ITS.

However, it was believed that unambiguous data of the type generated by a true experiment were necessary to justify the large amounts of funding required to set up these systems ($1-2 million per system). Information was needed to understand the conditions under which these systems could be useful: for whom, where, and how. Part of the urgency for valid data stems from a history of such systems being implemented and quickly falling into disuse. An experiment was needed to determine whether disuse was due to the hardware (faulty cameras and transmission equipment unable to provide suitable communication medium) or the software (the ways of using the system, as well as the reactions of the users).

A multilevel design was developed to respond to these information needs given the situational constraints. At the "macro" level, a quasi-experiment was constructed to assess ITS impact before, during, and after implementation. This design would measure changes over time in the utilization of health care communications. A number of threats to validity were inherent in this design; it was insensitive to determining whether hardware or software problems were responsible for ITS effects. To improve the sensitivity of the design, a series of "micro" level studies were incorporated into the ITS experiment. The micro studies tested specific hypotheses about the efficacy of interactive television as a medium of communiction (as opposed to face-to-face communications) between various users (such as physicians, patients, health worker teams) and for various purposes (such as patient education, case diagnoses, conferences, bedside visits). These studies were to be conducted in laboratory-like fashion with participants from the ITS hospitals as well as other settings randomly assigned to tested conditions.

The multiple level of design schedules a series of studies which essentially investigate the same problem, each yielding different information. The macro design generates data about the efficacy of the intervention over time; the micro design suggests the efficacy of the components of the system (Saxe & Fine, 1979).

SUMMARY

As should be obvious from the above examples, there is no single formula for designing social experiments. Researchers and planners must be flexible, creative, and eclectic in selecting randomization procedures to satisfy information needs. Design, in practice, is both a participatory process and one that has to be flexible enough to meet information needs and the special conditions under which a program is carried out.

Ethical Considerations

A variety of ethical problems and questions can be inferred from our discussion of social experimentation. One of the initial examples of social experimentation was the case of retrolental fibroplasia (Chapter 2). In that situation, where a failure to conduct experimental trials resulted in babies being subjected to a dangerous and untested medical procedure, it was probably unethical *not* to develop a rigorous experimental design (cf. Eisenberg, 1977). In other of the examples, such as sickle cell counseling, the ethical issues involved the questionable right to withhold or modify a treatment for research purposes. Ethical questions permeate every aspect of social experimentation, but nowhere are the issues as critical as they are in the design phase. A number of ethical dilemmas that relate to the selection of a design are discussed below.

WITHHOLDING TREATMENT

One such dilemma, especially important in true experiments, is the problem of constructing no treatment control groups. If a treatment is hypothesized to be of value, under what conditions is it fair to withhold the benefit, on a random or other basis, for the purposes of research? In mental health and counseling programs, individuals in no treatment conditions may experience prolonged psychological discomfort and disability. In educational programs, valuable resources may be made available to treatment group members and not to those in control conditions. Although there are many people outside of the mental health and education fields who are skeptical about the benefits of such programs (substantiating the need for research on them), research may be harmful to individuals placed in control conditions. The benefits to society of the research must be weighed against the cost to participants—especially those who are denied treatment (Rivlin & Timpane, 1975a; Warwick, 1978).

Although there is potential for abuse, there are also factors which can justify the use of no treatment control conditions. Experiments are usually of short duration and thus treatments are not actually withheld, just delayed. A delay strategy was used in the sickle cell counseling study, where individuals in the control condition merely received the test and treatment in a different sequence. For most counselees, there was no actual delay. Such circumstances, whenever they can be arranged, certainly reduce the ethical problems. It is also typical for treatment to represent a scarce resource. Kidney dialysis machines prior to the government's involvement in funding were scarce, and were often available only if the patient was wealthy (Saks, 1978). When this is the case, distributing a scarce resource in a random fashion may be the fairest allocation system (Wortman & Rabinowitz, 1979). Of course, the ethical standards that one should employ depend upon the situation. Especially in health-related interventions where a delay in a treatment may result in irreversible changes, different standards must be considered (Veatch, 1975).

CAUSING HARM

One defense of no treatment control conditions is that experiments are done precisely because it is not known whether the treatment is effective. Thus, constructing a no treatment control condition may not represent denial of a benefit. It is possible that just the opposite will occur and that a treatment may cause harm. Certainly direct harm was caused by the pure oxygen therapy used for premature babies. Harm could be caused in a new educational program if it made students unable to learn traditional concepts (a charge made by some against "new math" programs). In a counseling program, harm could be caused if participants' anxiety was raised (a possibility in genetic counseling) or if participants were taught maladaptive skills (the implication of McCord's 1978 follow-up of the Cambridge-Somerville Youth Project). Such harmful consequences may occur as unintended side effects of an otherwise effective program.

Since one would not knowingly cause harm, an important principle is to design into an experiment early detection of harmful consequences. The possibility of harmful treatments is an important reason for constructing control conditions. Even if one has data about responses in the absence of a new treatment, it is often useful to have a control condition that provides data from the same population, at the same point in time, and under the same conditions to detect problems with the treatment. It is also important to pilot-test or to construct a demonstration program before beginning a large-scale social experiment. Prior empirical work that does not attempt to satisfy all of the conditions of the experiment but allows for a test of the feasibility of the treatment and the measures can be useful in this regard.

RAISING EXPECTATIONS

Individuals involved in a social experiment may be informed about the treatment condition (or control condition) to which they have been assigned, or they may be told only that they are in a social experiment which involves many conditions and not told in which specific condition they are participating. In either case, individuals usually have some knowledge that a treatment is available, and that they might have access to it.

Depending on the nature of the problem being investigated, this knowledge of a treatment may unwittingly raise individuals' expectations about the treatment and its benefits. For example, research to evaluate the social services provided to labor union members was designed to assess the needs of workers, their perceptions of and responses to services available, and their perspectives on needed services (Fine & Akabas, 1981). However, it was important not to let the research be structured so that it implied delivery of services that would not be provided. By saying "What kinds of services would you like or need?" a researcher may unwittingly encourage respondents to think that they will receive the services mentioned. Respondents should be informed about the limits of the intervention and the research: what they can realistically expect and what is unlikely to emerge from their participation.

VIOLATING PRIVACY/RIGHTS

A less tangible ethical dilemma in social experimentation occurs when a procedure invades the privacy or otherwise violates the rights of the participants. An important distinction needs to be made between the ethics of an intervention (which might be implemented even if a social experiment were not conducted) and the ethics of the research. The most obvious way in which rights can be violated occurs when information collected about a participant, or information provided by the participant, is made public. Medical and school records and the responses to questionnaires evaluating a program are examples of information which, if released, could embarrass or otherwise harm a participant. Their release clearly violates legal and moral standards (cf. Capron, 1975). Although this is not a design issue per se, experimental procedures for collecting, maintaining, and analyzing data are important in determining the ethics of a study. For example, if one were to study an illegal activity like drug abuse, maintaining anonymity of records and selecting a design with the greatest safeguards against release of information would be extremely important. It may not be possible to conduct the experiment if appropriate safeguards cannot be provided.

Rights may also be violated by the use of deceptive procedures. Although it is less likely that deception would be used in social experimentation than in other forms of social research, participants are often unaware of certain features of the experiment (Bower & deGasparis, 1978). In drug experiments, it is common practice not to tell control group subjects that they are receiving an inert substance. Leading schizophrenic patients who are receiving placebos to believe that they are receiving symptom-reducing medication raises major ethical dilemmas (such as McGrath et al., 1972). In this and other situations, a crucial aspect of the experiment is to test the effect of participants' knowledge about the treatment. One way of avoiding ethical violations and ensuring internal validity in social experiments is to make the treatment and control conditions equivalent by providing the same information, and obtaining informed consent by stipulating conditions, for example, "While some of you will receive drug X, others will receive substance Y."

RESOLVING ETHICAL DILEMMAS

Some general strategies for dealing with ethical problems were offered above. Of course, it is impossible to describe all of the possible ethical problems that might be encountered and their resolutions. To resolve ethical problems, government agencies, numerous professional associations, and many concerned with ethical research practices have tried to develop guidelines (for example, American Psychological Association, 1973). These guidelines continue to be modified as more experience is gained in conducting social research. Some of the central features of these guidelines, as they apply to social experiments, are described below.

Informed consent. Perhaps the most widely accepted way of dealing with ethical dilemmas is to insure that participants in experiments have voluntarily agreed to participate after being informed about the nature of the experiment. Informed consent procedures include providing to potential participants a description of what will happen to them in the experiment, the known risks involved, what kinds of data will be collected, and under what conditions the data will be used. Such statements of informed consent usually guarantee the participant the right to leave the experiment at any time, without sacrificing any payments earned or other inducements. This principle is increasingly being enforced by law (affecting those who do research in institutions that receive federal funding), although its feasibility in social experimentation is considered problematic by some (Rivlin & Timpane, 1975a).

One reason it is difficult to apply informed consent to social experiments is that a treatment (or no treatment) condition is often assigned to an entire institution, not discrete individuals. When schools participate in a new educational program, informed consent is probably given by the school board, rather than individual students or parents. While students are the participants, they are generally not given an alternative to participation (short of dropping out of school). Another problem with the ability of subjects to "voluntarily" agree to participate is that very often, participants in experiments are members of powerless groups—for example, children, prisoners, or mentally disabled individuals (Kelman, 1972). Although individuals (or their guardians) may provide consent, it may be neither fully informed nor voluntary because they either did not understand what they were agreeing to or they were coerced. Participants in the New Jersey Negative Income Tax Experiment may not have understood the conditions of the experiment but may have felt compelled to participate because almost anything was better than the social stigma associated with welfare (Rossi, Boeckmann, & Berk, 1978; Warwick, 1978).

Weighing benefits and harm. Implicit in almost every ethical consideration is a weighing of the potential benefits to be derived from a study against the potential harm that might be caused to individuals or society (Rivlin & Timpane, 1975a; Warwick, 1978). Informed consent is only necessary when risks are involved and essentially is supposed to allow participants to make their own determination of whether the risks are worth the benefits. At least in the short term, the risk in the typical social experiment is to the participant, and the benefits to society. Of course, risks are often trivial (such as a few minutes of lost time) and the benefits, even to an individual participant, may eventually be substantial (such as new knowledge or elimination of a disease). As we have seen, individual responsibility for decision-making is often not achieved in social experiments. When there is a great potential for harm, when powerless subjects are involved, and when participants may not understand, it is necessary to involve others in the decision. The current practice is to establish advisory panels composed of scientists and representatives of the community to make determinations about the benefits and costs of conducting experiments (Rivlin & Timpane, 1975a; Warwick, 1978) prior to the introduction of informed consent.

Because almost every social experiment entails risks, the general rule is that great care should be exercised before deciding to conduct an experiment. At a very basic level, there is an obligation that the investigators be competent and that the data to be generated be useful. Beyond that basic obligation, it is generally assumed that every effort will be made to insure that risk is minimized and that participants are not in a worse condition at the end of the experiment than they were when they entered. This was the reason for the provisions of the health coverage which was at least as good as their preexperiment health insurance. Although it might have been useful to study how people cope with low levels of insurance (not confounded, as in the natural situation, by unemployment, social class, and so on), this would have created a serious ethical problem.

Undoubtedly, there are going to be occasions when substantial risks in an experiment are justified by the benefits. This is most obvious in the case of medical experimentation. It is clear that the retrolental fibroplasia experiment which uncovered the cause of the disease ran such a risk. The nurses who were asked to implement the treatment by lowering the oxygen given to new babies resisted because they thought that lowering the oxygen level would be dangerous (when, in fact, the high levels were dangerous). Although the dilemmas are usually not as clear in nonmedical social interventions, they do exist. Thus, in educational programs, while there are ethical problems in tampering with traditional instruction, the danger of *not* experimenting seems equally clear. It is only resolvable when broad consideration is given to the costs and benefits of experimentation and the costs and benefits of not experimenting (Eisenberg, 1977; Gilbert, Light & Mosteller, 1975; Mosteller, 1981).

Intervention vs. experimentation. A number of distinct ethical problems posed by social experiments, such as obtaining informed consent from an institution rather than the participating individuals, have been identified. One additional problem particular to social experimentation is that the features of the experiment (the design) may be less risky than the intervention itself. Thus, the content of a treatment and the ethical dilemmas it poses are often not under the control or influence of the social experimenter, who may only be able to influence the research component. The treatment may, in fact, already have been adopted as social policy and/or may be accepted as policy unless research indicates that it is ineffective or problematic. In these circumstances, it seems inappropriate to hold the experimenter accountable for the treatment. But if a potentially unethical or risky treatment is not yet policy, social experimenters may be ethically responsible for furthering use of the treatment—even for research purposes.

It may be useful to separate intervention and research for purposes of considering ethical dilemmas, despite our view of social experimentation as a collaborative venture. Thus, in the case of the sickle cell counseling programs, the potential risk to individuals of being made more anxious as a result of counseling had to be weighed against the benefits of their ability to make more knowledgeable parenting decisions and to cope with sickle cell disease. While these risks and benefits need to be considered, given that counseling has already been widely adopted they may not have to be considered as part of a decision about conducting the experimental study itself. However, the fact that the researcher is not directly responsible for the intervention does not take away the responsibility to document problems with the intervention and to alert others if problems exist. Nevertheless, thinking through these problems should lead to their quick identification and resolution.

Perhaps the central point is that social interventions will take place regardless of whether or not systematic testing and experimentation are built in. Very often, the decision may be between "fooling around with people" (Gilbert, Light & Mosteller, 1975) vs. systematically studying the intervention process. There are risks involved in experimentation, but there may be as many risks in not experimenting.

SUMMARY

Ethical dilemmas are an integral feature of social experimentation. If they are absent it may mean that the intervention is not very important (see Elms, 1972). Rather than trying to avoid such issues, the strategy advocated here is to develop designs which are sensitive to ethical problems. Social experimenters should work with planners, participants, and other interested parties to resolve inherent ethical dilemmas. The benefits and costs of experimentation must be carefully weighed and the risks of conducting the experiment, as well as *not* conducting the experiment, must be considered. By converting an intervention into an experiment, the research process may, in fact, expose some ethical hazards of the intervention before they get out of hand.

It should be acknowledged that whatever procedures are employed to deal with ethical problems, conflicts will arise. In addition, it will not be possible to develop universal rules for ethical conduct of social experiments. Although informed consent and reduction of risk should be primary concerns, social experiments will not be of much use if many participants refuse to consent or if useful treatments are abandoned because of potential risks. The experimenter, although dedicated to ethical treatment of individual program participants, also needs to consider the needs of society and the importance of carrying out experiments which can potentially improve our quality of life.

Maintaining the Integrity of Designs

Planning a social experiment and actually carrying it out are very different activities. A design should be selected to be flexible enough to adapt to the environment of a program. It is almost impossible to predict how individuals will respond to the operation of a program, which is a particular problem when true experimental designs are used and one attempts to control the assignment of participants to conditions. In such experiments, although they are often conceptually necessary and ethically feasible, "real world" conditions can play havoc with their execution.

It is not suggested that every design be maintained regardless of the costs, for there are clearly situations in which it is desirable to modify or prematurely terminate an experiment. Some problems of executing social experiments can be identified, however, and the knowledge of these problems can lead to designs which are easier to maintain. Following Conner (1977), who has analyzed a dozen social programs which were planned as true experiments, several features of the relationship between design and execution that require attention and reinforcement can be identified: characteristics of the assignment plan, researcher/program planner relationships, and implementation procedures.

ASSIGNMENT PLAN

The most obvious design element has to do with the plan for assigning participants (or other units) to conditions of the experiment. Conner distinguished between "fixed" and "flexible" assignment plans. In a fixed plan, those conducting an experiment assign randomization units to conditions without exception; that is, they follow a carefully prescribed randomization plan. In a flexible plan, some leeway is permitted and assignments are altered depending on the objective circumstances or their interpretation of the participants' condition.

An example of a fixed assignment plan is provided by the sickle cell counseling experiment described earlier in this chapter. In the counseling experiment, clients who agreed to participate in the experiment were assigned to a sequence of tests and counseling that was prescribed by the researchers; neither staff nor clients could change the assignment. Such a procedure helps to insure the integrity of the study design, but is not without problems. For example, such an inflexible approach might reduce the number of people willing to participate in the study (thereby limiting external validity); in addition, internal validity problems may arise because of differential attrition by condition ("subject mortality"). If the procedures actually create administrative problems, it is also likely that the staff of the program will find a way to subvert the design. Such was the case in the initial stages of the Kansas City Police Patrol Experiment (see Chapter 1) where police officers did not follow the revised patrol instructions.

An example of a study in which it was necessary to have flexible assignment is Ross and Blumenthal's (1975) test of court programs to rehabilitate individuals convicted of drunken driving (Conner, 1977). Ross and Blumenthal conducted the study in cooperation with the Denver court system. Judges were asked to assign penalties to all those convicted of drunken driving (and certain other motor vehicle violations) according to a random assignment schedule. One-month periods were selected at random and during each month (cycled three times), judges were to assign either fines, conventional probation, or rehabilitation (a driver reeducation course) to all cases. Judges were allowed to vary the severity of the sentence (for example, the amount of fine, length of probation, amount of education) and were also permitted to exempt certain cases based on their own judgment.

The unfortunate aspect of the exceptional cases provision was that it was used differentially. During months when fines were to be assessed, 94 percent of those convicted received fines; when probation was to be applied, only 68 percent of those convicted received probation; and, when rehabilitation was prescribed, only 48 percent received this sentence. Of the subjects who were included in the analysis (only those who received the treatment as scheduled), there were no differences between the three groups in terms of their subsequent driving behavior. It is impossible to determine if there was an interaction between characteristics of the exceptional cases and their responses to treatment conditions. For example, it may have been older drivers who were classified as exceptional (that is, more responsible); perhaps these individuals would have been most susceptible to changing their behavior in a rehabilitative program.

Although it is easy to critique Ross and Blumenthal for allowing flexibility in the random assignment plan, it was probably necessary given the context in which the experiment was carried out. The judges might not have agreed to participate if they were not given some latitude. This may often be the case and if one wants to carry out social experiments, flexibility needs to be built in. When such flexibility is necessary, its harmful consequences can be mitigated if one has data on the differences/similarities between the participants who were excused (or had their assignment to conditions altered) and those who participated according to the assignment plan.

Even with a predetermined assignment plan, "seepage" is likely. Conditions, particularly if situated in the same settings, are likely to blur. An intervention perceived to be valuable by participants may spread into the control conditions despite a predetermined assignment plan. Contamination is a serious threat to the validity of the data: If the conditions do not remain pure, comparisons are meaningless. While contamination may be interpreted as a measure of "success"—if the intervention was ineffective, it would not be adopted by the control condition—it seriously interferes with interpreting research results. Structures for "monitoring" seepage should be put in place; program implementers need to be alerted about the difficulties introduced by seepage, and told when they can share their knowledge and experience with the control group.

The people who administer social experiments are often uncomfortable with assignment plans, fixed or flexible. They may feel that some participants are being neglected or unduly deprived or that experimenting with some participants is unethical. The reservations and discomforts of the implementers about assessment should be acknowledged and discussed before instituting an assignment plan.

RESEARCHER/PROGRAM PLANNER RELATIONSHIPS

As the above discussion of implementation indicates, collaborative relationships among the various parties in social experimentation are crucial to the conduct of experiments. They may be especially critical at the design stage, where one tries to develop procedures which satisfy the various constituent groups. Unfortunately, it is not easy to describe the circumstances that best facilitate the development and maintenance of a design.

Conner (1977) divided the studies he analyzed into two groups: those in which the researcher was located within the organization that conducted the program (internal) and those in which the researcher was located in a separate organization (external). (There are also researchers who are external by contract but internal by loyalty.) There are several views about the "best" location for a researcher (Anderson & Ball, 1978; Satin & Saxe, 1979; Weiss, 1972). An "independent" research firm contracted by an intervention group to conduct research over a period of several years may feel some constraints. External researchers are not dependent on the program developers or sponsors, although they might be dependent on future contracts and referrals for continuing support for their positions. Internal researchers may have more power (for example, to control the assignment plan) and probably have more information about the programs.

Conner found that researchers located inside a program tended to have more success in implementing the randomization plan than researchers who were external. In the six studies having internal researchers, randomization was successfully implemented, while in the six studies in which the researcher was external, only half had successful randomization. Although internal researchers appeared to have more success, it is important to note that the researchers, regardless of location, must be powerful enough to be able to influence the appropriate assignment of participants to conditions. Conner's analysis is at variance with other efforts to assess the conditions for successful research (see Bernstein & Freeman, 1975). In a variety of social programs (not only those planned as true experiments), external researchers are more likely to develop rigorous (that is, true experimental) designs, perhaps because they have independent referents vis-à-vis program personnel.

An additional caveat, perhaps obvious, is that internal/external distinctions ignore differences between levels of power. In the studies described throughout this book, a variety of combinations of role and power have been illustrated. It is also important to take into account the role of the funding agency. In many cases, such as the Follow Through Planned Variations situation (see Chapter 3), the structure provided by the government had an important effect on the nature of the program and the experimental design.

In still other cases, the researcher and program administrator are one and the same. Such was the case in both the health insurance study (Newhouse 1974a, 1975a) and the Negative Income Tax Experiment (Rossi & Lyall, 1976). In each of these experiments, the program was developed for the purpose of developing a research study; thus, the researchers maintained control over randomization. Although the effectiveness of this approach and, in fact, the wisdom of large-scale experiments, is still not clear, it is one important model of researcher and planner relationships.

These issues of location, loyalty and power are problems of the researcher's identity. As a researcher, one is in a position to generate support for a program, to produce information that could terminate a program, to identify individuals or structures responsible for problems in a program, and /or to innovate strategies to improve the functioning of a program. The potential power of researchers is great, although actual power may be much less than the perceived power of the role. Research is still considered a mystery, an intimidation, or an irrelevancy to many program personnel. The "rub" comes when preliminary data suggest problems inherent in the intervention; for example, incompetence in program administration, needs for radical restructuring of the program, or needs for different distributions of resources. A researcher may discover that a job training program effectively trains youth, but that the corporations that sponsor the research are unwilling to hire the minorities being trained. Or, early patterns of the data on the impact of drug therapy may suggest that the intervention is dangerous to participants or is wasteful of their resources. Another researcher may read a press release in which preliminary results on a child abuse project are misquoted or taken out of context. Despite the criticisms offered, the program may remain intact. Ethical considerations may indicate a reexamination of the experiment

Researchers have a responsibility to report preliminary findings/distortions to their sponsors and to work collaboratively to determine routes of action. In the job training example, the intervention may have to be expanded to include training of the personnel officers in the corporation about Affirmative Action, with obvious implications for changes in the research design. The child abuse press release may prompt a second "corrective" press release which adds the criticisms to the praises of the program. The final example, in which preliminary data indicate the dangers or uselessness of drug therapy, may require termination of the entire experiment, or a redesign of the intervention and the research. Above all, responses should be generated collaboratively. To do so, researchers need to have clear a priori agreements with their sponsors/collaborators about their loyalty to the research (vs. the program), their obligations to the sponsors and the participants, and their commitment to science as well as the politics of the program. A contract specifying the roles and loyalties of all involved parties may prove a useful "backup" for researchers caught between conflicting loyalties and/or pressures. Such a contract can specify mutually agreed upon mechanisms for maintaining the integrity of the design, should potentially problematic data emerge.

IMPLEMENTATION ISSUES

Aside from "pure" design questions (such as the assignment plan) and questions of how the researcher-program planner should structure their relationship, there are a variety of other implementation-related issues. The procedures for instructing program personnel in the assignment plan and the information given to program participants are both important to the success of a planned experiment. They require the same kind of planning that the actual experimental design receives. Knowing when to modify or terminate an experiment may be crucial, both to collecting useful data and to insuring that further experimentation can be undertaken. These are only a sample of implementation issues, but they illustrate the types of problems that need to be addressed.

Program personnel. The training of program personnel is often ignored, but it should be obvious that design plans do not get implemented automatically. They often require the joint action of a variety of individuals and groups, although when the researcher actually conducts the study and has all the decision power, this may be less of a problem. However, when the researcher shares power or has complex relationships (either in terms of numbers of people or levels of relationships), this is a potentially significant problem.

Conner (1977), for example, analyzed the effect of the number of implementers on the actual conduct of the experiment. When, as in the drunken driver experiment, many implementers (in that case, the judges) are involved, it is difficult to maintain the integrity of the design. A particular difficulty is that implementers may act differently across conditions seriously limiting internal validity. In some cases, each implementer needs to be considered in a separate analysis (sometimes creating statistical problems) and the interaction between implementer and the intervention must be assessed. In some cases this factor can be systematically varied; in other cases, it requires an internal analysis (for example, one judge who favors fines, another who favors rehabilitation).

There are a number of other ways in which such problems may be handled. One would be to centralize the assignment plan: while different implementers are responsible for the assignment plan, they assign participants only in consultation with a central office or person. In a case where it is necessary to have a flexible plan, it might be necessary to set up a panel to review formally any exceptions to the assignment rules. A more direct solution, viable in certain cases, is to reduce the differences between conditions and thus the difficulty of gaining implementer assistance. While no treatment control groups are often necessary, this is not always the case. For some programs, systematically altering levels of the treatment variable may be all that is necessary. Such design features greatly simplify the implementation of the experiment.

Participant information. Many of the issues concerning what information is given to participants in social experiments were considered in Chapter 3. Earlier, the focus was on the differential effects of giving information to individuals in the treatment and control conditions. It was noted that in true experiments, internal validity could be threatened if information was provided because of such effects as compensatory rivalry and demoralization. In the health insurance study, for example, participants in all conditions knew that they were in an experiment and realized that their responses to the program might have an important impact on the development of national health policy. Clearly, in such a situation, there is not a great deal that can be done to reduce the effects of participant "hypothesizing." Importantly, the designers have built in a variety of control conditions that should enable them at least to estimate the effects of being in an experiment. It goes without saying that similar experiments should have such controls.

It should also be recognized that the problem of what information to give participants is a particular problem in experiments specifically designed as research studies. To the extent that experiments are conducted as a natural part of the development of social innovation, participants will not feel like "guinea pigs" and will not exhibit effects unique to the experimental situation. The more natural the conditions of the experiment and the longer the time that the experiment is conducted, the less likely it is that these effects will occur.

Modifying and terminating an experiment. Although extending the length of an experiment solves one aspect of the problem, it is equally important to consider how to modify the design once a study is under way, and how to terminate a study. In some cases (see Meier, 1972), the question arises as to how much data are necessary before the results of an innovation of great potential value are disseminated. Meier describes the case of the poliomyelitis vaccine: though it was quickly obvious that it was effective, much data had to be collected to "prove" its efficacy. This data collection process slowed the process of dissemination and has been an especially problematic issue in evaluating health care innovations (Mosteller, 1981). Although this problem is, in part, a policy question out of scientists' purview, in other cases (such as the polio vaccine), the researcher's informed opinion is very much needed.

While knowing how to balance costs and benefits of conducting research is difficult (cf. Office of Technology Assessment, 1980), it is a necessary component of social experimentation. One should not be hesitant to consider costs and benefits and, if necessary, to make changes during implementation. Especially when an experiment is found to be harmful to participants, it must be quickly terminated or modified. In such situations, the usefulness of additional data may be very limited. Such abuses may also make policy makers hesitant to allow further experimentation.

Conclusion

The practice of social experimentation and the planning of social interventions are undoubtedly complex. Despite the many obstacles and problems, however, solutions are possible. The problems of conducting experiments probably reflect the difficulty of the social issues themselves. Their resolution, through the collaborative action of many, is what can lead to significant new knowledge and better social interventions.

CHAPTER 8

MEASUREMENT PRACTICE

> *"The problem with insight, sensitivity, and intuition is that they tend to confirm our biases. At one time, people were convinced of their ability to identify witches. All it required was sensitivity to the markings of the devil. Clinical experience is not the same thing as empirical evidence."*
>
> Naomi Weisstein

In many ways, the issues in measurement are similar to those in design—it is a process which involves planning and selection. Measurement differs, however, because one may select many measures, whereas designs are more circumscribed. In practical terms, measurement is as limited as all other aspects of social experimentation. Financial resources are not bottomless and there are clear limits as to how much information can be collected from experimental participants. One must decide what types of information are most important and how they can be collected.

In Chapter 4 we described several measurement tools available to assess social behavior. A number of conceptual problems that underlie social measurement were also discussed. The present chapter focuses on the pragmatic issues of measurement—the selection and application of measurement tools. Just as the integrity of the design process must be maintained, so too must the actual measurement process be carefully conducted so that the intended effects are actually assessed.

Specification of Goals

Social interventions generally have multiple goals. As noted in Chapter 7, goals need to be clearly articulated. Measurement involves specification of the goals to be tested, the instruments to be used, and the people who should be involved in the assessment. This section describes how one determines which program goals to measure, how goals and indicators are operationalized, and implementation procedures for measuring the outcomes of social experiments.

CONCEPTUALIZING PROGRAM GOALS

The process of defining conceptual program goals can be a difficult process. Although it is often assumed that social programs from the start have an explicit set of goals, this may not always be the case. Social programs often develop out of the sudden availability of particular resources, or from political considerations the implications of which have not been considered. They are rarely guided by sophisticated hypotheses about human behavior. For this reason, the determination of conceptual goals requires the coordinated efforts of researchers, who understand ways in which goals can be measured, and planners, who may or may not understand the objectives of a program. Goals are important to understand in order to develop an appropriate design, and are equally important to develop the measures of outcome used in a social experiment.

Most social programs are designed to achieve multiple conceptual goals, which may be either implicit or explicit. A Community Mental Health Center (CMHC), for example, may have any one or all of the following objectives:

(a) to provide social support to deinstitutionalized patients;

(b) to increase public access to mental health services;

(c) to provide preventive mental health services;

(d) to offer outreach services to special populations.

Each goal requires its own research design and data collection procedure. If deinstitutionalization is the primary goal, a simple count of the numbers of people in large institutions versus the numbers at the community mental health centers might be sufficient. If outreach is the primary objective, interviews with community people might be necessary. Each goal suggests a methodological strategy. To best determine the measurement issues for a social intervention, one must consider its objectives and decide which are to be considered.

Not only do social programs begin with many objectives, but as they evolve over time, their objectives may change. For example, as domestic violence increasingly becomes a public concern, CMHCs are developing programs responsive to this issue. At the same time, a number of states are mandating that services to the deinstitutionalized be a central priority. With community, advisory board, legislative, and financial pressures competing and often conflicting, it is difficult to know how to measure the impact of CMHC "services." As priorities change, programs are redirected and data collection procedures must be modified accordingly. Decisions about measurement of program impact are rarely final.

What should be measured? While CMHCs represent a more complicated set of problems than most, they also embody many typical measurement problems. A systematic approach to the measurement task is offered by Stufflebeam's (1971) CIPP model of research. CIPP (an acronym for Context, Input, Process, and Product) organizes research so that it can inform social planners. It involves identifying four levels of research variables appropriate to measuring program impact. On the Context level, data are collected about the sites (location, facilities, people, history) used in the research. On the Input level, data are collected on the old and new resources of the program (technology, finances, lender-agency leakages, community alliances). On the Process level, data are collected on the implementation and administration of the treatment (Who runs the program? What do people know about it? What problems have developed?). On the Product level, data are collected to provide an overall assessment of program efficacy (Did the intervention work? Was there a reduction in mental health problems, dropouts, illness, domestic violence, truancy from school, and so on?). The model forces program researchers and administrators to clarify, before measurement begins, what information needs to be gathered and how it will be utilized.

The study of the interactive telecommunications system that was designed to improve delivery of health services in a rural environment (Saxe & Fine, 1979; see Chapter 7) employed the CIPP model to generate information about the functioning of the program and how individuals responded to it before, during, and after program implementation.

1. *Preimplementation.* On the Context level, data were to be collected about the environment: age, race, income and education of the professionals, staff, and patients who could potentially use the system. The Input level tapped information about the utilization of program and hospital resources relevant to program goals (for example, do professionals already have communication across several areas—telephone, conferences, centralized continuing education, curriculum development?).

2. *During and after implementation.* The Process level tells us how people feel about and interact with the new system, suggesting how the system is utilized and how it may be improved (for example, who is technology-phobic? Are some people "hogging" the system?). Finally, the Product level relates the outcomes of the system to the defined objectives (for example, do physicians contact each other more frequently because of the ITS? Is this positive use of their time, or is it wasteful? Have patient costs been inflated by the technology, or reduced?).

Stufflebeam offers this model as a way to conceptualize program goals and measure the comprehensive impact of a social program.

Unanticipated effects. While the CIPP model is a systematic way of looking at anticipated program impacts, the unanticipated effects of a program also need to be considered. All too often, research done on social interventions considers only the immediate, localized consequences of the intervention. The long-term impact and effects beyond the program are neglected. Social programs can be designed so that side effects of the intervention are also measured. These effects are often neglected because they are expensive to assess. Cook et al. (1975) describe the costs and benefits of broad and narrow models of research, which they call the *medical* and the *tailored* models of information gathering, respectively.

The medical model involves extensive research on program effects. Researchers study unanticipated as well as intended program effects. While it is most appropriate to apply this model to medical problems (where the dangers of unanticipated effects can be very important), it is also applicable to social programs. A perhaps unusual example is the "social program" that resulted from the 1978 New York City law mandating that dog owners clean up the waste left by their pets on streets and sidewalks (Jason et al., 1980). Although this law was not instituted as a social experiment, one could compare New York City to a similar city along the dimensions of (1) absolute amounts of dog waste left on the streets and sidewalks of the city, (2) numbers of dogs abandoned at the ASPCA, (3) numbers of stray dogs, and (4) the health consequences for children and others who might come into contact with dog waste. Such extensive information gathering would look at the expected outcome measures (item 1) as well as the rippling effects of the law (items 2, 3, and 4).

The medical approach involves collection of information beyond that necessary to determine whether or not the treatment achieved its original objective(s). A tailored model, alternatively, involves narrowly focused research designed to measure indicators of specified goals. For example, if the aim of the New York City law was primarily to reduce the absolute amount of dog feces on the streets, then that in itself would be the sole indicator of program success. The specific behavioral objectives defined prior to program implementation and unintended effects would probably be unassessed. A medical model better suits exploratory studies and studies in which there are potentially harmful outcomes for participants or others. The two styles are not mutually exclusive, however, and may best be utilized in conjunction with one another (especially in pilot research in which a large number of variables are assessed).

Problems. The impression should not be given that the determination of program goals and measurement procedures is an easy process. Typically, program goals are poorly delineated, and measurement procedures are difficult to develop. Below, three types of programs—broad-aim, long term, and "invisible indicator"—are described in which specific types of problems develop.

The objectives of broad-aim programs, designed for comprehensive, large-scale impact, are harder to articulate systematically and therefore harder to measure than those of more narrow, focused program. "Broad-aim programs . . . seem designed to frustrate a research person who feels s/he must know specifically what the program hopes to change in order that s/he may gather base line data" (Weiss & Rein, 1970, p. 236). A broad-based program designed generally to facilitate improved race relations in high schools is harder to define, in terms of expected impact, than a program aimed at encouraging racially integrated athletic clubs. Although the two may sound similar, what is expected from the second is clearer and more easily measured than the vague objective of the first.

Similarly, the objectives of long-term programs are more difficult to predict, and therefore more difficult to determine than those of short-term programs. The long-term program, requiring time and community involvement in order to flourish, may affect participants in a variety of unexpected ways which change over time. For example, a family health program designed not only to provide services, but also to influence the attitudes, behaviors, and knowledge of a community toward preventive health practices, may require a lot of time to have impact. Indicators of long-term success could include more frequent visits to the health clinic, spread of information through the community, more and earlier requests for reduced smoking programs, and/or more requests for nutrition classes. Unanticipated effects might include a reduced number of car accident deaths due to less drinking while driving and/or increased use of seat belts, or community lobbying for national health insurance. Because many of the long-term effects can not be anticipated, it is important to use data collection instruments that are sensitive to potential effects, and to be vigilant throughout data collection about unanticipated effects.

Accessible indicators of program objectives are obviously easier to measure than those which are inaccessible, such as drug use in the home or amount of cheating behavior in settings other than the one being tested. Drug use is certainly easier to monitor in a drug rehabilitation residential unit than in clients' homes or on the street. Yet insofar as the invisible information is necessary to determine program effectiveness, researchers and administrators need to find innovative ways to access such invisible information.

OPERATIONALIZING PROGRAM GOALS

Specifying program goals is but the first step in measurement. The succeeding steps involve their operationalization and measurement. One must formulate clear and tangible indicators of program impact—success, effectiveness, and nonimpact. Refining, or reducing, program hypotheses into measures of impact is a difficult process and one that inevitably involves some loss of information, but it is a necessary step in valid measurement of a program's impact.

Moving from a conceptual question to a simple indicator of readjustment often appears reductionistic. Operationalization sometimes leaves researchers with a sense of having compromised the goals of the program. However, the process is essential to the conduct of research. Without operationalization, information can not be collected systematically, clear measures of impact cannot be derived, and no inferences about program effectiveness can be made. Conceptual goals, once specified, must be operationalized in a manner satisfying to program research and administration.

Every conceptual goal can be operationalized in many ways. For example, the conceptual goal of helping the deinstitutionalized could be measured by:

(1) interviewing a sample of deinstitutionalized individuals about their adjustment and satisfaction;
(2) observing the daily social interaction of these individuals;
(3) monitoring patient records to note any changes in psychiatric symptoms or prescription drug usage; and/or
(4) surveying employers about their perceptions of the adjustment of deinstitutionalized individuals.

Because each method provides different data in response to a distinct aspect of the program goal (and it would probably be impractical to use all possible indicators), measures should be chosen in consultation with those interested in and affected by the program.

Some program administrators consider operationalization of goals an impossible, undesirable, or unreasonable task. A collaborative context—with researcher and administrator working together to create measurable indicators of program effects—makes the task more manageable. The conceptual understanding of the administration coupled with the scientific rigor of the researcher should generate operational indicators of program effectiveness (Weiss & Rein, 1970).

Operationalization requires movement from most general to most specific, from global to particular, abstract to concrete. Consider a social experiment on the impact of a family therapy program for adolescents labeled juvenile delinquents (Klein, Alexander & Parsons, 1977). The treatments tested included: (a) a family-based systems therapy group, (b) two control condition therapy groups, and (c) no treatment. The family-based treatment focused on clear, straightforward family communication, reinforcement of interpersonal behaviors, and contracting of the rights and responsibilities of the family members. The underlying assumption of the system's approach is that deviant behavior may be manifested by one family member, but is somehow supported by the entire family. Therefore, to the extent that change is possible, all family members need to be involved.

How, in such a situation, can treatment impact be measured? Operationally, how can one determine if families are encouraging or not encouraging healthy behavior? The researchers operationalized this concept in several ways. They looked at family communication patterns: the frequency of discussions and silences, as well as the frequency and nature of interruptions in family interactions. In a follow-up study, they examined the extent to which the identified delinquents in treatment and control conditions were recidivist and the number who had siblings referred to the courts. Results indicated that the family-based intervention resulted in a substantially lower recidivism rate for the original "juvenile delinquent" and a significantly lower sibling referral rate than other treatment conditions. Indicators of program success other than observation of intrafamily behaviors and utilization of court records could also have been used. Interviews could have been conducted with family members to measure satisfaction with family relations; school-related behaviors could have been used to test for any changes in academic performance; psychological tests could have been administered to detect personality changes. But given the theoretical interest in the family system, it was most reasonable to utilize the indicators that were selected by the researchers. These indicators—family communication patterns and sibling referral rates—reflect family system changes, not just changes in the individual deemed "deviant."

Consider another example: the Yoke Crest program designed to rehabilitate juvenile offenders (Silberman, 1975). Yoke Crest employs a strategy of positive and negative behavioral reinforcements in juvenile rehabilitation. How can rehabilitation success be measured? Assume that Yoke Crest aims to develop "better, more responsible citizens." This is hardly a controversial goal and few would question the inherent value of such a program. Yet the question remains, how can a "better, more responsible citizen" be recognized, much less measured? Is such a person one who is employed, married, active in community social groups, a religious devotee, or active in local politics? Is such a person one who stays off drugs, out of jail, or goes back to school? How can a "better, more responsible citizen" be defined?

Developing operationalizations would be the job of researcher and the administrator—they would compose a series of measurable indicators of such a citizen, while trying to hold their personal values in abeyance. The researcher-administrator team might decide operationally that a "model citizen" is one who can hold down a job for a three-month period, is satisfied (as measured by a life satisfaction scale), stays clear of drugs (as measured by physical check-ups, self-reports, and so on), and participates in personally enjoyable activities (such as "rap groups" at a drug center, volunteer work, reading, or music). Alternatively, the "model citizen" might be one who enrolls in a high school equivalency program, returns to live with parents or another member of their family, regularly participates in drug counseling sessions (once a month), attends church or other community group activities, and is willing to work with a younger drug addict undergoing rehabilitation.

Regardless of what operational definition of the treatment goal is selected, it must be determined jointly by researchers and administrators. If these individuals have discrepant visions of program success, there may be conflict, especially if the data according to one suggest the program to be effective, while the data according to the other indicate program failure.

Operationalizing program goals, although easier in some contexts than in others, provides for the most meaningful assessment of program effectiveness. If program goals remain vague or are not operationalized, the results of the social experiment will be disputable and frequently not interpretable (Cook & Gruder, 1978). The probability that data will be used in decision-making is directly related to the quality of the data collected. If goals have not been operationalized, chances are that the information does not respond to a particular problem. This lessens the chance that the data will influence policy or program decisions.

RELATING MEASURES TO GOALS

Because the conceptual goals of a social program are diverse, one usually develops a variety of operational indicators to be measured in a variety of ways. The use of multiple outcome measures rather than a single indicator of program impact provides researchers and administrators the opportunity to understand the "holistic" impact of a social program. If the knowledge, attitudes, behaviors, and perceptions of participants are all measured, the effective pieces of the program can be distinguished from the ineffective pieces. Take, for example, a family planning course taught by an obviously uncomfortable or puritanical instructor. Although this instructor may effectively teach the facts about the varieties of birth control procedures available, implicit messages about the "inappropriateness" or even "dirtiness" of discussing such issues may also be transmitted to students. Such a program may increase student knowledge, but it also models negative attitudes toward human sexuality.

If such an experimental program were measured solely in terms of knowledge acquired, the course might look effective, while the fact that distorted attitudes were transmitted in the class would not be identified by the measurement procedures. In a similar vein, imagine two family planning courses, one with an emphasis on biology and contraception and the other stressing personal values, attitudes, and students' feelings about sexuality and parenting. If both classes were researched in terms of the (1) amount of scientific knowledge gained, and (2) amount of personal reflection on sexuality and pregnancy, the first class might look more knowledgeable, while individuals in the second class might have gained more social maturity. Both effects are important to assess so that classes combining both perspectives can be developed if that is the goal. Reducing the number of unwanted pregnancies may require that adolescents not only learn the facts of life but also explore their own feelings and attitudes toward sexuality and parenting. Because it is not sufficient to teach just the facts to induce change (Lewin, 1951), both kinds of outcome measures are valuable. On the other hand, it may be that there is no "truth" as to which class would better benefit the students and each may offer distinct benefits. It is necessary to utilize appropriate indicators of program effectiveness to identify such outcomes.

It is important to collect information on attitudes towards interventions, as well as behaviors affected, if only in order to distinguish and understand the difference between the principles of a treatment itself and its administration. What can be said about a program that fails as implemented? Should it be deemed a total failure, with recommendations not to replicate it in other sites, or should the implementation be attempted in other sites with any appropriate change?

Consider the all-too-frequent situation in which a community opposed to integration is forced to integrate its schools. In such a situation, resistance and negative feelings are modeled for students and cannot help but undermine the programs designed to facilitate interracial relations (such as human relations groups, minority history courses, and multiracial social events). In this case, using only behavioral outcome measure (such as the numbers of students working in racially integrated groups or amount of cross-racial socializing) might incorrectly suggest the failure of the integration program. If additional attitudinal information were collected, one might learn that the students received the message, explicitly or implicitly, that the program was not good, or that the students recognized their parents' or others' negativism and modeled themselves accordingly. If both kinds of information were available in this case, then one could make the determination that the implementation failed, and the program itself was never actually tested. Of course, it may also be that such forms of integration do not work and that the student internalizes the community's view. In an effort to distinguish the success or failure of a program from the success or failure of its implementation, however, multiple outcome measures will generate a clear picture of "what's going on" and "what causes what."

Qualitative vs. quantitative measures. The difference between qualitative and quantitative measures can be characterized by the different styles of journalists and scientists, respectively. Journalists document the personal experiences of a few people and report these stories as snapshots of reality. Scientists often collect short-answer quantified information from many people to provide a representative, though less detailed, perspective on the event (Snow, 1971). How can social researchers, interested in both the detailed individual experience and the overall quantifiable impact, obtain meaningful useful information from individuals in a social experiment? Should we interview some key, accessible people about their impressions, as the journalist might, or should a number of individuals be randomly selected and their experiences quantitatively assessed? Our suggestion is that a combination of quantitative and qualitative data can furnish researchers and administrators with the most complete knowledge about a social program (see Chapter 5).

Qualitative data, as noted in Chapter 5, includes all information that is descriptive and nonstructured, and typically is used to provide insight into the *unique* experience of each respondent. Responses to open-ended questions, a stream of consciousness transcript, and running chronologies about an event are generally qualitative in nature. Quantitative data, on the other hand, include numerical or categorical responses to questions, providing information about *commonalities* across individuals and/or groups of individuals. The same concept can be investigated in a qualitative way: "Having participated in the program, could you make some suggestions as to how you might improve it?" or a quantitative way: "To improve this program, would you . . .

    (a) add more staff,
    (b) reduce staff size,
    (c) change staff, or
    (d) none of the above?"

The information resulting from open-ended questions is undoubtedly richer than quantitative data, but more limited for analytic purposes. Qualitative data allow respondents greater latitude of response, but they limit the analysis strategies. Quantitative data have the opposite problem because they restrict respondent responses, although they are more amenable to easy analysis.

In an ideal world, quantitative and qualitative data collected on the same program confirm each other, demonstrate common issues, and illuminate identical problems. Yet this is often not the case; the two methods frequently generate contradictory findings. In these instances, the qualitative information can usually help researchers discern the meaning of the quantitative results (Campbell, 1974, 1979). The two modes of questioning are both critical to capturing full and complete responses: they elicit distinct kinds of information and are by no means redundant.

Long-term vs. short-term measures. Most social programs have both short- and long-term outcomes: social experiments should, when possible, measure both. Unless both kinds of effects are documented, the full impact of a program may be misinterpreted (Weiss, 1972).

Immediate effects are, of course, more easily measured than long-term effects. This is true for a number of reasons, not the least of which is the availability of participants for short-term testing, and the loss of participants over time (this was a particular problem in the sickle cell counseling experiment). People may drop out of programs, move from the area, forget to leave forwarding addresses, or die. Measuring long-range effects under these circumstances is quite difficult. A study conducted in Eugene, Oregon, measured the short- and long-term consequences of a juvenile rehabilitation program and encountered many of these problems in an attempt to "follow-up" individuals who had participated in the program some years earlier. Friends, neighbors, and employers were questioned about the whereabouts of the sought after participants; researchers frequented favorite "hangouts" to try to find the boys; welfare rolls and social security files were used in the search. The effort paid off: the "find" rate was 75 percent of the original group (Rothbart & Frease, 1965). The Cambridge-Somerville Youth Study (McCord, 1978) is another good example: more than 30 years after the study began, researchers were able to locate almost all of the initial participants (or ascertain that they were deceased).

It is somewhat easier to conduct a study over time with an intact experimental population. The infant day care study (Kagan, Kearsley & Zelazo, 1977) involved monitoring infant behavior over the course of two years. Children—33 in day care, 67 in home care control conditions, and 16 mixed (part-time home and part-time outside care)—were tested over time on many outcome measures. The study investigating the developmental consequences of day care could not logically be conducted on a short-term basis; it had to be conducted across time. This requirement, however, was relatively easily met because at least some of the infants were enrolled for the necessary period of time in the day-care facility.

Most social intervention research, as might be imagined, is limited to short-term outcome measures, often because of the time and financial constraints of long-term research (Fine & Goldman, 1979). In addition, some programs require short time frames so that dissemination of information and their impact can be quickly demonstrated. In such circumstances, measures should be developed which can predict future outcomes. In educational programs, for example, researchers usually develop tests which (perhaps through other research) are known to correlate with later performance.

Implementation

How does one go about collecting data? The process is not as easy to describe as one might think. Collecting data is not like picking grapes off a vine—the data in social experiments are changing and sensitive to how they are picked. Who collects the information, how is it collected, and what kinds of information are gathered all color the results.

ARTIFACTS

Numerous factors influence data collection procedures—some intentionally, some unintentionally. Many of these influences are measurable, while others are not. For example, one such factor concerns how respondents feel about and accordingly respond to research when they know they are being studied.

The experience of being researched affects the resulting information. As Orne (1962) has noted, *demand characteristics* are built into the research process. Independent of the effects of participating in a social program, individuals who know they are "being watched" tend to act differently than individuals who do not know they are being watched—hence, the viewers' enjoyment in watching naive individuals on Candid Camera. Knowing that research is being conducted can cause individuals to alter their responses to interviews or questionnaires in varied ways (Rowan, 1974):

(1) Some respondents provide data in which they praise the program, despite apparent program failure, for fear that a bad report would cause program funds to be withdrawn, the institution to become impoverished, or their jobs be lost.
(2) Some respondents will be extremely critical of the program, using the data to retaliate or "get back" at the institution or administration—a sabotage tactic.
(3) Some respondents may create attitudes about the program just so they can partake in the research—they fabricate opinions merely to participate.
(4) Some may feel obligated to say nice things just because they are being asked about the program.

Researchers must try to measure responses that reflect authentic perceptions of intervention activities and distinguish those responses that are rooted in feelings about the institution or the program administrators from feelings about the program. Data about the program and the institution should be collected separately.

Some of the methods for insuring the collection of valid data from participants have to do with the nature of the measuring instrument (as discussed in Chapter 4). Other considerations have to do with the research context and the nature of the questions being asked. Although it is true that individuals alter their responses if they know they are being studied, it is also true that researchers themselves can bias the research process.

The so-called interviewer expectancy effects are the least conscious and thus the most difficult to correct of researcher biases. Sudman and colleagues (1977) discovered that interviewers who expected respondents to underreport information had a greater number of respondents who did, in fact, underreport their behaviors (particularly in sensitive areas such as sexuality). Somehow, interviewers' anxiety about asking the questions was conveyed to the respondents and resulted in underresponses. Such expectancy effects suggest to respondents "You don't want to tell me this, right?" Because interviewers appear to share with respondents expectations of the difficulty or the sensitivity of particular questions, it is difficult to measure the extent of the bias introduced (Singer & Kohnke-Aguirre, 1979). The bias of interviewer expectancy can be minimized, however, if interviewers are trained so that they feel comfortable with questions that probe for sensitive material.

More overtly, however, interviewers influence respondent data by asking leading or vague questions. When collecting information, researchers should let the respondents provide the information, and not guide, lead, or distort the responses. Attitude items must be unambiguous; all terms should be precise and explicit. The question, "Have you ever been abused by your husband or lover?" is ambiguous because it does not provide a clear definition of the word abused. Is the question referring to psychological abuse, verbal abuse, or sexual abuse? Does it include hitting, slapping, punching, threats, use of weapons? It is critical that each person respond to questions with the same impression of what is being asked. If a researcher is interested in each respondent's own definition of abuse, an open-ended question should be used. To produce unambiguous data, every term in a questionnaire or interview must be clearly specified, or follow-up questions used to pinpoint the respondent's meaning (Roiser, 1974).

The Art of Asking Questions (Payne, 1951), describes the precision necessary for a "workable" questionnaire. Pitfalls include implied alternatives, loaded questions, and taking for granted knowledge of respondents. Implied alternatives (a way of leading respondents) are questions that imply that only two responses are appropriate to a question. "Would you consider people who resisted the military draft to be men of moral conscience or cowards?" Implied alternatives limit the range of responses available to respondents, and therefore force them to make choices that may not accurately reflect their true attitudes.

In much the way that implied alternatives produce misleading information, questions which suggest taken-for-granted knowledge also introduce potential data problems. If a question were asked about the expected impact

of a remedial educational program "such as DORO," it is likely that many
would answer even if they did not know what DORO was (and in this case,
"DORO" is a fabrication). In a survey of any kind, questions which take for
granted respondent knowledge are, for this reason, problematic. The resulting data represent fabricated or "appearance" opinions or attitudes. Gill
(1974) got 70 percent of his respondents to make judgments about the
fictitious "Metallic Metals Act" by asking them their impressions of the
Act, without asking if they were familiar with it. Respondents are reluctant
to volunteer that they are unfamiliar with a program, act, or organization
with which an interviewer obviously thinks they should be familiar. Accordingly, respondents have perfected the art of "faking it" in order to "save
face." (So, if you want to demonstrate that a majority of your respondents
are familiar with the program being researched, ask them about their impressions of the program. This will guarantee a higher, if inaccurate, rate of
community familiarity than if they are asked if they have ever heard of the
program.)

If one is more interested in documenting true estimates of familiarity with
a particular program, it is important that this information be tapped in a way
that is unobtrusive and does not convey to respondents that they *should* be
familiar with the program. For example, to determine the extent of public
knowledge of the Outreach drug abuse problem at Bluehill Hospital, one
might ask community residents "What options are available, locally, for
citizens with a drug problem?" or "Do any local hospitals offer drug treatment programs? (if yes, which ones)?" rather than "What do you think of
the Outreach drug abuse program at Bluehill Hospital?"

DATA GATHERERS

Who should collect data about a social program or intervention? It is
desirable, although often not possible, to employ researchers who are
"blind" to the conditions; that is, researchers who are unaware of the
intervention or condition of the respondent, and/or ignorant of the hypotheses of the study. This precaution can reduce the potential biases introduced
by the researchers.

A critical question, as was noted earlier in terms of design, is whether data
collectors should be internal or external to the program (Anderson & Ball,
1978; Weiss, 1972). This question has long been debated in the social
research literature. Researchers internal to the program are an asset in that
they are familiar with the respondents and knowledgeable about the program,
and may therefore be more trusted in the interview. An internal data collector,
on the other hand, may have difficulty being "objective." An individual
internal to the program may have an investment in collecting data that make

the program look good or look bad. In some cases, an internal researcher may be less trusted in an interview because of these "connections."

There are costs associated with external data collectors as well. While external data gatherers are objective, fresh, and in some ways naive about the program, they are unfamiliar with the people, unlikely to recognize program nuances, and may be oblivious to subtleties in the research process. Whether to use an internal or an external data collector is a decision that should be made independently for each social experiment.

Additional data collector decisions concern researcher-respondent interaction. Should an attempt be made to match researchers and respondents on gender, age, and race? Should researchers be multilingual? Trained in dealing with stressful situations? These questions should be considered as one embarks on research. One way to decide is to conduct small pretests for these methodological alternatives.

PREPARING FOR DATA COLLECTION

Respondents who are going to be interviewed or surveyed should be contacted in advance to (1) secure their participation, (2) arrange an appointment, and (3) encourage interest. Participating in research can be viewed as a chore or an interesting experience; often the difference depends on how the research is initially presented to the participant.

A cover letter explaining the sponsors, purpose, and procedures of the research is helpful. Promising anonymity may be attractive for some; promising personal credit may be appealing for others. Of course, this promise must be kept. The feasibility should, when possible, be determined by some form of a pilot test.

When conducting social experiments, it is not always easy to secure participation. Obviously when large-scale social experimentation is undertaken this is less of a problem; at least it is as much a problem for social planners as it is for the researchers. Usually, there is no "best" way to secure participation. Offering payments or pledging a contribution to an organization will work in some cases but not in others. Another approach is social pressure, which can take a number of forms. One can approach a group and invite them to agree to participate as a group. Alternatively, one can request that formal or informal leaders secure groups' participation. Or, one can use social categories to "catch" respondents, such as "I am interviewing all of the key participants in this program and would be interested in including you in the sample" (Richardson, Dohrenwend & Klein, 1965). The strategy one employs is, of course, closely tied to the design goals of the experiment.

It should be recognized that research participants deserve something in return for their participation. Whether they are paid, provided a service, or acknowledged as individuals, their participation must be reciprocated in some way. The failure to do so may be unethical and, as well, may make the participants less willing to provide useful data.

DATA COLLECTION METHODS

As was described in Chapter 4, data come in many forms. They can be extracted from records or collected through observation, tests, or interviews/questionnaires. Because every mode of data collection has its unique advantages and disadvantages, some cautions are appropriate to each.

Data extracted from archives, or records, need to be examined carefully. One must be sure that the record keeping procedures are updated and equivalent across sites and that the same piece of information really means the same thing in different settings. For example, researchers in medical clinics might be interested in "no show" rates. One must be sure that across sites a "no show" means the same thing: does it include people who just fail to meet their appointments or people who cancel and/or reschedule? Shared understandings of the information are critical for archival analyses.

Data collection through observation similarly has to meet standardized criteria. Decisions have to be made about whether or not the observers should participate or remain unobtrusive. Either way, observers should employ common indicators of particular behaviors, and establish reliability in their observations. One coder's "smile" must be comparable to another coder's definition of a "smile." It must be decided, with observational techniques, how standardized the data must be. Should observations be structured so that only particular behaviors are coded (Bales, 1951, 1958), or open-ended so that the flow of interaction is monitored?

Interviews and questionnaires can also be administered in a variety of ways. They can be conducted face-to-face or over the telephone; individually or with a group. Each method has distinct features. Face-to-face interviews are considered more personal and less inhibiting, and are more likely to elicit respondent cooperation than are telephone interviews. Information that is particularly sensitive is often best collected in a face-to-face setting. Data on income, sexuality, and drug use, for example, may be retrievable only after personal rapport has been established. The telephone, however, is obviously a much cheaper method of collecting large-cale information and appropriate for many kinds of surveys (Groves, 1979). The costs and benefits must be considered in determining the most effective methodology for any piece of research.

WHEN THE INFORMATION IS NOT AVAILABLE

Nonresponse is a problem inherent in the conduct of social experiments and is particularly problematic when individuals have agreed to participate in the experiment but do not want to provide data. Some people do not want to complete questionnaires or do not show up to take tests. Participants may refuse to provide information for their own records or may deny researchers an interview. Although such refusals have to be respected, they introduce biases into the data that need to be identified. The usual procedure is to determine whether the respondents differ from nonrespondents in some systematic manner.

Research on antibiotic prescription practices of physicians was conducted as a true experiment so that half of the physicians were interviewed in person and half received the questionnaire in the mail (Shosteck & Fairweather, 1979). The results of the experiment indicate that the nonresponse to the mail survey (25 percent) far surpassed the nonresponse to the personal interview (7 percent). The mail survey, however, elicited a much lower refusal rate and a much lower number of ineligibles. The authors concluded, after a follow-up study, that the high response rate for the "mail" method included, in fact, both refusals and ineligibles. Who falls in the nonresponse group, and what bias results, can be determined in a follow-up study in which those who do not respond are interviewed about their eligibility for participation in the research.

Response rates are central to social experimentation. It is important to collect a representative spectrum of participants to respond, and to document the characteristics of those individuals who choose not to participate. If the results of social experiments are to be generalizable (to avoid threats to external validity), the biases in the data need to be understood and corrected when possible.

Problems with response rates are exacerbated in longitudinal or follow-up studies. It is critical when undertaking a long-term study to collect sufficient information from the participants initially, so that long-term follow-up can be facilitated by information about family, relatives, friends, and work (Rothbart & Frease, 1965). The McCord (1978) follow-up of juveniles who had received counseling in the 1940s had a remarkably high response rate. If one is pursuing such research, information must be collected that will aid in tracking down individuals who may be difficult to find.

ETHICS

In addition to what information is collected and how it is collected, it is critical for researchers to recognize ethical principles inherent in data collection. The collection of information, as has been noted, is an intervention in and of itself. Those administering the intervention, the program administrators and researchers, must take responsibility for its consequences. Asking individuals about their experiences may involve an invasion of privacy, and therefore must involve some contracting about how confidentiality will be dealt with, and should be followed by a "check-up" interview.

Collecting information entails a formal or informal contract between researcher and respondent. It should include an understanding of what information is being collected and why, in addition to information that is supplied about the intervention itself. Professional guidelines stipulate ethical considerations and procedures in data collection (American Psychological Association, 1973). Most importantly, informed consent must be obtained to collect, store, and use the participant's data (Barber, 1967).

As part of establishing informed consent, confidentiality must also be negotiated. In many instances, respondents will want their data to remain anonymous so that no one has access to information about their personal opinions, behaviors, or thoughts. Such a request must be respected by researchers. If it is impossible to respect this or information cannot be collected anonymously, respondents must be informed and given the opportunity to withdraw. Once respondents are promised confidentiality, measures must be taken to insure that this promise is kept.

A further ethical consideration, relevant to outcome measures, involves the accurate representation of the information collected. It is unethical to misquote a respondent, take comments out of context, or document selectively what has been reported. Accurate and fair note taking, record keeping and/or observations are critical to credible and morally respectable scientific research. Researchers have a commitment to their respondents, as well as to the program administrator, the public, and the scientific community (Rivlin, 1971).

Finally, a note about a "check-up" on respondents. It is often the case that information collected from respondents is sensitive. Whether an individual takes a test, completes a survey, or participates in an interview, the experience itself, or the thoughts or images it stimulates, may be disruptive or disturbing to the respondent at some later point in time. Social researchers may need to provide a referral list of services to participants who are in need of help (legal, economic, or counseling), and to administer a follow-up phone call or visit to check on the respondent. It is the researcher's responsibility to make sure not to affect respondents in an unhealthy or disruptive manner.

Conclusion

All of the issues raised in this chapter ultimately must be dealt with jointly by researchers and program planners. A researcher alone cannot decide to use only measures of subjective impressions and exclude behavioral data. Nor should a planner alone decide that questionnaire methods are the best means of collecting information. The researcher, familiar with research procedures and methods of collecting data, can contribute technical knowledge and expertise to the selection of outcome measures. The program official, familiar with the context of interest, the kinds of information needed for decision-making, and the probable reaction of participants can contribute contextual knowledge to the process. Independently, neither can determine adequately the outcome measures; together they should generate a viable model of information gathering.

CHAPTER 9

UTILIZING THE RESULTS OF SOCIAL EXPERIMENTATION

"Nothing in science has any value to Society if it is not communicated"

Anne Roe, *The Making of a Scientist*

Ideally, social experiments generate information that is utilized to improve social interventions and ameliorate social problems. It is assumed that the utility of a social experiment is measured by its ability to influence policy decisions about a social intervention. Whether at the local or national level, an experiment's usefulness is presumed to depend on the degree to which its results are put to work in changing and improving social policy. Actually, the utilization of results from a social experiment can be conceptualized more broadly. One's use for research findings might be to provide better information to members of Congress when they are making complex decisions (such as whether there should be continued federal aid for battered women's shelters). An equally important research use is to help raise public consciousness on vital, often elusive social issues (for example, that child abuse is a pervasive social problem). A continuum of outcomes, from identifying a problem to enacting specific policy changes, may be considered to cover the gamut of uses for applied research (Weiss, 1979).

Like most aspects of the social research process, utilization in our view is an interactive process. If research results are to be employed meaningfully, the information must be presented in relevant ways and in forms that can be understood by those audiences who might be interested in the experiment (Weiss, 1977b). This requires an exploration of and response to the information needs of the various audiences. Collaborative involvement of researchers, practitioners, policy makers, and consumers can optimize the interpretation and application of results. In a social experiment, responsibility goes beyond the actual collection and analysis of data. It involves systematic planning to assure fullest possible utilization of results.

What Is Utilization?

Much criticism has been leveled at social research and experimentation for not fulfilling its promise of generating utilizable knowledge (Goodwin, 1975; Patton, 1978). Critics often point to the few documented instances in which specific research was used in developing social policy directly. Social experimentation has been grandiose in its promises to generate unequivocal information about the impact of social interventions; however, few demonstrable policy changes can be traced to research findings. Even staunch advocates of social experimentation are willing to concede this point (cf. Weiss, 1977b).

Applied social research is generally regarded as underutilized (Abt, 1979; Lindblom & Cohen, 1979; Weiss, 1977a, 1977b) because policy makers and those responsible for social programs are often viewed as uninterested or unimpressed by research results. This perception of underutilization arises from a narrow view of what is considered utilization and a wider view of the actual problems that arise in applying research findings. Our conception of utilization is somewhat broader. Social experiments are not necessarily designed to answer particular policy questions; rather, they can help us understand the effects of social interventions and social problems, and generate knowledge for improving social conditions. The application of research findings toward a particular policy or to a general set of social understandings is assumed to be a slow process. The most important function of research may be to highlight the inadequacy of present interventions and to suggest alternative approaches. Research does not supplant the process of making judgments and decisions.

EQUIVOCALITY: AN OBSTACLE TO UTILIZATION

Direct utilization of results is often regarded as essential, but some aspects of social experimentation unfortunately limit this outcome. The principal problem is that experiments often indicate that a specific intervention is not efficacious or indicate complex conditions under which an intervention might be successful. Gilbert, Light and Mosteller (1975) have found that true social experiments (because of the rigor of their research designs) are paradoxically more likely than less rigorous designs to reveal limited effectiveness of new treatments. Although planners may want unambiguous, positive findings about their programs, research often shows that social programs have equivocal effects. Some aspects of an intervention may prove effective while others do not, or the program may prove to be beneficial only to certain populations. Good research will identify such complexities, but not always to the appreciation of program sponsors.

The Head Start program had equivocal value, according to the initial Westinghouse Ohio State University evaluation study (Cicerelli et al., 1969). As a summer experience for disadvantaged children, it was not an effective educational program. But as a full-year program, it did reduce the short-term academic gap between Head Start students and a control group. Head Start was documented as a significant nutritional, health, and social intervention for economically disadvantaged preschoolers, and, in the short run, a contribution to academic progress. The question suggested by these data is "Was Head Start a success?" The answer is "yes," if particular outcome measures are selected. But the data did suggest that under certain conditions Head Start did not improve certain outcomes and this left some audiences dissatisfied about the program (Datta, 1976). The most reasonable implication of the initial data was that the program should be extended; that small doses of help to participants were insufficient.

Findings derived in the Kagan et al. (1977) study of infant day care had similarly equivocal conclusions. The results of that experiment showed that working-class Chinese children, after participating in an innovative day-care program, exhibited cognitive improvements, and were less anxious in novel situations. This finding did not hold for Caucasian children. The study documented the value of day care for some children and the lack of negative effects for others. These findings substantiated some changes that may result from involvement in day care and by finding no negative effects helped establish its acceptability. In a society with increasing numbers of working mothers, day care can be useful, nonharmful places for children. The Kagan et al. experiment allowed for documentation of some positive and no negative outcomes. It did not, however, provide definitive evidence of the intervention's effectiveness.

Rigorous social experimentation is unlikely to indicate only positive outcomes; moreover, most findings require qualifications. It should be recognized that the scientific model underlying experimentation tends to indicate skepticism. Careful testing is bound to yield both positive and negative effects. Identifying the parameters of impact of a social intervention may be the primary goal of experimentation. However, social experiments, in identifying these limits, may paradoxically make the utilization of data more difficult by adding to the complexity of the situation.

To prepare for the inevitability of complex findings, it should be realized that even those of undisputable impact do not satisfy all audiences. Different constituencies have different needs for information, different biases, and differential abilities to utilize the results of a social experiment. For example, responses in the early 1970s to the Head Start study varied widely. Parents who were very satisfied with the program were disturbed by the negative reports of the program. Elliott Richardson, then the Cabinet Secretary responsible for the program, had a similar reaction. He thought that the evidence indicated it was useful and supported Head Start's continuation. Daniel Moynihan, President Nixon's advisor at that time and a critic of many OEO programs (he thought they were based on incorrect assumptions), subscribed to the negative portrayal of the Head Start program. Many legislators, interesting in cutting the budget, were hoping for negative results. All of these actors constituted critical audiences for utilization. Their needs and biases must be acknowledged. Because conclusions drawn from most data are likely to be ambiguous, great potential exists for desirable findings to be "read into" data. This demonstrates the need for careful planning of the dissemination of research findings.

ENLIGHTENMENT: A METHOD OF UTILIZATION

A significant component of utilization, applicable to all audiences but often neglected in relevant discussions, is what Weiss (1977a) calls "enlightenment." Results of social experimentation, whether equivocal or not, can provide a new perspective on any new framework for conceptualizing a social problem or intervention. Using enlightenment as an indicator of utilization, the findings of a social experiment contribute to the pool of knowledge that informs decision-making. Knowledge generated from social experiments accumulates and incrementally adds to public and professional ways of thinking about social problems. At some opportune political or conceptual point, this knowledge culminates in a new definition or understanding of the social problem (perhaps similar to what Kuhn, 1970, has described as a "scientific revolution").

Weiss found evidence of the enlightenment function in a study conducted on the extent to which mental health research is utilized in decision-making. Reactions were solicited from health policy decision makers (in federal, state, and local agencies) to summaries of 50 mental health experiments. The single most important factor in determining the usefulness of research was the degree to which the findings "challenged the status quo." Usefulness was not, as intuitively expected, related to the direct applicability of the finding, but the degree to which the finding actually changed ways of thinking. Results which challenged usual ways of viewing a problem brought the research to the attention of policy officials. Such research was perceived as having the greatest influence on policy.

Similar findings have been obtained by Patton (1978), who interviewed government officials responsible for health programs. According to Patton, these decision makers rarely took action on the basis of just one piece of information (that is, one study). But, as evidence accumulates, in part from systematic research, policy decisions evolve in directions that draw from the research. Results collect until patterns emerge. Caplan, Morrison, and Stambaugh (1975), in a similar vein, found that government officials use the "concepts, perspectives, and generalizations" provided by social research as a central part of the policy-making process.

This position leads to the conclusion that one can assess the utilization of social experiments in different ways. There are specific uses of the results of social experimentation (such as changing a particular policy decision), as well as nonspecific uses (for example, policy makers learning about a new perspective on a problem). In the following sections, some ways are described for utilizing the results of a social experiment.

Planning Utilization

In order to plan for optimal utilization of a social experiment, several features of the experimental situation need to be considered. Relevant audiences must be identified, utilization goals must be formulated, and strategies for utilization developed. Although no clear-cut formula is available for successful utilization, these elements seem important.

Planning for the design and the utilization of a social experiment should be considered one and the same process. A rigorous design is meaningless if the data are not used. A well-planned utilization strategy is impotent if the data are weak. To illustrate a comprehensive and thorough planning process, consider the case of the FREESTYLE evaluation conducted by the University of Michigan's Institute of Social Research (1980). FREESTYLE is a television series designed to change children's sex-role stereotypes through "Career Awareness." The series was developed to present "nontraditional" role models for children to change attitudes and behaviors of young boys and girls, aged 9 through 12.

In the complex design of the project, seven cities were involved. In some cases the program was shown at school, in others the program "stood on its own." The design also called for equivalent numbers of male and female viewers, representation of black, Hispanic, and white viewers; and included students in grades 4, 5, and 6. Conditions were varied to include at-school viewing, with and without a supplemental reader; at-home viewing, with and without parental involvement, and control groups.

It was decided, a priori, that involvement of potential utilizers of information (policy makers, parents, teachers, "experts"), along with other gatekeepers, was essential for successful implementation and utilization of the experiment. Contact was made with project sponsors at the National Institute of Education and representatives of other agencies, such as the Public

Broadcasting Service (PBS). Local school district administrators, teachers, and the show's producers were invited to consider what evaluation questions needed to be answered, and how the information could subsequently be used.

The program was elaborate: $4 million were spent, 268 teachers were involved, and 7000 students viewed the program. The results, though complicated, suggest that viewing FREESTYLE did influence the children's beliefs and attitudes about adult sex roles, in terms of employment and family roles. The program was less successful, however, in modifying children's self-interests in nontraditional directions.

Utilization and dissemination plans were equally thorough: PBS had a contract to telecast the series, schools could acquire the tapes of the programs, teacher guides were printed, and opportunities to purchase the series were publicized. Nonetheless, according to the evaluators, "The system that created FREESTYLE is 'out of the business.' " Funding for production has dried up, the PBS broadcasts are near an end, schools are unlikely to have funds to purchase the tapes, teacher guides are in short supply, and requests to purchase the series are yet to be heard from.

Utilization is a complex process which is unfortunately difficult to track because there are no good outcome measures that demonstrate the extent to which research findings have been utilized. One must often develop a plan for utilization recognizing that the plan may be compromised and that a researcher ultimately may exercise little control over the time, place, or circumstances in which the study's findings will be used, ignored, or distorted. No single approach can be regarded as the best way to plan utilization. One needs to look to various approaches and potentials. A first step in this "attention" process is identifying the various audiences for whom the results of a social experiment are relevant.

AUDIENCES

Results must be publicized so they can be understood and used by numerous audiences. A good social experiment has various constituent groups who may be interested. In practice, one focuses on the information needs of these specific groups. For example, in a study on early intervention for newly disabled workers, results were fed back to a variety of interested audiences: union members and leadership, and staff of the disability unit in the Health and Security Plan. Interest in the study was also expressed by insurance company representatives, medical practitioners at health maintenance organizations, and federal and state agencies concerned with needs of disabled workers. Psychologists and other human services providers also made known their interest in the data to help them substantiate values of early intervention and prevention strategies. Each group had a distinct area of interest in the findings: cost-effectiveness outcomes for insurance carriers, physical and mental health outcomes for the medical practitioners, and workers' relationships to worksites for agency representatives. The translation of these findings had to be matched to the needs of each group. Four audiences can be identified as critical targets for disseminating the results of any social experiment: policy makers (social planners), researchers, practitioners, and the public. Each group presents somewhat different utilization needs and must be dealt with in a distinct way (Akabas, Fine & Yasser, in press).

Policy makers. Policy makers, at one level, use results of social experiments to make informed decisions about modifying, replicating, or terminating a social program. Does police presence matter in deterring crime? Does Head Start reduce the academic gap over time? Is day care a custodial, social, or educational experience? The results of an experiment that suggest "under the following conditions Head Start is effective" or "given attitudinal outcome measures, FREESTYLE works" are often considered unsatisfactory to policy makers interested in concrete, unambiguous conclusions.

At other points, policy makers need to set the general priorities, but do not make specific decisions for programs and policy. Policy makers have recently been interested in information about the impact of plant closings on workers. Empirical evidence is accumulating and demonstrates negative economic, social, physical, and psychological impact of plant closings on workers and their families. Such facts enlighten policy makers about the effects of economic crises (Kasl & Colb, 1980). Indications of increased suicide, domestic violence, and substance abuse (of drugs, alcohol) rates following a plant closing may be crucial to policy development. Policy makers who are aware of these consequences may be more willing to support programs that save existing plants, rather than expending funds to resolve the problems that result from closings. Obviously, such information should be collected far in advance of deadlines, so that policy makers have the time to recognize the needs present and act upon them.

An example of complex results which need to be simplified for utilization purposes is illustrated again by Head Start compensatory education programs (Datta, 1976). As described in Chapter 2, the program was criticized in an initial report (Cicirelli et al., 1969). According to this analysis, Head Start did not appear to improve academic abilities of the participating children when they attended first and second grades. Because these findings disconfirmed educational expectations for the program, as well as parents' and teachers' impressions, the report generated a great deal of controversy (see Datta, 1976; McDill, McDill, & Sprehe, 1972; Williams & Evans, 1969). Policy makers were faced with decisions about continued funding and possible expansion of the program. A number of important questions were raised. As part of this decision-making process, policy makers assessed the validity of conclusions drawn from the experiment and the extent to which this information could be generalized.

While some regarded the Head Start study as a failure (because of subsequently identified methodological problems and negative program results), in some respects it had enormous impact. Public awareness of the need for compensatory education and preschool programs was raised, and a wide range of educational policy decisions made prominent (Datta, 1976). Consistent with the study's recommendations, Head Start was extended as a full-year program, and a recommendation was adopted that the program continue on an experimental basis (rather than implemented on a nationwide basis). These decisions were made with substantial involvement by policy makers who carefully reviewed the study's data, methodology, and attending controversies. The lesson, however, may be that utilization is not as simple as deciding to continue or discontinue a social innovation. Utilization involves critical analysis, interpretation, and public critique, which may result in complex changes to the program.

The Health Insurance study (Newhouse, 1974a, 1974b) was similar to Head Start research because of its enormous potential impact on the entire U.S. health care system. Considering the controversial nature of the study's underlying social problem (that of the financing of U.S. health care), divergent audiences await the findings, eager to interpret or disrupt them in ways that might support their self-interests. Although some professional groups may encourage a negative perspective on National Health Insurance, others concerned with broad access to health care will interpret the results in a more positive light. Clearly, the larger the problem, the more controversy will be generated about it, and the greater the readiness of some policy makers to request and possibly make use of the information. Despite the potential importance of social experimental data, researchers need to maintain perspective on the value of their contribution—data represent only one input into the policy-making process. Politics, economics, and social conditions influence these decisions to an even greater extent. Nonetheless, data that are rigorous, valid, and respectable should be promoted and translated so as to influence policy. The key to effective utilization will be the development of data that are in fact and in presentation as valid and relevant as possible.

Researchers. The researcher audience represents a second important target in utilization planning and contributes at least two functions in illuminating results of social experiments. First, as translators of data to policy, researchers can explain the results of experiments to various constituencies. Without researchers serving in this translator function, direct utilization by other audiences may be constrained. Second, as critics, researchers formulate questions about the results of an experiment. They develop lists of alternative explanations, identify problems of the methodology, and question assumptions of the study. These tasks—critical to experimentation—should, of course, be addressed by those who have initiated experiments as well as other researchers.

Campbell and Erlebacher's (1970) critique of the methodology used in and reanalysis of the Head Start study is a poignant example of researchers who serve as critical audiences for social experiments. Through an analysis of the study's internal validity, Campbell and Erlebacher revealed a spurious assumption of the Westinghouse report: that the Head Start students and controls were initially comparable. Using regression analyses that controlled for inequities in social class between the two groups, Campbell and Erlebacher revealed the actual extent of the impact of Head Start on economically disadvantaged preschoolers.

Researchers' critiques can reformulate a study's conclusions, and therefore serve an important function in the utilization process. Although some might not consider a critique to be an effective form of utilization (because it does not directly lead to a policy or program change), we would argue that it is a necessary step in the utilization of results of social experiments. In fact, if a critical review is not present, there should be reluctance to use the results of the experiment. A critical review can add credence to study results.

The role of a researcher is not simply to criticize, but to untangle the complexity of research results. Increasingly, the government turns to outside groups such as the National Academy of Sciences and to in-house groups such as the Office of Technology Assessment (part of the U.S. Congress) to evaluate particular research efforts and problems. Although there may be important changes in the next ten years, both the government and private agencies have developed prodigious capabilities for such translation.

Practitioners. The extent to which the findings of a social experiment result in the implementation of a new or changed program, or are translated into policy, partially depends on practitioners in relevant fields. Teachers and educational administrators represent some important audiences for and carriers of information about the Head Start study. Physicians and health planners are a prime target for the results of the health insurance study. Information can be applied directly by practitioners to improve their abilities to provide services and improve their service systems. In the cases of Head Start and the health insurance experiments, practitioners may be the best utilizers of the data. The knowledge of teachers of programs that enhance learning by disadvantaged students and the recognition by physicians of the link between the availability of health services and health can significantly affect practice.

Practitioners are not merely vital appliers of data to policy, but can also contribute to interpretation and development of improved interventions. In order to do so, practitioners must be aware of the results of relevant experiments and how these have been interpreted and critiqued by researchers and policy makers. Involvement of practitioners can only be insured by including them in utilization planning.

One social experiment conducted by a private research company, Abt Associates, tested the cost and effectiveness of program variations in a national sample of day-care centers (Travers and Goodson, 1980). While each center's student/teacher ratio was expected to affect the children's academic and social outcome measures, it did not. However, the size of the group did. In small groups, children were more likely to be praised, supported, and comforted; they were less likely to engage in passive observation or mindless chattering, and, importantly, received improved test scores. Across three geographic regions (Atlanta, Detroit, and Seattle), group size was a significant program variable in day care. Practitioners could utilize such information to modify their programs toward greater effectiveness by introducing smaller working and learning groups. Practitioners are likely to be the most direct utilizers of new knowledge, and consequently the most appropriate persons to test the applicability of such knowledge (Mayo, 1980).

The public. For pragmatic as well as ethical reasons, the public constitutes a critical, though typically neglected, utilization audience. Social experiments are designed to perform tests of social interventions and to inform social policy. The public is the generally understood beneficiary of such research. Work conducted under the rubric of social experimentation is undertaken for the public good. These results, for the most part, have significant consequences for the public. The health insurance study, for example, will provide important information for the public which ultimately will decide whether or not to support such a program. Withholding or concealing research findings is unethical given the fact that public moneys support most social experiments. Although social research and the principles which underlie social experimentation are often applied in proprietary organizations, many of the same considerations apply. Adherence to ethical guidelines and open reporting of findings are expected, if not mandatory.

The public serves as consumers of and participants in social experiments. As participants, they provide the data that researchers and planners need in order to determine the impact of any social program, and represents potential interpreters of the results. To illustrate by hypothetical example, consider a study being conducted to assess adolescents' attitudes toward Jews. The data, on cursory glance, indicate that most adolescents harbor negative attitudes. However, when one presents the data to the participants and asks them to explain the finding, the students became bewildered. It may be that none of them know what a Jewish person is. If such is the case, their data are obviously of questionable validity, although this fact would not have come to light if their feedback was not solicited. Similar identification of the problems of interpretation might come to light when data are shared with any "public" group.

STRATEGIES

Utilization has many targets, and aims to accomplish many purposes for each group. Diverse strategies can be employed to achieve these aims. To raise public consciousness ("enlighten" them) about the education of disadvantaged preschoolers (Head Start), one may wish to *link* community representatives into a data-utilizing coalition of community resources (for example, industrial, mental health, union, physical health, education, governmental, and clergy representatives). Or, after testing a previously untested assumption about police patrolling (as in the Kansas City Police Patrol experiment), one may choose to *disseminate* the findings and solicit nationwide responses. To generate public and professional support for socialized models of financing health care (the health insurance study), one may develop *advocacy* strategies for data utilization. Or, to inform relevant persons about the benefits of educational television programs (for example, *Sesame Street*), one may sponsor *educational* forums for data utilization. Each aim suggests an alternative utilization strategy. The strategies are not exclusive of each other and the interconnection of approaches is probably crucial.

Linkage. Essential to effective utilization is the establishment of linkage. This means implicitly relating empirical findings to policy questions; and connecting producers of results to potential consumers. Linkage converts the results of an experiment into potential policy fodder for specified target audience(s).

Some maintain that research findings must be linked to action, that is, provide clear action implications. Others suggest that the policy makers be linked to knowledge producers (Caplan, Morrison & Stambaugh, 1975; Lippitt, 1976). This follows the collaboration model between researchers and planners that has been advocated throughout. When collaboration is lacking, a gap between research and action hinders the application of the research. Hoole (1978) notes that research findings, to be utilized, should be linked to particular decision-making concerns, and that social research should be tailored to specific policy questions. Linkages between research and action, research producer and policy maker, and/or research findings and decisions, are necessary for meaningful utilization of research findings.

Establishing linkage involves collaboration—among researchers, planners, policy makers, and consumers. Honest, open sharing of information facilitates the utilization of results. Sharing of perspectives and biases, as well as joint involvement, promotes data interpretations that reflect research and program concerns. It should help to provide answers to both policy and theoretical questions. Because each audience has a different perspective, it is essential that the utilization plan take into account the need for inputs from various audiences, recognizing the power distributions among these groups.

Lake (1977) describes the optimal collaboration relationship as one characterized by reciprocity; a two way flow of information; by openness to
receive evaluations and feedback; and by realistic expectations of the data by
researchers and planners. Also important are clear role boundaries between
researcher and planner; equal power and minimal threat; open confrontation
of differences; and the involvement of all relevant parties. Without such
collaboration, the opportunity is enhanced for misunderstanding and misin-
terpretation.

Dissemination. Dissemination involves sharing the results of a study with
relevant audiences. The aim of dissemination is to raise public and/or
professional consciousness about a social issue, and to suggest alternative
strategies for resolving the problem. Dissemination of information may involve publications, conferences, educational techniques, and public media.
Dissemination begins the process of reconsidering assumptions about social
problems and utilizing an experiment's results. In the case of the Negative
Income Tax experiment, dissemination helped policy makers, researchers,
the public, and practitioners to dispel the myth that public assistance creates
disincentives to work.

Advocacy/lobbying. A utilization strategy more directly tied to policy is
that of advocacy or lobbying. The literature on the use of such strategies is
not extensive (probably its use is frequently undocumented). Advocacy/
lobbying can be easily illustrated. A nationwide survey (essentially a nonexperimental design) assessed the impact of the Vietnam War on men of the
Vietnam era (Vietnam Era Research Project, Center for Policy Research,
1979). The study compared Vietnam veterans (both those who were in
combat and those who were not) with age-matched men who did not serve. It
was mandated by the U.S. Congress through the Veterans Administration in
order to evaluate the need for expanded veterans benefits and policy changes
in the treatment of Vietnam era veterans. The study (even a preliminary
report of it) has been the focus of great interest by veterans' groups. Investigators and funding agencies (the National Institute of Mental Health and the
Veterans Administration) are dealing with various groups that want to use
the results for advocacy purposes (see New York Times editorial, October
13, 1979).

Despite the already high degree of impact, some caution is indicated.
Because conclusions are often equivocal, they can be used "promiscu-
ously." Groups organized to support the militray draft and those organized
against it can use the same findings to promote their opposing views. Because this study is federally funded, data are in the public domain: anyone
has legal access to them. At this point, the dissemination/utilization process
is less controlled. But researchers are responsible to men who participated in
the study and to society to be sensitive to how the data are used. They must

acknowledge criticism, but also respond to analyses and /or interpretations that they believe are misleading.

Education and training. Yet another strategy for utilization occurs through formal and informal education and training (Chin & Benne, 1976). This strategy is underutilized but nevertheless important. When results of an experiment are complex or when interpretation is not clear, educational efforts may be useful to inform audiences about the results. One could easily imagine a training program for day-care workers in which the finding about reduced group size is translated into a program strategy to optimize the children's social interactions and cognitive gains (Travers, 1980). In fact, a significant outcome of the Westinghouse study of Head Start involved an extensive parent-child education program in which parents were trained for involvement in compensatory education programs (Datta, 1976). Education and training offer mechanisms through which results of social experiments can be transmitted to the next generation of "practitioners." Teachers, physicians, police officers, and others need to be educated about the results of social experiments and given the opportunity to utilize them. The form these educational programs take can vary as much as the nature of these interventions.

Media coverage. The mass media, whether newspapers or radio and television, are important for dissemination of study results, but they can affect the utilization of results in various ways. By trying to simplify results and present uncomplicated research findings, media representatives can present somewhat distorted conclusions of research studies. Although such distortion is certainly something researchers should worry about and strive to prevent, media representatives should nevertheless be encouraged to utilize research findings. While the communications media can sensationalize and dangerously distort the actual community impact of any problem (headlines may read, "Homocide! Suicide! Battering!"), the attention given to social problems through such coverage is crucial for public involvement (Marsiniak, 1980). Researchers/social planners should take active and much needed roles in understanding media perspectives and influencing the clarity with which results are reported (Saxe, 1979).

CONSEQUENCES

There are consequences in the use of each utilization strategy. Direct utilization, as perhaps was the case with Head Start (Datta, 1976), represents only one of many potential outcomes. Further funding for research may result, as in the case of the Negative Income Tax Experiment (Rossi & Lyall, 1976). A program also may be terminated, as in the Performance Contracting Experiment (Gramlich & Koshel, 1975); or an expanded variation may be developed, as with Follow Through and Head Start (Datta,

1976). Dissemination and utilization may encourage secondary analyses like the Cook et al. (1975) examination of the *Sesame Street* data, or merely policy consideration of the results, as in the Kansas City Patrolling Experiment (Kelling et al., 1976).

Utilization Issues

Our vision of pluralistic social experimentation encompasses diverse perspectives and disciplines which collaborate in design, interpretation, and planning for utilization. Utilization, as we have noted, is not a static process. There is neither one single interpretation of an experiment nor a single utilization approach. Utilization evolves through processes of interpretation, criticism, reinterpretation, formulation of new research questions, and so on.

It is likely that the more significant the social experiment, the more controversy will surround its findings. A significant experiment will arouse multiple interest groups, each representing its own set of priorities and reading the data in a different way and thereby suggesting distinct policy recommendations. The extent to which cross-group conflict facilitates or inhibits utilization remains an empirical question. It is difficult to predict which factors will lead to utilization. Obviously, the nature of the results is critical. If the results support a policy or program that is well accepted, the results will probably be welcomed and channeled toward program development. If, as is perhaps more frequently the case, results indicate no effects or reveal problems with the program, they may threaten the survival of the program. To the extent that the results are clear and unexpected (for example, if they directly challenge the status quo) it is likely that they will have direct impact. Research results are traditionally ambiguous and often do not reveal anything very surprising, but they can help planners understand and consider alternatives that may have more demonstrable impact.

The enlightenment function of data utilization should be reemphasized. The data from an experiment, while not immediately useful, may be applied when results are combined with results of other studies and, perhaps, when the *zeitgeist* has changed. A problem emerges with research findings that are inconsistent with the zeitgeist, the current social policy context. One such difficult research finding suggests that juveniles who are arbitrarily released without sanction for criminal behavior are less likely to get involved in subsequent criminal trouble. Those who receive the most severe sanctions are most likely to be criminally recidivist (Shannon, 1980). While judges intuitively release some juveniles, the judicial system is not presently likely to release juveniles as a way to reduce recidivism rates. This is obviously a finding whose day has yet to come, although it has been proposed in different forms many times before (see Sommer, 1976). Precocious findings such as this represent only one of the interesting issues that emerge when one considers the utilization process. The next section examines the role of criticism in the utilization process, resistance to utilization, inappropriate utilization, and responsibilities to respondents.

CRITICISM

In the discussion of researchers as an audience, it was suggested that critiques of experiments serve an important role. Although true, it is also clear that critiques of a research study can polarize interest groups, make resolution of different views more difficult, and force people to "throw the baby out with the bathwater" (Sobel, 1978); that is, the results may be ignored because of the controversy that surrounds them. For researchers who ascribe to scientific views of problems, criticism is seen as a natural part of the knowledge-generating process. For planners, perhaps, criticism is seen as less natural. It is assumed to reflect widespread disagreement with the intervention and its chosen strategies (Weiss, 1972).

A social experiment may receive criticism either of the assumptions on which the experiment is founded or the methods by which the experiment is conducted. While these are not independent categories of criticisms, they reflect different types of reaction. They require a somewhat different strategy if their impact on the utilization of the experiment is to be positive.

Assumptions. It is more difficult to respond to criticisms of the assumptions of a program or of research, as exemplified by Aaron's (1978) critique of the Great Society programs. Aaron maintained that Great Society antipoverty programs were rooted in spurious assumptions that poverty is an inescapable "caste" (see Chapter 8). While his criticisms contribute enormously to enlightening us about poverty, and the views which molded many of the programs of the 1960s, it became unclear how to utilize results of studies plagued by spurious assumptions. Specific findings about various Great Society training and educational programs are deeded irrelevant in this context.

Nonetheless, such critical analyses of assumptions help in the development of new types of programs that more closely match actual needs. For example, the assumption was questionable that Head Start should predominantly serve an educational function. Head Start was documented as a valuable nutritional, health, and social growth experience, with some academic benefits. A broadened set of expectations for Head Start substantiate its effective operation and would mold research that could make the program more useful in reaching broadened aims.

Methodology. Methodological criticisms are, perhaps, somewhat easier to respond to than critiques of programmatic assumptions. When such criticism is directed at internal validity problems, there are usually data which can support or refute the alternate explanation. If data are unavailable, other data can be found to determine whether an alternate explanation is feasible.

The controversy described in Chapter 3 over the results of the Follow Through planned variations (Anderson et al., 1978; House et al., 1978; Stebbins et al., 1978) illustrates some of these issues. The criticism of the initial assessment of Follow Through focused on confounds in the original design, as well as low power of the design (Chapter 5). Critics reanalyzed some of the original data, highlighting important differences that were minimized by the original researchers. In response, the original researchers presented other data to substantiate the lack of significant differences for the program, challenging the critics to provide data to reconfirm their alternate explanation.

Regardless of the critique of a social experiment, the most important point to be grasped is that criticism is natural, as well as needed, in the utilization process. In some cases, criticism can be responded to immediately; in other cases, criticisms may be so debilitating that all aspects of the data are called into question. In either case, criticism will help to develop the appropriate use of the experiment.

RESISTANCE TO UTILIZATION

For many reasons, program planners, policy makers, and participants may be reluctant to utilize, or even to disseminate, research findings. Results that indicate administrative incompetence or corruption may be suppressed. Data documenting program ineffectiveness or favoring the withdrawal of federal funds may be silenced (Campbell, 1973). Program inertia or laziness (Campbell, 1971; Hoole, 1978) may interfere with research utilization and may blunt the impact of findings. Programs which are run in a conservative and rigid fashion or programs that are barely surviving may be structurally resistant or reluctant to risk change.

Utilization may also be resisted for less defensive, even good reasons. The data themselves may be perceived as inadequate. Data collected too early may camouflage program impact. For example, results from a social experiment on community knowledge and utilization of an innovative dentistry program indicated that the community was largely unaware of the program (Fine & Goldman, 1979). The problem, however, was in the timing of the research. Community awareness of the program was actually just beginning to flourish when the data were being collected. The research probably took place several months prematurely. Consequently, the data inaccurately indicated less community familiarity with the program than was actually the case. It may have been best not to disseminate such information. In this case, premature dissemination of the "low community awareness" finding might have discouraged community utilization, and worked against both future funding of a worthwhile program and against the "public good."

While premature release of findings can introduce problems, the decision not to disseminate is often manipulative and may facilitate public ignorance rather than public good. For example, policy makers concerned with lowering taxes and minimizing government's role in health care would be reluctant to disseminate findings that validate citizen's demands for national health insurance. A social experiment that demonstrates that health is improved across social class when national health insurance is available may increase public pressure on the government to fund comprehensive and equitable national health insurance programs. Dissemination and utilization of research requires a willingness on the part of policy makers to take action based on the results and to provide for consumers. When policy makers are unable or unwilling to provide such services, research findings may be deceptively shelved.

Dissemination of information often introduces new options to the public. When the public is made aware of policy alternatives or informed of the value of particular social resources, it is more likely to demand access (Fine, 1979). Relative deprivation (Crosby, 1976) occurs when individuals feel that their entitlements fall short of their attainment. Dissemination of information that demonstrates the value of national health insurance and reveals that the United States and South Africa are the only two industrialized countries that do not provide national health insurance could lead U.S. citizens to feel deprived and angry. Such findings are likely to inform the public in ways that exacerbate public demands for social change.

INAPPROPRIATE USE OF RESEARCH FINDINGS

Research findings can sometimes be utilized in an irresponsible or inappropriate manner. As indicated above, premature dissemination of results in a social experiment can lead to contamination of experimental conditions (see Chapter 3). Early release of information of negative results may induce unnecessary participant panic or promote an unnecessary climate of crisis. Untimely dissemination can also instigate unnecessary changes in policy. Utilization must be timed and planned in such a way as to insure maximum benefits and minimal costs.

One inappropriate use of data involves violations of confidentiality. All dissemination and utilization strategies need to be designed so that individual rights to privacy are held intact, and anonymity and confidentiality respected.

A frequent misuse of experimental findings involves taking research findings out of context or presenting them in distorted form. For example, in 1960, the American Medical Association sponsored a study aimed at discrediting plans to expand government support of medical care for the aged. Senior citizens' perceptions of their need for government sponsored health benefits were surveyed. No racial minorities or institutionalized persons were interviewed; and the sample was weighted to overrepresent upper economic groups. The results, as reported, indicated that 68 percent of those surveyed said they could pay for a medical emergency costing $1000 and 90 percent said they enjoyed good health. The researchers concluded that the population of senior citizens in the U.S. indicated no need for government assistance for health care. The Foundation for Voluntary Welfare, the sponsoring foundation, was delighted and widely disseminated the information. They did so without specifying the nature of the sample (which was not representative of the aging population) and without pointing to the methodological limitation of their conclusions. Such reporting has been considered unethical management of research findings (Cain, 1976).

In another example, interpretations may be advanced that distort the actual findings of the study. For example, neighborhood youth resources centers (NYRC) were developed in Philadelphia to provide adolescents in high crime areas with social and vocational outlets. The differential arrest rates for target and nontarget boys suggest that NYRCs can benefit these youth. Target area boys were less likely to be arrested than controls and NYRCs were the cause of attenuated arrest rates. This was a potentially important finding with a number of political ramifications. Imagine the reaction, however, of a hypothetical city council unwilling or unable to commit moneys to expansion of the NYRC concept. The council might want to suppress the data entirely or provide a reinterpretation so that it appears to the public that expanding NYRCs citywide would be an unreasonable policy. The council could account for the reduced arrest rates by suggesting that police in the target areas know about the NYRCs and therefore were negligent and irresponsible (regarding arrests) compared to police in nontarget areas. The low arrest rates would be attributable to the fact that target-area police were making fewer arrests, not to the effectiveness of the NYRCs. Both of these examples illustrate what Patton (1978) reminds researchers and program planners to take into account: the political context of social research.

A further misuse of research findings concerns the tendency to overgeneralize. A study conducted in Seattle tested the effectiveness of hidden cameras placed in small businesses with the objective of deterring crime (Hidden Camera Project, NILECJ, 1978). The cameras proved to be very effective in improving "clearance" rates for robbery arrests. Does this mean that all small businesses in cities such as New York City, Chicago, Los Angeles, should install hidden cameras? To what extent can these findings be generalized? The success of this technique might be limited to high risk robbery locations or to cities where extra resources and special police attention are allocated to the target areas. Such a program might not be cost-effective in a big city, with its many transients and no finances or resources provided to the police department for apprehending suspects. For reasons such as this, no social experiment should be considered the critical experiment. Each enlightens us further as to the value and limits of new technology. Replication in varied sites is necessary for valid generalization. Overgeneralization is poor use of research, and probably poor policy.

RESPONSIBILITIES TO RESPONDENTS

Collecting data involves taking pieces of information from individuals for research purposes. What do respondents get from this exchange? Dissemination of information serves as one method for repaying the public for its cooperation and, as noted earlier, becomes an ethical responsibility. Researchers and planners need to assume some responsibility for the public effects of dissemination. The consequences of such dissemination on program morale, hiring and firing decisions, violations of confidentiality, potential for misuse or distorted interpretations, or for re-funding decisions must always be considered.

Because of these privacy precautions, concerns for political security, and fear of criticism, planners might be tempted to underdisseminate study findings, which consequently results in underutilization, posing serious ethical consequences. To *not* report that a program is inefficacious or has harmful consequences is irresponsible. Withholding negative results, for example, that a new drug for heart attack victims has serious side effects (New York Times, December 8, 1980) is unethical and illegal. Covering up problems, such as sexual harassment in a vocational training program for women in nontraditional careers, is a dangerous example of nonutilization. Dissemination must be direct and honest, aimed to inform, not demoralize or immobilize the public. Successful dissemination should instigate more research, action, and reformulated research questions.

Utilization should be an open process. It is unwise policy and unethical practice to utilize only those aspects of data which might be considered safe, or those pieces which support existing programs or ideas. Using only politically beneficial pieces of information compromises the research findings. Taking findings out of context is also a violation of the integrity of the research project and of the trust that has been given social researchers. Any tampering pragmatically reduces the usefulness of results.

Conclusion

In an ideal situation, social research findings will be comprised of sound and meaningful data utilized widely. It is hoped that the information reflects valid data and is responsive to the problem and context. Utilization must be tailored to various audiences and should present clear information, explicit action implications, and reflect an understanding of the sociopolitical environment. It is a difficult, but necessary, process.

SECTION IV

CONCLUSION

CHAPTER 10

PROMISE AND PROBLEMS OF SOCIAL EXPERIMENTS

"Understanding . . . is not a foundation for action if the terms in which a problem is 'understood' tend toward acceptance of the status quo."

Alice Rossi, 1973

Social experimentation, as we have emphasized throughout, is a way of thinking about and organizing the study of social problems. It is a system of logic based on principles of science that suggests a state of mind, and much as a methodology. While social experimentation incorporates procedures which one can apply in technological fashion to the study of social interventions, the technology is secondary in importance to the approach represented by experimentation. It is not suggested that careful attention to details of experimental design and measurement and analysis is unnecessary. These details are clearly critical for valid experimentation, but significant only within a broad context.

This broad context incorporates, in part, the perspectives of social scientists, social planners, and others involved in and affected by social experiments. Social experimentation, if it is to be carried out successfully, requires each constituency to become involved in the process. This, in turn, requires understanding by each group about how their information needs are related to the conduct of a total experiment. While details of social experimentation need not be shared by all affected by an experiment, the perspective offered by social experimentation—principally, the value of testing and developing valid information—does need to be understood. This shared understanding is a precursor to meaningful collaboration. It is essential if we are to go beyond the isolated use of social experimentation and in the direction of an experimenting society.

Thus, social experimentation should be a part of the thinking not only of social scientists. If social experimentation is to be useful to society, it needs to be part of the way of thinking of policy makers, social program administrators, and those affected by social interventions. Social program administrators and policy makers and those affected have more input about the conduct of these interventions than do social researchers. If experimentation is to be conducted, joint action with researchers will be essential. Social experimentation requires a different approach, not only in the design of studies, but in the critical and systematic evaluation of ideas.

Alice Rossi's quotation suggests that experimentation of any sort is valuable only so far as it expands understandings and confronts traditional assumptions and conceptualizations of social problems. Social experiments can be conducted to confirm our assumptions about problems and test the legitimacy of present approaches. Inherent in the concept of experimentation is the testing of innovative ideas. Rather than serving an accountability function for society, social experimentation should derive from "generative" theorizing about social problems (cf. Gergen, 1978). It should produce and cultivate new ideas for interventions as well as test proposed ones.

Many social experiments described in previous chapters have been used to test remedies for social ills and generate new understandings of social behavior. The large scale educational experiments described (Head Start, Follow Through), as well as such studies as Kagan, Kearsley, and Zelazo's (1977) day-care experiment, represent attempts to explore new social arrangements. In part, the experiments are tests of these arrangements; they also test important concepts about human development. These studies have not ended research on educational interventions and, in fact, have probably been responsible for generating a host of new ones.

Goodwin (1975) in his discussion of social research and the social welfare system noted that the use of experimental methods has been underappreciated in policy formulation. Although in part he supports the expanded use of experimentation, Goodwin offers words of caution. Experimental methods, he says, should be applied to developing broadened models, rather than to reinforcing predetermined, or self-fulfilling, designs. The former outcome is possible only when one tests different administrative arrangements for a program and challenges the assumptions underlying the system.

Social experimentation, in essence, introduces a way of conceptualizing change in the social world, coupling methodological considerations with generative policy ideas. It is a process that ideally incorporates historical insight, philosophy, and policy-mindedness into scientific methodology. In designing responsive social policy we need to coordinate information from history, social, and political interactions (Lindblom & Cohen, 1979), as well as scientific input. Our view, perhaps understated up to this point, is that scientific input is a necessary but certainly not a sufficient component of responsive policy formulation. Many other components along with research and policy should be regarded as evolving. The design and implementation of a social experiment is merely one point in the policy formulation process. In the best of circumstances, it is not the last step. Policy strategies can be determined by integrating various inputs; they must evolve in response to changes in the nature of society, social problems, and institutions. Policy derived from social experimentation which has been held static over time represents in our framework, a contradiction in terms. Social experimentation over time should change continually to update policies which prove inappropriate, outdated, or moot.

We do not believe that an experimenting society is a present reality, at least not in the United States and other Western societies. Discrete elements of the experimenting society exist; as evidenced by increases in the number, scope, and diversity of social experiments that are being conducted. Other signs are present as well. We are moving toward the systematic application of social experimentation. The interest in applied social research in general, and the concern of policy makers for this work, are obvious signs. On the local level, too, small-scale experiments are abundant—in alternate energy forms, child care arrangements, and work schedules, to name a few. Despite this optimistic view, it is important to note that the concept of an experimenting society, though perhaps not a radical idea, is problematic. We now consider both the promises and difficulties faced by an experimenting society. First, we describe in more detail than earlier our vision of an experimenting society and its potential for addressing difficult social problems and conditions. Next, we critically examine the concept of an experimenting society and the use of social experimentation in policy formulation. The goals of this discussion are to summarize some of the key concepts that we have tried to present throughout this volume and to provide some perspectives on the actual use of social experimentation in society.

The Promise of an Experimenting Society

While our debt to Donald Campbell (1969, 1971) as a leading proponent of an experimenting society should be obvious, he is not alone among social scientists who have explicitly dealt with the concept of social experimentation. Others (such as Boruch & Riecken, 1975; Rivlin, 1971) have also called for increased social experimentation. Several prestigious policy "think tanks" have launched major efforts to improve the use of social experimentation (such as the Brookings Institution, the Social Science Research Council). While many—even those not directly concerned with social policy—have advocated rigorous research on social problems, Campbell's approach is distinguishable from others (who share his experimenting society view) in that he embedded social experimentation within the broad framework of how society functions vis-à-vis social policy.

In Campbell's (1971) view, social experimentation is appropriate and much needed as a response to society's problems. Interventions designed to respond to social problems too often are blocked by the inertia of social institutions. In effect, it is easier to maintain the status quo, perhaps to study it (passively collect data), than it is to experiment with new solutions. Programs are neither started nor maintained and terminated, with adequate (scientific) consideration of impacts. The proposals of the the conservative Reagan Administration appear to represent such an approach to policy.

Until recently, we had begun to witness the slow incorporation of social research into policy decisions. Evaluation research, an increasingly important component of social programs, is very often conducted to understand and determine the impact of social programs (Freeman, 1977; Perloff, Perloff & Sussna, 1976; Rentz & Rentz, 1978; Rutman & DeJong, 1976; Wortman, 1975). Although evaluation research has received a major impetus in recent years from governmental and social agencies (Rossi, 1979), the viability of the model is not yet clear. Evaluations are frequently flawed by validity threats and it is unclear that evaluation information is actually utilized (Alkin, Daillak, & White, 1979; Bernstein & Freeman, 1975; Weiss, 1977b). One explanation of the nonutilization of evaluation research results is that many evaluations try to determine "success" or "failure," usually from end product indicators; evaluations assume that value judgments can be made (that is, decisions about what is good versus what is poor). This may be a naive conception of the use of the social sciences (see Berk & Rossi, 1977; Saxe & Fine, 1980).

A further problem is that evaluation traditionally implies a separate and post hoc research effort from program activities. This can result in poor quality or unusable research being done as evaluation. Design and measurement are processes that require planning, without which threats to validity may be difficult to control. In part, the post hoc nature of evaluation research is an historical accident. Much of the current field grew out of efforts to understand Great Society programs and to use budget analysis procedures to determine if money was well spent (House, 1978). Evaluation components were designed by independent individuals in units separate from program activities, so as to maintain the "objectivity" of the audit and assessment function; hence, the concern we have described at a number of points about internal vs. external researchers. This approach to evaluation, unfortunately, violates the realization that in order to collect methodologically sound data, the intervention and the research need to be developed concurrently.

An additional problem with the policy application of evaluation research has been the assumptions which mold our social interventions. These are the same assumptions underlying our evaluations of the intervention. Evaluation designs, frequently attached at the tail end of social interventions, do not test basic assumptions which support the intervention, and therefore frequently contribute little to a new knowledge base, and may even introduce spurious evidence of program impact (Aaron, 1978). Assumptions about the root of a problem, such as poverty, or about an appropriate intervention, such as work incentive programs, can cater to misleading notions about social programs (Mitroff & Bonoma, 1978). Because social interventions are often developed by a group of individuals sharing a common perspective and disciplinary identification, they may elicit effects which go unexpected, unnoticed, and unmeasured (Goodwin, 1975). For example, a work training program that aims to change people and not structures may promote employment for trainees, but may also create large displacement in the labor pool. While successful from an educational perspective, its economic consequences are not likely to be effective.

Social experimentation as a collaborative activity engaged in by social researchers, planners, and others challenges assumptions that underlie many traditional policy responses to social problems. Alternatives can be tested and explored. There is no need to accept one policy decision as final. Assessments of new interventions can be as wide or narrow as the researcher-planners would like them to be. The emphasis should focus on change, by exploring the costs and benefits of alternatives, rather than by determining the success or failure of a particular program. The value of social experimentation is, implicitly, that no one policy is permanent and that change is expected. Social experimentation assumes that policy must be modified, checked, and balanced as society evolves. Its most expedient model favors evolving policy and assumes that change is inherent and critical to the progression of policy.

Campbell (1971) proposes an experimenting society as an expanded way of viewing the place in society of evaluation research. In the experimenting society, program planning (and idea development) is integrated into evaluation. Campbell's vision emphasizes action in contrast to thinking through and simulating possible solutions to social problems. In the experimenting society "action research" (Ketterer, Price, & Polister, 1980; Lewin, 1948; Sanford, 1970) plays a prominent role. Action research is the way in which some have characterized researchers' involvement in actual social problems. Unfortunately, because action research has usually required that researchers deliver the treatment as well as design and measure outcomes, it has not yet gained wide usage (Sanford, 1970). The experimenting society, in which social researchers collaborate with social planners, offers a potential for resolving this difficulty.

The experimenting society will be a society which affords prominence to scientific values. The willingness to accept or reject new ideas founded on empirical verification and validity principles is central to this value system. The scientifically based value system of the experimenting society acknowledges the need for special policy to mature out of dialectical processes of concept formulation, rigorous testing, analysis, and concept reformulation. The experimenting society calls for a narrowing gap between social science knowledge and social policy. This gap will not close merely by structures which impose and regulate the use of social science data; rather, it will come about by the widening application of scientific logic to the study of social problems (Bunker, 1978).

HOW IT MIGHT OPERATE

How would the experimenting society operate and how would it differ from the current state of policy affairs? Some predictions or possibilities are offered regarding the ways in which the experimenting society might differ from our current policy-making system.

The "overadvocacy" trap. A good illustration of the difference between current policymaking and the experimenting society can be drawn from Campbell's (1969) description of the "overadvocacy trap." This results when program administrators and policy makers become advocates and publicly identify with particular *solutions* to social problems. Social experimentation offers an alternative political strategy. A scientific as well as generative approach to problem solution would be for policy makers to be committed to social problems and not their solutions—and thus free to explore multiple programmatic responses. Adopting the former position results in exaggerated claims of the effectiveness of particular solutions and in blindness to anomalous data about the effects of the proposed solution. When political figures advocate particular solutions, they often find it difficult to change positions—even when the data do not substantiate the value of the program. Advocating the importance of the problem and expressing a willingness to accept all sound data is tantamount to a call for adopting the hypothesis testing frame of mind and enlightened skepticism about proposed solutions.

It might be difficult to imagine policy makers adopting a nonadvocacy system. It is no more difficult to understand how problems currently are approached. As noted in the earlier discussion of the health insurance experiment (see Chapter 7), various insurance plans had been proposed (over a long period of time), yet no agreement has been reached in adopting a particular plan. The illogic of the overadvocacy trap should be obvious. Various political leaders have made publicly clear their positions on national health insurance. Each has developed plans to solve the most critical national health problems. At least at this time, it does not seem possible that these individuals—many of whom concur on the need for a better system of assuring the availability of health care—will come to agreement on an actual solution. Because of the intransigence of those advocating particular plans, no solution has been reached. The present political climate may not make it possible for a comprehensive insurance system to be adopted. Certainly it might be preferable for the leaders involved to explore openly the efficacy of various solutions.

Science and the broader context. A further distinguishing feature of the experimenting society will be the demystification of science. Principles and logic of science will form part of the context of social and political realms. Language and approach will be neither mystical nor foreign. In much the same way that science will affect social policy, policy and society will influence the approach and hypotheses of scientists. Participants in the experimenting society will include all of us, whereas present participants in today's world of policy formulation are limited to the political and academic elite (Aaron, 1978).

This feature of the experimenting society, as noted by Campbell (1971), marks an important development of current modes of policy formulation. One way of viewing the experimenting society is as a structure for providing systematic input from individuals to social planners. As members of society, we will all be affected by, if not involved in, numerous social experiments. Such involvement will heighten each individual's potential contribution to policy formulation, and provide an opportunity for consumers of social services to share positions on social issues.

Because our assumption is that policy in the experimenting society would be more fluid and less static than in our current political realm, we anticipate that individual contributions will potentially have greater impact. Outcome measures, consisting of both "hard" indicators of program impact as well as "soft" measures of participant satisfaction, recommendations, and perceptions will influence policy formulation. Responsive structural changes will emerge from data interpretation. Just as polling and other forms of survey research have become pervasive aspects of our society, as an "active" variant of this referenda process, social experimentation can play an important role in obtaining public input on social issues.

NOTE FOR THE EXPERIMENTING SOCIETY

In case we have not been sufficiently explicit, we should again state our reasons for advocating an experimenting society. The experimenting society would give social scientists a greater role in policy formulation. We also think that it would improve the development of social policy and contribute to the solution of social problems. An experimenting society offers, in essence, one of the best ways for social scientists to conduct useful research. It seems to us a way to insure that research would actually be utilized in serving society.

Our position in advocating an experimenting society is not intended as a disguised effort to establish social scientists as "high priests" of society. Rather, we think that the most important impact of social experimentation should be to further the use of social scientists as "methodological servants" (Campbell, 1973) of the society. Social scientists' expertise is only one component in the decision-making system. As noted in Chapter 1, society is becoming more technologically and interpersonally complex. We need increasingly sophisticated methods to understand the implications of changes. Our society is inherently pluralistic and depends on the input of large numbers and types of people in order for policy to be developed. Our advocacy of an experimenting society is not meant to exclude other approaches; in a pluralistic system, it would clearly represent only one way of developing understandings (Lindblom & Cohen, 1979).

In terms of the potential of an experimenting society to accommodate sound social research, rationales and implications seem clear enough. If ethical and valid true experiments are to be conducted, it seems essential for policy makers and those involved in the development of social programs to participate collaboratively. We must recognize, as theorists diverse in individual orientation as Skinner (1971) and Dewey (1957), that society already intervenes in people's lives. Coupling the experimental model with the development of social policy, as is proposed in the concept of an experimenting society, allows us to determine whether particular interventions are justified, whether resources are being directed in appropriate ways, and whether our understandings of social problems are accurate, current, and responsive to the people (see Rivlin, 1971). We can gain critical information about these interventions and whether they should be continued (although, clearly, social experimentation can function as only one complement of the usual decision mechanism). Without the collaborative involvement of social researchers and policy makers, it seems impossible to conduct the types of empirical analyses that can inform the most important social policy decisions of the day.

Even if good social research were possible under the current set of circumstances (where an experimenting society does not really exist), it seems unlikely that the findings of social experiments would be appropriately utilized. The policy-making structure is not yet familiar enough, nor supportive enough, of the approach to facilitate their widespread application. There is today public pressure for scientific input in public policy. It is too easy, as noted at several points, to raise methodological and conceptual problems with any single piece of research. The potential for being misunderstood by policy makers who have their own frames of reference is too great when decision makers do not have "ownership" or direct involvement in the formulation of research. Unless social policy makers transfer their advocacy from a particular program solution to advocacy for the social problems themselves, and for social research on intervention strategies, it seems unlikely that they will recognize all available information.

Thus, an experimenting society does not advocate particular programs, but seeks instead to improve the development of understandings of and solutions to social problems. The development of an experimenting society is a way to improve the conduct of social research, and hence its utilizability. Of course, despite our advocacy, we want to promote a scientifically skeptical frame of reference. In the next section, we will describe some problems in adopting the social experimentation perspective.

Problems With the Experimenting Society

As should be obvious, the more widespread the use of social experimentation, the more society will fundamentally alter the way it formulates policy and develops social intervention. If, in fact, this change is as plausible as we think, it is necessary to consider critically the implications of developing an experimenting society. Although we think the positive aspects of social experimentation far outweigh the negative, there are clearly problems and dangers inherent in adopting this perspective. A number of problems have been identified in the literature and these, as well as other issues, are described.

SCIENTIFIC LOGIC

Throughout this book, we have argued that scientific logic can provide a helpful perspective in developing understandings of social problems; at least this has been our hypothesis. It is important to examine this hypothesis critically and to assess whether social experimentation is the appropriate model for applying scientific logic. One important conceptual issue is whether society's problems are amenable to empirical analysis—especially analysis characterized by experimental research. Scientific logic may be inadequate to answer the most pressing problems of society. There also may be good theoretical reasons for not trusting empirical analyses of these problems.

One prominent critic of social experimentation (at least, the greater use of and reliance on it) has been Guttentag (1977). According to Guttentag, we have moved into a postindustrial society characterized by human, professional, and technical services; a communal society in which collaborative decisions between individuals and groups are society's most important feature (see also Bell, 1976). From Guttentag's perspective, the experimental model—which was, perhaps, an adequate scientific perspective for our industrial society—is inadequate to help heterogeneous groups make decisions and integrate multiple emergent objectives.

According to Guttentag, the choice of a design for a research study (which is central to social experimentation) represents only a small part of the social decision-making process. More important in her view is the paradigm, or the way in which one chooses to view the problems and integrate diverse ideas about the problems. Guttentag's preference is the use of a paradigm which is decision-oriented. She suggests a model based on Bayesian statistics that permits the use and cumulation of reasoning, at least ideally. Bayesian analysis is designed to facilitate synthetic reasoning and is responsive, at any point in time, to the decision needs of the program administrators.

Another philosophical argument against social experimentation has been offered by Mitroff and his colleagues (Mitroff & Bonoma, 1978; Mitroff & Turoff, 1974). The essence of their argument is that the experimental model does not take into account the way in which a problem has been conceptualized. While an experimental design can aid in decision-making, the model does not really aid in challenging this image once the "right" conceptual image has been chosen for the study. This parallels the issue of faulty assumptions addressed at several points in the book. Furthermore, there is no such thing as a "pure" or "true" experiment, in the sense that alternative explanations are always present. No experiment, or experimental design, can really verify or prove false a hypothesis.

Experimentation cannot always be done, nor is it always necessary. Answers to questions about social intervention are often obvious, sometimes they are not important enough to warrant the resources of a social experiment; in other cases, data may already be available but not used because of value differences. Implicit in the work of Guttentag, as well as Mitroff and his colleagues, is a recommendation that one should not rely too much on experimentation. This is probably an admonishment worthy of attention.

However, our current policy structure bifurcates funding for social research and for social programs so that each develops virtually independent of the other. While battered women's shelters are funded (inadequately) without reasonable provision for research, research on the topic is often conducted independent of action. The social experimentation model introduces a different kind of integration of research and action, with implications for funding, program development, and research.

With respect to funding, social experimentation, by incorporating research and program development, reduces some duplication of spending. With respect to program development, social experimentation builds in an evolving dynamic intervention nourished by research. With respect to research, social experimentation examines individuals and structures in action—as they experience change and can envision different (if not better) life circumstances. So, although additional monies to investigate abstract social problems may be a notion resisted by activists, the social experimentation model incorporates these traditionally dramatically opposed positions. It profits the program, the research, the participants, and the financing.

PRACTICAL PROBLEMS

Many other potential problems lurk in the experimental model, especially as it applies to the development of actual social programs. Weiss and Rein (1970), for example, have argued that social programs with broad aims cannot be sufficiently standardized to consider the treatment of a single independent variable. To illustrate this position, they use a hypothetical program called the Neighborhood Benefit Program (NBP). The NBP is designed to change existing community institutions to be more useful to citizens, particularly to underprivileged youth. There are many targets of the program, including different groups within the community, and it is difficult, a priori, to know what interventions will affect which group. Although collecting data about the program's impact is critical, ambiguous treatment makes it difficult to implement the design. The units to which the program is directed cannot be identified as randomized units. Also, while the program might be held constant across conditions in order to satisfy research criteria, this consistency could hinder program development (stifle its experimenting with new interventions). If this were done merely to serve the needs of researchers, it would be infeasible.

In cases where such difficulties are overcome, other serious problems persist. Gramlich and Koshel (1975) evaluated an experiment in educational performance contracting. Performance contracting is a strategy for providing educational services. Business firms are hired to run schools, and often these private concerns are offered financial incentives to meet performance objectives (such as raising student test scores "x" points). It was an attempt to apply an economic market place concept to an educational environment.

The experiment, conducted in randomly selected treatment and control group schools, proved unsuccessful on a number of grounds. Data from achievement tests of reading and mathematics, as well as attendance records, indicated that the students in the business-run schools did not gain in any measurable way compared with students in traditional educational environments. Although some gains were noted in test scores of students in business-run schools, these were offset by poorer attendance records.

While the experiment was relatively straightforward, according to Gramlich and Kochel, it encountered difficulties at almost every stage. These difficulties cast doubt on the use of experimental methods in such settings. There were problems, for example, in determining what information should be tested and how the school districts and schools for the study should be selected. Although the problems of this experiment may have merely reflected the expected tensions between social researchers and planners, this study documented the difficulty of developing social policy, even when research is applied. An important, and as yet unanswerable, question is to what extent these problems could be avoided if the "experimenting ethic" were widespread, accepted, and institutionalized.

The widespread implementation of a social experimentation would raise additional problems, actual or potential. Rossi (1979), for example, has posed the question of whether social experiments can ever be done in timely enough fashion to be useful. Rossi suggests that the government's willingness to fund a social experiment usually does not occur until it is ready to enact a new policy for a particular problem. While exceptions clearly exist to this rule (such as Follow Through; see Chapter 3), Rossi's hypothesis is probably accurate in many cases. He asserts that social experiments, if they are to realize the promise of progressive research, should precede correspondent policy by a decade. How can such research be conducted in substantial precedence to policy formulation? One solution is that social experiments derive funds from institutions other than those associated with a particular government administration. For some social experiments to actualize their potential in instigating change, their financial base may have to be independent of government structures.

Rossi also raises a technical question about "hardware" vs. "software" programs. He implies that social programs made up primarily of "hardware" (technology) are more easily implemented in a standardized manner, and more easily measured in a systematic way, than are "software" (human services) interventions. In other words, technological or economic interventions stripped of heavy administrative baggage are more amenable to standardized implementation than social programs, which are usually heavily reliant on interpersonal relations, training modules, and/or educational components. He concludes, therefore, that labor programs may not be amenable to social experimentation; and that programs involving extensive social interactions may be more difficult to implement as true experiments than more quantitative, technical interventions.

Another potential problem is that social experiments will manipulate and measure people and not structures; that social experiments will inherit the conservative assumptions of many social programs that people should be the targets of intervention. Such programs—like assertiveness training for women workers or reducing the minimum wage for youth—focus on changing the victims of social problems rather than on examining the structural and economic root of social problems (Jahoda, 1981). Social experiments, if they can escape the assumptions that underlie social programs, can lead to actual social change.

Finally, we must humble our assumption that social experimentation and pluralism can easily coexist. Social experiments could easily be taken to illogical extremes, so that empirical "answers" are mindlessly applied to all problems. Models of the "best" day-care program, educational technique, or transportation system could be derived and applied universally, without recognition of individual, group, or geographic differences. Social experiments, if abused, could obfuscate pluralism, generating and applying the same social program to all. While this is possible, it is hoped that this is improbable, because research should be able to demonstrate the specific conditions under which interventions have particular impacts. Incorrect use of methodology, although inconsistent with the spirit of social experimentation (that of evolving social policy) is, of course, possible. Easy answers, however, are unfortunately not impossible and misuse must be considered.

HAS IT WORKED?

As important as a conceptual analysis of the adequacy of social experimentation is an analysis of the empirical evidence of its history, thus far. Can we, at this stage, really say that social experiments have provided better and more useful facts than other forms of research and policy analysis? On an even more basic level, can it be shown that social experiments have really provided us with *any* useful information? These are, unfortunately, deceptively simple questions, ones that are inherently subjective. Readers will have to make their own decision based on their analyses of the social experiments discussed throughout this volume. It is doubtful that any fair assessment will be clear-cut. Even our own conclusions are mixed.

Some of the most important social experiments of recent decades, such as the Negative Income Tax experiment, *Sesame Street,* Cambridge-Somerville Youth Study, and the Kansas City Police Patrol Experiment, all have serious methodological and utilization problems. The Negative Income Tax experiment not only was terminated prematurely, its conclusions were not expected (Rossi & Lyall, 1975). *Sesame Street,* though successful, may not have been as successful as first suspected (Cook et al., 1975). In fact, the decisions for continued government support were probably based on erroneous assessments by the experimenters. The Cambridge-Somerville Youth Study has similarly been shadowed by controversy for a long period of time (McCord, 1978; Sobel, 1978). There are clearly both good and bad reasons for continuing youth programs, but because the intervention took place so long ago, it is unclear at this time how much relevance the data of the study have on public policy.

Jahoda (1981) warns of the potential for social experiments to raise unimportant questions, even at the point of their conception. Her concern is that social science curiosities, as a rule, become aroused only after world events have created a problem, after entrenched positions have been taken and policies instituted. "However their unanticipated consequences are skillfully demonstrated by research, results come too late to make a difference " (p. 190).

This caution is of particular significance to social experimentation. While we pride ourselves on forward-looking research, Jahoda, Rossi, and others remind us that our social experiments are often the fruits of the same assumptions that have molded social policy, and are rarely either of a new genre or radical in structure or vision. If social experiments can realize the vision we set forth, the tasks of designing the intervention and the methodology will require time, effort, serious collaboration, and criticism.

However, it may be misleading to emphasize the problems and difficulties of these experiments. These all represent preliminary efforts for the experimenting society. They are expected to encounter difficulties in conceptualization and implementation. As noted in a previous chapter, while the original Negative Income Tax experiment did not provide answers that policy makers could use directly, it did serve two important functions. One was that major changes in the welfare system had not been made, and the lack of persuasive evidence based on the NIT was clearly an important factor in this decision. Second, as Lynn (1978) has noted, we now have data from the other follow-up welfare experiments that indicate that the original ideas were incorrect. Perhaps the most important value of an experiment is to save us from adopting erroneous policies (see also Gilbert, Light & Mosteller, 1975). In essence, the research identified a direction we should not take. As well, it helped us design better follow-up research which could inform policy.

Another serendipitous advantage of true experimental methods has been described by Kushler and Davidson (1979). They argue that, in many instances, social interventions are most important in that they halt deteriorating conditions rather than absolutely improve conditions. Without a valid comparison group, an intervention may appear to have no effect. Only in light of a comparison group that provides evidence of deterioration can one approximate the importance of the social intervention. A 1977 study by Davidson illustrates this point. Testing an innovative program for diverting adolescent offenders, random assignment was instituted to one of two experimental conditions or to a control condition of routine court processing. Participants in both experimental conditions indicated no change in level of involvement with the courts or school truancy; they did not get better because of the program. There was, however, a dramatic increase in both court appearances and truancy in the control condition. Only through randomization and comparisons across groups could this prevention of social deterioration have been documented. In the absence of control group information, one would have assumed that treatment program had no impact.

The most important point may be that a social experiment, despite the use of comparison groups and classical statistical techniques, may not be best viewed as a decision tool, but as significant input. Nothing in our complex social world is linear, unidimensional, or univariate (McGuire, 1973); intervention can be blanketly labeled "good" or "bad." Aspects of all social programs work to some extent; some aspects of all social programs do not work to some extent. If modest goals are adopted for social experiments—simply to help us realize what has happened and to inform our evolving understanding process—we can agree on a qualified statement that social experimentation does work.

FIT WITH SOCIETY

Temporarily putting aside scientific concerns with conceptual clarity and empirical verification, one must also consider the implications of a social experimenting society as a realistic model. In effect, we want to question whether this is a practical model for society and for the development of social policy.

A central issue is whether society is ready for social experimentation. Is it, in fact, reasonable for policy makers to assume other postures than an advocacy approach to both problems and their solutions? This seems hard to assess because, if you will pardon our use of terminology, we do not have any experimental evidence. Although it seems clear that policy makers will at least have to understand the neutral position of the scientist in considering alternative approaches, not a great deal of data is available about how this might be implemented. It is also unclear, if one examines the settings in which scientists play policy roles, whether scientists are able, because of their background and perspective, to make better judgments than other individuals who maintain an advocacy role.

There is some evidence (Zuniga, 1975) that the scientific model is insufficiently broad to incorporate the concerns of society. Zuniga is an experimentally trained psychologist who worked to implement social change in Chile during the three years of the Unidad Popular Government. According to Zuniga, it requires an act of faith to assume that scientific research could contribute to the policy development. It also requires a humbling regard for the subordinate character of scientific paradigms within broader frames of philosophical and political reference.

While an experimenting society will not come about easily or without problems, it seems clear that it is an approach that could be and is being tried, at least in specific areas of societal functioning. Some aspects of the model are inconsistent with how society needs to function. These seem to be problems that can be dealt with; dealt with, that is, if an experimenting society is instituted within a supportive social structure and under a widely held value system. This value system would need to include, as a central component, the willingness and interest of individuals from diverse backgrounds and perspectives to join with one another to collaborate, for social, rather than individualistic, good. These goals would be the development and implementation of social programs which meet society's pressing needs to deal fairly with their citizens and to promote human welfare.

Final Thoughts

Perhaps the most important idea to leave behind is that social experimentation is an evolving process. As one societal solution is adopted, the problem changes and requires a new answer. As Will Rogers noted, "Today's solution is tomorrow's problem." Discovering effective police practices may mean overloading prisons and the justice system; establishing battered women's shelters may create a pool of "domestically independent," but unemployed, women; national health insurance might result in an overburdened health care system.

Social experimentation, then, provides no long-term solutions. It is, however, one type of response to a larger societal problem: limited resources and inequitable access to power among people. In Chapter 1, we discussed the increasing numbers and growing complexity of social problems for which programs are being developed. As problems multiply and move into the public domain, the pool of resources is shrinking. Funds, personpower, and space do not come from bottomless pits. California's adoption of Proposition 13 and other similar state and federal initiatives are evidence of the public's resistance to sponsorship of unlimited social programs (Mushkin, 1979).

Social experimentation is a rational strategy for determining the effectiveness of solutions to problems. It should lead to programs being sponsored for their efficacy and value. It is clearly a different way of viewing social problems and responses. The dearth of resources mandates a more rational, criterion-bound mode of decision-making. Social experimentation represents one aspect of such a method. It is a process accessible to researchers and social planners, one designed to match better policy information needs and research products.

The experimenting society, then, is a response to a societal problem. This is not a weakness, but rather a reality of the model. It might happen, for example, that as social experiments become more normative, and collaborative an assumed component of social research, that new problems will emerge. Social planners and researchers may overcollaborate to the extent that critical objectivity is sacrificed; social experiments testing similar programs may yield discrepent results; the findings of "no difference" may be used to terminate social programs rather than to explore alternatives. The process, as we envision it, is such that new issues will surface. The examples and the concerns described in this book will quickly become outdated. One indicator of the effectiveness of this text will be the length of time before these ideas sound old-fashioned to participants in the Experimenting Society.

> *A good question is never answered. It is not a bolt to be tightened into place, but a seed to be planted toward the hope of greening the landscape of idea. The difference between a seed and an inert speck can be hard to see, but only one of them will grow and return itself in kind and be multiplied.*

> John Ciardi

References

Aaron, H. J. *Politics and the professors: The Great Society in perspective.* Washington, DC: Brookings Institution, 1978.

Abrams, R. I. Not one judge's opinion: Morgan v. Hennigan and the Boston Schools. *Harvard Educational Review,* 1975, *45,* 5-16.

Abt, C. C. (Ed.) *Problems in American social policy research.* Cambridge, MA: Abt Books, 1979.

Acland, H. Are randomized experiments the Cadillacs of design? *Policy Analysis,* 1979, *9,* 223-241.

Akabas, S., Fine, M., & Yasser, R. Putting secondary prevention to the test: A study of an early intervention strategy with disabled workers. *Journal of Prevention,* in press.

Alkin, M. C., Daillak, R., & White, P. *Using evaluations: Does evaluation make a difference?* Beverly Hills, CA: Sage, 1979.

American Psychological Association. *Ethical principles in the conduct of research with human participants.* Washington, DC: APA, 1973.

Anderson, S. B., & Ball, S. *The profession and practice of program evaluation.* San Francisco, CA: Jossey-Bass, 1978.

Anderson, R. B., St. Pierre, R. G., Proper, E. C., & Stebbins, L. B. Pardon us, but what was the question again? A response to the critique of the Follow Through evaluation. *Harvard Educational Review,* 1978, *48,* 161-170.

Asch, S. E. Effects of group pressure upon the modification and distortion of judgments. In H. Guetzkow (Ed.), *Groups, leadership, and men.* Pittsburgh, PA: Carnegie Press, 1951.

Babbie, E. R. *Survey research methods.* Belmont, CA: Wadsworth, 1973.

Bales, R. F. *Interaction process analysis: A method for the study of small groups.* Cambridge, MA: Addison-Wesley, 1951.

———*Personality and interpersonal behavior.* New York: Holt, Rinehart & Winston, 1958.

Ball, S., & Bogatz, G. A. *The first year of Sesame Street: An evaluation.* Princeton, NJ: Educational Testing Service, 1971.

Banta, D., Beheny, C., & Willems, J. *Toward rational technology in medicine: Considerations for health policy.* New York: Springer, 1981.

Barber, B. Experimenting with humans. *Public Interest,* 1967, *6,* 91-102.

Bar-Tal, D., & Saxe, L. (Eds.) *The social psychology of education: Theory and research.* Washington, DC: Hemisphere Publishing, 1978.

Bell, D. *The coming of post-industrial society.* New York: Basic Books, 1976.

Benedict, R. *The chrysanthemum and the sword.* Boston, MA: Houghton-Mifflin, 1946.

Bennis, W. G., Benne, K. D., Chin, R., & Corey, K. E. *The planning of change* (3rd ed.). New York: Holt, Rinehart & Winston, 1976.

Berk, R. A. Discretionary methodological decisions in applied research. *Sociological Methods and Research,* 1977, *5,* 317-333.

Berk, R. A., & Rossi, P. H. Doing good or worse: Evaluation research politically re-examined. *Social Problems,* 1977, *23,* 337-349.

Bermant, G., Kelman, H. C., & Warwick, D. P. (Eds.), *The ethics of social intervention.* Washington, DC: Hemisphere, 1978.

Bernstein, I. N., Bohrnstedt, G. W., & Borgatta, E. F. External validity and evaluation research. *Sociological Methods & Research,* 1975, *4,* 107-134.

_____ & Freeman, H.E. *Academic and entrepreneurial research: The consequences of diversity in federal evaluation studies.* New York: Russell Sage Foundation, 1975.

Blalock, H. M *Causal inferences in non-experimental research.* Chapel Hill, NC: University of North Carolina Press, 1964.

Bock, R. D. *Multivariate statistical methods in behavioral research.* New York: McGraw-Hill, 1975.

Boeckmann, M. *The contribution of social research to social policy: A study of the New Jersey income maintenance experiment and the family assistance plan.* Unpublished doctoral dissertation, John Hopkins University, 1973.

Boruch, R. F. On common contentions about randomized field experiments. In R. F. Boruch and H. W. Riecken (Eds.), *Experimental testing of public policy: The proceedings of the 1974 Social Science Research Council Conference on Social Experiments.* Boulder, CO: Westview Press, 1975.

_____ & Gomez, H. Sensitivity, bias and theory in impact evaluation. *Professional Psychology,* 1977, *8,* 141-434.

_____ McSweeney, A. J., & Soderstrom, E. J. Randomized field experiments for program planning, development and evaluation: An illustrative bibliography. *Evaluation Quarterly,* 1978, *4,* 655-695.

_____ & Riecken, H. W. (Eds.) Experimental testing of public policy: The proceedings of the 1974 Social Science Research Council Conference on Social Experiments. Boulder, CO: Westview Press, 1975.

Bower, R. T., & deGasparis, P. *Ethics in social research: Protecting the interests of human subjects.* New York: Praeger, 1978.

Boydstun, J. E., Sherry, M. E., & Moelter, N. P. Patrol staffing in San Diego: One- or two-officer units. In T. D. Cook & Associates (Eds.), *Evaluation studies review annual, Vol. 3.* Beverly Hills, CA: Sage, 1978.

Brock, T. C. Designs for corrective advertising. In L. Saxe (Chair), *Improving utilizability of psychological research through evaluation research strategies.* Symposium presented at the meeting of the American Psychological Association, Toronto, August, 1978.

Brown, P. G. Informed consent in social experimentation: Some cautionary notes. In A. M. Rivlin and P. M. Timpane (Eds.), *Ethical and legal issues of social experimentation.* Washington, DC: Brookings Institution, 1975.

Bunker, D. R. Organizing to link social science with public policy making. *Public Administration Review,* 1978, *6,* 195-208.

Burdick, S. Researching problems of battered women. In I. Frieze (Chair), *Perspectives on the problems of battered women.* Symposium at the meeting of the Association of Women in Psychology. Pittsburgh, PA, March 1978.

Burns, E.M. *Health services for tomorrow: Trends and issues.* New York: Dunellen, 1973.

Byar, D. P., Simon, R. M., Friedewald, W. T., Schlesselman, J., DeMets, D. L., Ellenberg, J. N., Gail, M. H., & Ware, J. H. Randomized clinical trials: Perspectives on some recent ideas. *New England Journal of Medicine,* 1976, *295,* 74.

Cain, L. The AMA and the gerontologist: Uses and abuses of "A Profile of the Aging: USA." In G. Sjoberg (Ed.), *Ethics, politics and social research*. Cambridge, MA: Schenkman, 1967.

Calder, R. The focused group technique and qualitative research in organizations. In E. Lawler (Ed.), *Organizational assessment*. New York: John Wiley, 1980.

Campbell, D. T. Factors relevant to the validity of experiments in social settings. *Psychological Bulletin*, 1957, *54*, 297-312.

———Reforms as experiments. *American Psychologist*, 1969, *24*, 409-429.

———Considering the case against experimental evaluation of social innovations. *Administrative Science Quarterly*, 1970, *15*, 110-113.

———*Methods for the experimenting society*. Paper presented at the meetings of the American Psychological Association, Washington, DC 1971.

———The social scientist as methodological servant of the experimenting society. *Policy Studies*, 1973, *2*, 72-75.

———*Qualitative knowing in action research*. Kurt Lewin address presented at the American Psychological Association, September, 1974.

———"Degrees of freedom" and the case study. In T. D. Cook & C. S. Reichardt (Eds.), *Qualitative and quantitative methods in evaluation research*. Beverly Hills, CA: Sage, 1979.

———& Erlebacher, A. How regression artifacts in quasi-experimental evaluations can mistakenly make compensatory education look harmful. In J. Hellmuth (Ed.), *Disadvantaged Child*, 1970, *3*.

———& Stanley, J. C. *Experimental and quasi-experimental designs for research*. Chicago, IL: Rand McNally, 1966.

Cannell, C. F., & Kahn, R. L. Interviewing. In G. Lindzey and E. Aronson (Eds.), *Handbook of social psychology, Vol. 2* (Rev. ed.). Reading, MA: Addison-Wesley, 1968.

Caplan, N., Morrison, A., & Stambaugh, R. J. *The use of social science knowledge in policy decisions at the national level*. Ann Arbor, MI: Institute for Social Research, 1975.

Capron, A. M. Social experimentation and the law. In A.M. Rivlin and P.M. Timpane (Eds.), *Ethical and legal issues of social experimentation*. Washington, DC: Brookings Institution, 1975.

Chapin, F. S. *Experimental designs in social research*. New York: Harper & Brothers, 1947.

Chapman, J., & Gates, M. *The victimization of women*. Beverly Hills, CA: Sage, 1978.

Chin, R., & Benne, K. D. General strategies for effecting changes in human systems. In W. G. Bennis, K. D. Benne, R. Chin, and K. E. Corey (Eds.), *The planning of change* (3rd. ed.). New York: Holt Rinehart & Winston, 1976.

Cicirelli, V. G. et al. *The impact of Head Start: An evaluation of the effects of Head Start on children's cognitive and affective development*. Vol. 1. Report to the U.S. Office of Economic Opportunity. Columbia, OH: Westinghouse Learning Corporation and Ohio University, 1969.

Cochran, N. Grandma Moses and the "corruption" of data. *Evaluation Quarterly*, 1978, *2*, 363-374.

Cohen, D. K. The value of social experiments. In A. M. Rivlin and P. M. Timpane (Eds.), *Planned variation in education: Should we give up or try harder?* Washington, DC: Brookings Institution, 1975.

Coleman, J. S. Response to Professors Pettigrew and Green. *Harvard Educational Review*, 1976, *46*, 217-224.

Coleman, J. S., Campbell, E. Q., Hobson, C. J., McPartlan, J.M., Mood, A. M., Weinfeld, F. D., & York, R. L. *Equality of educational opportunity*. Washington, DC: U.S. Government Printing Office, 1966.

College Entrance Examination Board. *On further examination: Report of the Advisory Panel in the Scholastic Aptitude Test Score Decline*. New York: CEEB, 1977.

Congressional Research Service. *Legislative oversight and program evaluation*. Washington, DC: U.S. Government Printing Office, 1976.

Conner, R. Selecting a control group. *Evaluation Quarterly,* 1977, *1,* 195-244.

Cook, T. D., Appleton, H., Conner, R. F., Shaffer, A., Tomkin, G., & Weber, S. J. *"Sesame Street" revisited*. New York: Russell Sage Foundation, 1975.

_____ & Campbell, D. T. The design and conduct of quasi-experiments and true experiments in field settings. In M. D. Dunnette (Ed.), *Handbook of industrial and organizational psychology*. Chicago, IL: Rand McNally, 1976.

_____ & Campbell, D. T. *Quasi-experimentation: Design and analysis issues for field settings*. Chicago, IL: Rand McNally, 1979.

_____ & Gruder, C. L. Metaevaluation research. *Evaluation Quarterly,* 1978, *2,* 5-51.

_____ & Levitan, L. C. Reviewing the literature: A comparison of traditional methods with meta-analysis, *Journal of Personality*. 1980, *48,* 449-472.

_____ & Reichardt, C. S. (Eds.) *Qualitative and quantitative methods in evaluation research*. Beverly Hills, CA: Sage, 1971.

Cronbach, L. J., Ambron, S. R., Dornbush, S. M., Hess, R. D., Hornik, R. C., Phillis, D. C., Walker, D. F., & Weiner, S. S. *Toward reform of program evaluations: Aims, methods and institutional arrangements*. San Francisco, CA: Jossey-Bass, 1980.

Crosby, F. A model of egoistical relative deprivation. *Psychological Review,* 1976, *83,* 85-113.

_____ Bromley, S., & Saxe, L. Recent unobtrusive studies of black and white discrimination and prejudice: A literature review. *Psychological Bulletin,* 1980, *87,* 546-563.

Crowne, D. P., & Marlowe, D. *The approval motive*. New York: John Wiley, 1964.

Dalkey, N. C., & Helmer, O. An experimental application of the Delphi method to the use of experts. *Management Science,* 1963, *102*.

Datta, L.-E. The impact of the Westinghouse/Ohio evaluation of the development of project Head Start: An examination of the immediate and longer-term effects and how they came about. In C. C. Abt (Ed.), *The evaluation of social programs*. Beverly Hills, CA: Sage, 1976.

Davidson, W. Diversion program for juvenile offenders. *Social Work Research and Abstracts,* 1977, *13,* 40-49.

Dentler, R. A., & Scott M. *Schools on trial: An inside account of the Boston Desegregation Case*. Cambridge, MA: Abt Associates, 1981.

Deutsch, S. J. Lies, damn lies, and statistics: A rejoinder to the comment by Hay and McCleary. *Evaluation Quarterly,* 1979, *3,* 315-328.

_____ & Alt, F. B. The effect of Massachusetts' gun control law on gun-related crimes in the city of Boston. *Evaluation Quarterly,* 1977, *1,* 543-568.

Deutscher, I. Public issues or private troubles: Is evaluation research sociological? *Social Focus,* 1976, *9,* 231-238.

Dewey, J. *Reconstruction in philosophy*. Boston, MA: Beacon Press, 1957.

Doron, J. *Intimate violence: A study of injustice*. New York: Columbia University Press, in press.

DuBois, P. A test of Pueblo Indian Children. *Psychological Bulletin,* 1939, *36,* 523.

Eisenberg, L. The social imperatives of medical research. *Science,* 1977, *198,* 1105-1110.

Eisenberg, L., & Micklow, P. L. The assaulted wife: "Catch 22" revisited. *Womens Rights Law Reporter,* 1977, *3,* 138-139.

Ellul, J. *The Technological Society*. New York: Alfred Knopf, 1964.

Elmore, R. F. Design of the Follow Through experiment. In A. M. Rivlin and P. M. Timpane (Eds.), *Planned variation in education: Should we give up or try harder?*. Washington, DC:

Brookings Institution, 1975.

Elms, A. *Social psychology and social relevance*. Boston: Little, Brown, 1972.

Eysenck, H. F. An exercise in mega-silliness. *American Psychologist*, 1978, *33*, 517.

Fairweather, G. W., & Tornatzky, L. G. *Experimental methods for social policy research*. Elmsford, NY: Pergamon, 1978.

Ferber, R., & Hirsch, W. Z. Social experimentation and economic policy: A survey. *Journal of Economic Literature*, 1978, *16*, 1379-1414.

Festinger, L. *A theory of cognitive dissonance*. Stanford, CA: Stanford University Press, 1957.

Fienberg, S. E., Larntz, K., & Reiss, A. J. Redesigning the Kansas City Preventive Patrol experiment. *Evaluation*, 1976, *3*, 124-131.

Fine, M. The battered women: Examining the social context. In I. Frieze (Chair), *Perspectives on the problems of battered women*. Symposium at the meetings of the Association of Women in Psychology, Pittsburgh, March, 1978.

———Options to injustice: Seeing other lights. *Representative Research in Social Psychology*, 1979, *10*, 61-76.

———An injustice by any other name . . . *Victimology*, 1981, *6*, in press.

———& Akabas, S. Combining experimental design with archival, survey and interview methods: Evaluation research in trade unions. In R. Conner (Ed.), *Methodological advances in evaluation research*. Beverly Hills: Sage, in press.

———Akabas, S., & Bellinger, S. Cultures of drinking: A worksite perspective. *Social Work*, in press.

Fine, M., & Blackman, J. *The battered woman*. Paper presented at Second National Conference in Needs Assessment. Louisville, KY, March, 1978.

———& Goldman, H. *Evaluation research and the one year educational innovation: Examining the paradox*. Unpublished manuscript, Columbia University, 1979.

———& Laufer, R. *Social health and the Vietnam generation*. Paper presented at the American Sociological Association, Boston, 1979.

———& Saxe, L. Evaluation research and psychology: Toward synthesis. In L. Saxe (Chair), *Improving utilizability of psychological research through evaluation research strategies*. Symposium presented at the meeting of the American Psychological Association, Toronto: August, 1978.

Fineberg, H. V., & Hiatt, H. H. Evaluation of medical practices: The case for technology assessment. *New England Journal of Medicine*, 1979, *301*, 1086-1091.

Fiorina, M. *Congress: Keystone of the Washington establishment*. New Haven, CT: Yale University Press, 1977.

Fisher, R. A. *The design of experiments* (7th ed.). New York: Hafner, 1960

Frank, J. D. *Persuasion and healing: A comparative study of psychotherapy* (Rev. ed.). Baltimore, MD: John Hopkins University Press, 1973.

Fraser, D. W., & McDade, J. E. Legionellosis. *Scientific American*, 1979, *241*, 82-101.

Freeman, H. E. The present status of evaluation research. In M. Guttentag and S. Saar (Eds.), *Evaluation studies review annual, Vol. 2*. Beverly Hills, CA: Sage, 1977.

Gay, J., & Cole, M. *The new mathematics and the old culture*. New York: Holt, 1967.

Gayford, J. Wife battering: A preliminary survey of 100 cases. *British Medical Journal*, 1975, *1*, 194-197.

Gelles, R. *The violent home: A study of physical aggression between husbands and wives*. Beverly Hills, CA: Sage, 1972.

Gergen, K. J. Social psychology as history. *Journal of Personality and Social Psychology*, 1973, *26*, 309-320.

Gergen, K. J. Toward generative theory. *Journal of Personality and Social Psychology*, 1978, *36*, 1344-1356.

Gilbert, J. P., Light, R. J., & Mosteller, F. Assessing social innovations: An empirical basis for policy. In C. A. Bennet and A. A. Lumsdaine (Eds.), *Evaluation and experiment: Some critical issues in assessing social programs*. New York: Academic Press, 1975.

_____McPeak, B., & Mosteller, F. Progress in surgery and anesthesia: Benefits and risks of innovative therapy. In J. P. Bunker, B. A. Barnes, and F. Mosteller (Eds.), *Costs, risks and benefits of surgery*. New York: Oxford University Press, 1977.

Gill, S. How do you stand on sin? *Time,* March 14, 1947, 72ff.

_____Glass, G. V., McLean, L. D., & Walker, D. F. No simple answer. Critique of the Follow Through evaluation. *Harvard Educational Review,* 1978, *48,* 128-160.

_____McGaw, B., & Smith, M. L. *Meta-analysis in social research*. Beverly Hills, CA: Sage, 1981.

Goldberg, S., & Lewis, M. Play behavior in the year old infant: Early sex differences. *Child Development,* 1969, *40,* 21-31.

Goodwin, L. *Can social science help solve national problems? Welfare: A case in point*. New York: Free Press, 1975.

Gordon, G., & Morse, E. V. Evaluation research. *Annual Review of Sociology,* 1975, *1,* 339-361.

Gordon, R. L. *Interviewing: Strategies, techniques and tactics* (Rev. ed.). Homewood, IL: Dorsey Press, 1975.

Gramlich, E. M., & Koshel, P. P. *Educational performance contracting: An evaluation of an experiment*. Washington, DC: Brookings Institution, 1975.

Greenfield, P., & Bruner, J. Culture and cognitive growth. In J. S. Bruner (Ed.), *Beyond the information given*. New York: Norton, 1973.

Groves, R. Actors and questions in telephone and personal interview surveys. *Public Opinion Quarterly,* 1979, *43,* 206-217.

Guttentag, M. Evaluation and society. *Personality and Social Psychology Bulletin,* 1977, *3,* 31-40.

_____& Struening, E. L. (Eds.) *Handbook of evaluation research, Vol. 2*. Beverly Hills, CA: Sage, 1975.

Hammond, S. W., & Fox, H. W., Jr. *Congressional staffs: The invisible force in American lawmaking*. New York: Free Press, 1977.

Hampden-Turner, C. *Sane asylum*. San Francisco, CA: San Francisco Book Co., 1976.

Hastorf, A. H., Polefka, J., & Schneider, D. J. *Person perception,* (2nd ed.). Reading, MA: Addison-Wesley, 1978.

Hay, R. A., & McCleary, R. Box-Tiao time series models for impact assessment: A comment on the recent work of Deutsch and Alt. *Evaluation Quarterly,* 1979, *3,* 277-314.

Heider, F. *The psychology of interpersonal relations*. New York: John Wiley, 1958.

Hendrick, C. Social psychology as an experimental science. In C. Hendrick (Ed.), *Perspectives in social psychology*. Hillsdale, NJ: Lawrence Erlbaum, 1977.

Hidden Camera Project. National Institute on Law Enforcement and Criminal Justice. *Exemplary Projects,* 1978.

Holsti, O. R. *Content analysis for the social sciences and humanities*. Reading, MA: Addison-Wesley, 1969.

Hoole, F. W. *Evaluation research and development activities*. Beverly Hills, CA: Sage, 1978.

House, E. R. Assumptions underlying evaluation models. *Educational Researcher,* 1978, *7,* 4-12.

_____Glass, G. V., McLean, L. D., & Walker, D. F. No simple answer. Critique of the Follow Through evaluation. *Harvard Educational Review,* 1978, *48,* 128-160.

Huff, D. *How to lie with statistics*. New York: W. W. Norton, 1954.

Hughes, R. N. Education Could Pay. *New York Times,* March 15, 1979.

Huxley, A. *Brave new world*. New York: Harper & Row, 1946.

Illich, I. *Medical nemesis*. New York: Random House, 1976.

Jahoda, M. Work, employment and unemployment. *American Psychologist*, 1981, *36*, 184-191.

Jason, L. A., McCoy, K., Blanco, D., Zolik, E.S. Decreasing dog litter: Behavioral consultation to help a community group. *Evaluation Review*, 1980, *4*, 335-370.

Jones, B. The advocate, the auditor and the program manager. *Evaluation Review*, 1980, *4*, 275-306.

Kagan, J., Kearsley, R. B., & Zelazo, P. R. The effects of infant day care on psychological development. *Evaluation Quarterly*, 1977, *1*, 109-142.

Kagan, J., Kearsley, R. B., & Zelazo, P. R. *Infancy: Its place in human development*. Cambridge, MA: Harvard University Press, 1979.

Kaplan, A. *The conduct of inquiry*. Scranton, PA: Chandler, 1964.

Kasl, S., & Colb, S. Some mental health consequences of plant closing and job loss. In L. Ferman and J. Gordus (Eds.), *Mental health and the economy*. Kalamazoo, MI: W. E. Upjohn Institute, 1979.

Kelley, H. H. The process of causal attribution. *American Psychologist*, 1973, *28*, 107-128.

Kelling, G. L., Pate, T., Dieckman, D., & Brown, C. E. The Kansas City Preventive Patrol Experiment: A summary report. In G. V. Glass (Ed.), *Evaluation studies review annual*, *Vol. 1*. Beverly Hills, CA: Sage, 1976.

Kelman, H. C. The rights of the subject in social research: An analysis in terms of relative power and legitimacy. *American Psychologist*, 1972, *27*, 989-1016.

Kerlinger, F. N. *Foundations of behavioral research* (2nd ed.). New York: Holt, Rinehart & Winston, 1973.

Kershaw, D. N. Issues in income maintenance experimentation. In P. H. Rossi and W. Williams (Eds.), *Evaluating social programs: Theory, practice and politics*. New York: Seminar Press, 1972.

Ketterer, R. F., Price, R. H., & Polister, P. E. The action research paradigm. In R. H. Price & P. E. Polister, (Eds.), *Evaluation and action in the social environment*. New York: Academic Press, 1980.

Kidd, R. F., & Saks, M. J. What is applied social psychology? An introduction. In R. F. Kidd and M. J. Saks (Eds.), *Advances in applied social psychology, Vol. 1*. Hillsdale, NJ: Lawrence Erlbaum, 1980.

Klein, N., Alexander, J., & Parsons, B. Impact of family system intervention on recidivism and sibling delinquency: A model of primary prevention and program evaluation. *Journal of Consulting and Clinical Psychology*, 1977, *3*, 469-474.

Klineberg, O. *Negro intelligence and selective migration*. New York: Columbia University Press, 1935.

Kohlberg, S. L. Development of moral character and moral ideology. In M. C. Hoffman (Ed.), *Review of child development research. Vol. 1*. New York: Russell Sage Foundation, 1964.

Kruglanski, A. M. The human subject in psychology experiments: Fact and artifact. In L. Berkowitz (Ed.), *Advances in experimental social psychology, Vol. 8*. New York: Academic Press, 1975.

Kuhn, T. *The structure of scientific revolutions* (2nd ed.). Chicago, IL: University of Chicago Press, 1970.

Kushler, M., & Davidson, W. Using experimental designs to evaluate social programs. *Social Work Research and Abstracts*, 1979, *15*, 27-32.

Lachenmeyer, C. W. Experimentation—a misunderstanding methodology in psychological and socio-psychological research *American Psychologist*, 1970, *25*, 617-624.

LaFrance, M., & Mayo, C. *Moving bodies: Nonverbal communication in social relationships*. Monterey, CA: Brooks/Cole, 1978.

Lake, D. *Dissemination and utilization of evaluation research*. Unpublished manuscript, 1977.

Lancy, D. F. The classroom as phenomenon. In D. Bar-Tal and L. Saxe (Eds.), *The social psychology of education: Theory and research*. Washington, DC: Hemisphere Publishing, 1978.

Larson, R. C. What happened to patrol operations in Kansas City? *Evaluation*, 1976, *3*.

Levitan, S. A., & Wurzburg, G. *Evaluating federal social programs: An uncertain art*. Kalamazoo, MI: W. E. Upjohn Institute for Employment Research, 1979.

Leviton, E. C., & Cook, T. D. What differentiates meta-analysis from other forms of review. *Journal of Personality*, 1981, *49*, 231-236.

Lewin, K. *Field theory in social science*. New York: Harper, 1951.

_____ *Resolving social conflicts*. New York: Harper, 1948.

Lindblom, D. E., & Cohen, D. K. *Usable knowledge: Social science and social problem solving*. New Haven, CT: Yale University Press, 1979.

Lippitt, R. The process of utilization of social research to improve social practice. In W. G. Bennis et al. (Eds.), *The planning of change*. (3rd ed.) New York: Holt, Rinehart & Winston, 1976.

Loftus, E. Impact of expert psychological testimony on the unreliability of eyewitness identification. *Journal of Applied Psychology*, 1980, *65*, 9-15.

Luborsky, L., Singer, B., & Luborsky, L. Comparative studies of psychotherapy: Is it true that "everyone has won and all must have prizes"? *Archives of General Psychiatry*, 1975, *32*, 995-1008.

Lynn, L. E., Jr. A decade of policy developments in the income maintenance system. In T. Cook and Associates (Eds.), *Evaluation studies review annual, Vol. 3*. Beverly Hills, CA: Sage, 1978.

Macht, L. B. Mental health programs, past, present, and future: Bases for evaluation. In E. W. Markson, and D. F. Allen, (Eds.), *Trends in mental health evaluation*. Lexington, MA: D. C. Heath & Co., 1976.

Mahoney, B. S., & Mahoney, W. M. Policy implications: A skeptical view. In J. A. Peckman & P. M. Timpane (Eds.), *Work incentives and income guarantee*. Washington, DC: Brookings Institution 1975.

Marciano, T. D. Middle-class incomes, working class hearts. *Family Process*, 1974, *13*, 489-502.

Marsiniak, D. *Plant closings: Community impact*. Paper presented at the Rural Mental Health Training Conference, Lansing, MI, 1980.

Martin, D. *Battered wives*. New York: Pocket Books, 1977.

Maslow, A. *Motivation and personality*. New York: Harper & Row, 1954.

Mayo, C. Training applied social researchers. In C. C. Abt (Ed.), *Problems in American social policy research*. Cambridge, MA: Abt Books, 1980.

_____ & LaFrance, M. Toward an applicable social psychology. In R. F. Kidd and M. J. Saks (Eds.), *Advances in applied social psychology (Vol. 1.)*. Hillsdale, NJ: Lawrence Erlbaum, 1980.

McCain, G., & Segal, E. M. *The game of science* (3rd ed.). Monterey, CA: Brooks/Cole, 1977.

McCain, L. J., & McCleary, R. The statistical analysis of the simple interrupted time-series quasi-experiment. In T. D. Cook and D. T. Campbell (Eds.), *Quasi-experimentation: Design & analysis issues for field settings*. Chicago: Rand McNally, 1979.

McCord, J. A thirty-year follow-up of treatment effects. *American Psychologist*, 1978, *33*, 284-289.

McCord, W., & McCord J. *Origins of crime*. New York: Columbia University Press, 1959.

McDaniel, G. L. Evaluation problems in Follow Through. In A. M. Rivlin and P. M. Timpane (Eds.), *Planned variation in education: Should we give up or try harder?* Washington, DC:

Brookings Institution, 1975.

McDill, E. L., McDill, M. S., & Sprehe, J. T. Evaluation in practice: Compensatory education. In P. H. Rossi and W. Williams (Eds.) *Evaluating social programs: Theory, practice and politics*. New York: Seminar Press, 1972.

McGuire, W. J. The yin and yang of process in social psychology: Steven Koan. *Journal of Personality and Social Psychology,* 1973, *26,* 446-456.

McGrath, S. D., O'Brien, P. F., Power, P. J., & Shea, J. R. Nicotinamide treatment of schizophrenia. *Schizophrenia Bulletin,* 1972, *5,* 74-76.

McKillip, J. Impact evaluation of service programs. *Evaluation Quarterly,* 1979, *3,* 97-104.

Meier, P. The biggest public health experiment ever: The 1954 field trial of the Salk poliomyelitis vaccine. In F. Mosteller et al. (Eds.), *Statistics: A guide to the unknown*. New York: Holden-Day, 1972.

Merton, R. K. *Social theory and social structure*. (Rev. ed.). Glencoe, IL: Free Press, 1957.

Metfessel, N., & Michael, W. A paradigm involving multiple criterion measures for the evaluation of effectiveness of school programs. *Educational and Psychological Measurement,* 1967, *27,* 931-943.

Michelson, S., et al. *A review of the Abt Associates, Inc. evaluation of the Special Impact Programs.* (Community Services Administration). Cambridge, MA: Center for Community Economic Development, 1977.

Middlemist, R., Knowles, E., & Matler, C. Personal space invasions in the lavatory: Suggestive evidence for arousal. *Journal of Personality and Social Psychology,* 1976, *34,* 541-547.

Mitroff, I., & Bonoma, T. V. Psychological assumptions, experimentation, and real world problems: A critique and an alternative approach to evaluation. *Evaluation Quarterly,* 1978, *2,* 235-260.

_____ & Turoff, M. On measuring the conceptual errors in large scale social experiments: The future as decision. *Technological Forecasting and Social Change,* 1974, *6,* 389-402.

Mosteller, F. Innovation and evaluation. *Science,* 1981, *211,* 881-886.

Moynihan, D. P. *Maximum feasible misunderstanding*. New York: Free Press, 1970.

Mushkin, S. J. *Proposition 13 and its consequences for public management*. Cambridge, MA: Council for Applied Social Research, 1979.

Nagel, E. *The structure of science*. New York: Harcourt, 1961.

Newhouse, J. P. Design for a health insurance experiment. *Inquiry,* 1974, *2,* 5-27.(a)

Newhouse, J. P. *The health insurance study —a summary* (R-965-1-OEO). Santa Monica, CA: Rand Corp., 1974.(b)

Nunnally, J. C. *Psychometric methods*. New York: McGraw-Hill, 1978.

_____ & Wilson, W. H. Method and theory for developing measures in evaluation research. In E. L. Struening and M. Guttentag (Eds.) *Handbook of evaluation research, Vol. 1*. Beverly Hills, CA: Sage, 1975.

Office of Technology Assessment. *The implications of cost-effectiveness analysis of medical technology*. Washington, DC: Government Printing Office, 1980.

Olson, D. *The politics of legislation: A congressional simulation*. New York: Praeger, 1976.

Orne, M. T. On the social psychology of psychological experiments: With particular reference to demand characteristics and their implications. *American Psychologist,* 1962, *17,* 776-783.

Pagelow, M. Institutional response to battered women. In I. Frieze (Chair), *Perspectives on the problems of battered women*. Symposium at the meetings of the Association of Women in Psychology. Pittsburgh, March 1978.

Panlu, L., Chen, H. C., & Chow, L. P. An experimental study of the effect of group meetings on the acceptance of family planning in Taiwan. *The Journal of Social Issues,* 1967, *23,* 171-177.

Parloff, M. B. Can psychotherapy research guide the policy maker? A little knowledge may be a dangerous thing. *American Psychologist*, 1979, *34*, 296-303.

Patton, M. Q. *Utilization-focused evaluation*. Beverly Hills, CA: Sage, 1978.

_____ Grimes, P. S., Guthrie, K. M., Brennan, N. J., French, B. D., & Blyth, D. A. In Search of impact: An analysis of the utilization of federal health evaluation research. In C. H. Weiss (Ed.), *Using social research*. Lexington, MA: Lexington Books, 1977.

Payne, S. *The art of asking questions*. New York: Norton, 1951.

Perloff, R., Perloff, E., & Sussna, E. Program evaluation. *Annual Review of Psychology*, 1976, *27*, 569-594.

Pettigrew, T. F., & Green, R. L. School desegregation in large cities. A critique of the Coleman "White Flight" thesis. *Harvard Educational Review*, 1976, *46*, 1-53.

Pillemer, D. B., & Light, R. J. Synthesizing outcomes: How to use research evidence from many studies. *Harvard Educational Review*, 1980, *50*, 176-195.

Popper, K. *The logic of scientific discovery* (2nd Ed.). New York: Harper Torchbooks, 1968.

Powers, E., & Witmer, H. *An experiment in the prevention of delinquency*. New York: Columbia University Press, 1951.

President's Commission on Mental Health. *Report to the President, 1978*. Washington, DC: U.S. Government Printing Office, 1978.

Rentz, C. C., & Rentz, R. R. Evaluating federally sponsored programs. *New Directions for Program Evaluation*, 1978, *2*.

Richardson, S., Dohrenwend, B., & Klein, D. *Interviewing: Its form and functions*. New York: Basic Books, 1965.

Riecken, H. W., & Boruch, R. F. (Eds.). *Social experimentation: A method for planning and evaluating social intervention*. New York: Academic Press, 1974.

_____ & Boruch, R. F. Social experiments. *Annual Review of Sociology*, 1978, *4*, 511-532.

Risman, B. J. The Kansas City Preventive Patrol experiment. *Evaluation Review*, 1980, *4*, 802-808.

Rivlin, A. M. *Systematic thinking for social action*. Washington, DC: The Brookings Institution, 1971.

_____ & Timpane, P. M. (Eds.), *Ethical and legal issues of social experimentation*. Washington, DC: Brookings Institution, 1975.(a)

_____ *Planned variation in education: Should we give up or try harder?* Washington, DC: Brookings, 1975.(b)

Robbins, A. Ethical standards and data archives. In R. F. Boruch (Ed.), *New Directions for Program Evaluation: Secondary Analysis*, 1978, *4*, 7-18.

Roethlisberger, F. J., & Dickson, W. J. *Management and the workers*. Cambridge, MA: Harvard University Press, 1939.

Roiser, M. Asking silly questions. In N. Armistead (Ed.), *Reconstructing social psychology*. Baltimore, MD: Penguin Books, 1974.

Roos, L. L., Roos, N. P., & McKinley, B. Implementing randomization. *Policy Analysis*, 1977, *4*, 547-559.

Roos, N. P. Contrasting social experimentation with retrospective evaluation: A health care perspective. *Public Policy*, 1975, *23*, 274-257.

Rosenhan, D. L. On being sane in insane places. *Science*, 1973, *179*, 250-258.

Rosenthal, R. *Experimenter effects in behavioral research*. New York: Appleton-Century-Crofts, 1966.

_____ Combining results of independent studies. *Psychological Bulletin*, 1978, *85*, 185-193.

_____ & Rosnow, R. L. *The volunteer subject*. New York: John Wiley, 1975.

_____ & Rubin, D. B. Interpersonal expectancy effects: The first 345 studies. *The Behavioral and Brain Sciences*, 1978, *3*, 377-415.

Ross, H. L., & Blumenthal, M. Some problems in experimentation in a legal setting. *American*

Sociologist, 1975, *10,* 150-155.

Rossi, P. H. Field experiments in social programs: Problems and prospects. In G. M. Lyons (Ed.), *Social research and public policy.* Hanover, NH: University Presses of New England, 1975.

———Issues in the evaluation of human services delivery. *Evaluation Quarterly,* 1979, *3,* 573-599.

———Boeckmann, M., & Berk, R. A. Some ethical implications of the New Jersey-Pennsylvania Income Maintenance experiment. In B. Bermant, H. C. Kelman, and D. P. Warwick (Eds.), *The ethics of social intervention.* Washington, DC: Hemisphere Publishing, 1978.

Rossi, P., & Lyall, K. C. *Reforming public welfare: A critique of the negative income tax experiment.* New York: Russell Sage Foundation, 1976.

Rothbart, G., Fine, M., & Laufer, R. *Finding and interviewing the Vietnam veteran.* Paper presented at the American Association for Public Opinion Research, Roanoke, VA, 1978.

———& Frease, D. *The problems of contacting respondents in a folow-up study.* Unpublished manuscript, University of Oregon, 1965.

Rowan, J. Research as intervention. In N. Armistead (Ed.), *Reconstructing social psychology.* Baltimore, MD: Penguin Books, 1974.

Roy, M. (Ed.). *Battered women.* New York: Van Nostrand Reinhold, 1977.

Rutman, L., & deJong, D. *Federal level evaluation.* Ottawa, Canada: Centre for Social Welfare Studies, Carlton University, 1976.

Ryan, W. *Blaming the victim.* New York: Vantage, 1972.

Saks, M. J. Social psychological contributions to a legislative committee on organ and tissue transplants. *American Psychologist,* 1978, *33,* 680-690.

———& Hastie, R. *Social psychology in court.* New York: Van Nostrand Reinhold, 1978.

Sanford, N. Whatever happened to action research? *Journal of Social Issues,* 1970, *26,* 3-23.

Saretsky, D. G. The OEO P.C. Experiment and the John Henry Effect. *Phi Delta Kappan,* 1972, *53,* 579-581.

Satin, D. G., & Saxe, L. The Deacon's masterpiece: Methodological and role complexities in the evaluation of an interdisciplinary mental health education program. *Evaluation and Program Planning,* 1979, *2,* 285-295.

Saxe, L. On making the media more attractive to psychologists. In D. Winter (Chair), *Psychology and the media: Defining and improving our relationship.* Symposium presented at the Meetings of the American Psychological Association, Toronto, August, 1978.

———*The evaluation of sickle cell counseling programs.* Unpublished manuscript. National Institutes of Health, 1979.

———(with Yates, B., & Newman, F.). *The efficacy and cost-effectiveness of psychotherapy* (Background paper #3: The implications of the cost-effectiveness of medical technology). Washington, DC: U.S. Government Printing Office, 1980.

———& Fine, M. Expanding our view of control groups in evaluations. In L. Datta and R. Perloff (Eds.), *Improving evaluations.* Beverly Hills, CA: Sage, 1979.

———& Fine, M. Reorienting social psychology toward application: A methodological analysis. In L. Bickman (Ed.), *Applied social psychology annual.* Beverly Hills, CA: Sage, 1980.

———& Lake, D. G. *Evaluation methods in interdisciplinary health team education.* Unpublished manuscript, Boston University, 1978.

Schlenker, B. R. Social psychology and science. *Journal of Personality and Social Psychology,* 1974, *29,* 1-15.

Schofield, J. W. School desegregation and intergroup relations. In D. Bar-Tal and L. Saxe (Eds.), *The social psychology of education: Theory and research.* Washington, DC: Hemisphere Publishing, 1978.

Scriven, M. The methodology of evaluation. In *Perspectives on curriculum evaluation (Ameri-*

can Educational Research Association monograph series on curriculum evaluation). Chicago, IL: Rand McNally, 1967.

_____Goal-free evaluation. In R. House (Ed.), School evaluation: The policies and the process. Berkeley, CA: McCutchan, 1973.

_____Evaluation bias and its control. Occasional Paper #4, Kalamazoo, MI: The Evaluation Center, Western Michigan University, 1975.

Sechrest, L., & Associates (Eds.). Evaluation studies review annual, Vol. 4. Beverly Hills, CA: Sage, 1979.

Seidman, D., & Couzens, M. Getting the crime rate down: Political pressure and crime reporting. Law & Society Review, 1974, 8, 457-493.

Shannon, L. W. Assessing the relationship of adult criminal careers to juvenile careers. In C. C. Abt (Ed.), Problems in American social policy research. Cambridge, MA: Abt Books, 1979.

Shostak, A. Blue collar stress. Reading, MA: Addison-Wesley, 1980.

Shosteck, H., & Fairweather, W. Physician response rates to mail and personal interview surveys. Public Opinion Quarterly, 1979, 43, 206-217

Silberman, M. Yoke Crest: An alternative to prison. Project DS 340-73E. Governor's Justice Commission of Pennsylvania, 1974.

Silverman, W. The lesson of retrolental fibroplasia. Scientific American, 1977, 236, 100-107.

Singer, E., & Kohnke-Aguirre, L. Interviewer expectation effects: A replication and extension. Public Opinion Quarterly, 1979, 43, 245-230.

Skinner, B. F. Beyond freedom and dignity. New York: Knopf, 1971.

Sloane, R. B. Stevens, F. R., Cronin, A. H., York, N., & Whipple, K. Psychotherapy versus behavior therapy. Cambridge, MA: Harvard University Press, 1975.

Smith, M. L., & Glass, G. V. Meta-analysis of psychotherapy outcome studies. American Psychologist, 1977, 32, 752-756.

_____Miller, T. I. The benefits of psychotherapy. Baltimore, MD: Johns Hopkins University Press, 1980.

Snow, C. P. The two cultures and a second look. New York: Cambridge University Press, 1963.

_____Public affairs. New York: Charles Scribner's Sons, 1971.

Sobel, S. B. Throwing the baby out with the bathwater: The hazards of follow-up research. American Psychologist, 1978, 33, 290-291.

Sommer, R. The end of imprisonment. New York: Oxford University Press, 1976.

Spitzer, W. O., Sackett, D. L., Sibley, J. C., Roberts, R. S., Gent, M., Kergin, D. J., Hackett, B. C., & Olynich, A. The Burlington randomized trial of the nurse practitioner. New England Journal of Medicine, 1974, 290, 251-256.

Stake, R. Measuring what learners learn. Urbana, IL: Center for Instructional Research and Curriculum Evaluation, University of Illinois, 1971.

Stebbins, L. B., St. Pierre, R. G., Proper, E. C., Anderson, R. B., & Cerva, T. R. An evaluation of Follow Through. In T. D. Cook and Associates (Eds.), Evaluation studies review annual, Vol. 3. Beverly Hills, CA: Sage, 1978.

Stern, P. C., & Gardner, G. T. Psychological resources and energy policy. American Psychologist, 1981.

Stobaugh, R., & Yergin, D. (Eds.). Energy future: Report of the energy project at the Harvard University Business School. New York: Random House, 1979.

Strauss, M. A sociological perspective on the prevention and treatment of wifebeating. In M. Roy (Ed.), Battered women. New York: Van Nostrand and Reinhold Co., 1977.

Stromsdorfer, E. E., & Farkas, G. Introduction. Evaluation studies review annual, Vol. 5. Beverly Hills, CA: Sage, 1980.

Struening, E. L., & Guttentag, M. (Eds.). Handbook of evaluation research. Vol. 1. Beverly Hills, CA: Sage, 1977.

Student. The Lanarkshire milk experiment. *Biometrika,* 1931, *23,* 398.

Stufflebeam, D. L. Alternative approaches to educational evaluation: A self-study guide for educators. In W. J. Popham (Ed.), *Evaluation in education: current applications.* Berkeley, CA: McCutchan, 1974.

———Foley, W. J., Gephart, W. J., Guba, E. G., Hammond, R. L. Merriman, H. O., & Provus, M. *Educational evaluation and decision making.* Itasca, IL: F. E. Peacock Publishers, 1971.

Suchman, E. *Evaluative research.* New York: Russell Sage Foundation, 1967.

Sudman, S. *Applied sampling.* New York: Academic Press, 1976.

———Bradborn, N., Blair, E., & Stocking, C. Modest expectations: The effects of interviewers prior expectations response. *Sociological Methods and Research,* 1977, *6,* 177-182.

Thurow, L. C. *The zero-sum society: Distribution and the possibilities for economic change.* New York: Basic, 1980.

Toffler, A. *Future shock.* New York: Random House, 1970.

———*Third wave.* New York: Random House, 1980.

Travers, J., & Goodson, B. D. *Research results of the national daycare study.* Cambridge, MA: Abt Associates, 1980.

U. S. Senate Committee on Human Resources. *Cost, management and utilization of human resources program evaluation.* (October 6 & 27, 1977). Washington, DC: Government Printing Office, 1978.

Varna, M. Battered women: Battered children. In M. Roy (Ed.), *Battered women.* New York: Van Nostrand Reinhold Co., 1977.

Veatch, R. M. Ethical principles in medical experimentation. In A. M. Rivlin and P. M. Timpane (Eds.), *Ethical and legal issues of social experimentation.* Washington, DC: Brookings Institution, 1975.

Vietnam Era Research Project (1979) *The psycho-social adjustment of Vietnam era veterans to civilian life.* Working paper submitted to the Veterans Administration, V101(134)P610.

Waldo, G. P., & Chiricos, T. G. Work release and recidivism: An empirical evaluation of a social policy. *Evaluation Quarterly,* 1977, *1,* 87-108.

Walker, L. Treatment alternatives for battered women. In J. Chapman and M. Gates (Eds.), *The victimization of women, Vol. 3.* Beverly Hills, CA: Sage, 1978.

Warheit, G. J., Bell, R. A., & Schwab, J. J. *Planning for change: Needs assessment approaches.* Rockville, MD: National Institute of Mental Health, 1974.

Warwick, D. P. Ethical guidelines for social experiments. In G. Bermant, H. C. Kelman, and D. P. Warwick (Eds.), *The ethics of social intervention.* Washington, DC: Hemisphere Publishing, 1978.

Webb, E. J., Campbell, D. T., Schwartz, R. D., & Sechrest, L. *Unobtrusive measures: Nonreactive research in the social sciences.* Chicago, IL: Rand McNally, 1966.

Weber, S. J., & Cook, T. D. Subject effects in laboratory research: An examination of subject roles, demand characteristics, and valid inferences. *Psychological Bulletin,* 1972, *77,* 273-293.

Weick, K. E. Systematic observational methods. In G. Lindzey and E. Aronson (Eds.), *Handbook of social psychology. Vol. 2.* (Rev. ed.). Reading, MA: Addison-Wesley, 1968.

Weiss, C. H. *Evaluation research: Methods of assessing program effectiveness.* Englewood Cliffs, NJ: Prentice-Hall, 1972.

———Evaluation research in the political context. In E. L. Streuning & M. Guttentag (Eds.), *Handbook of evaluation research.* Beverly Hills, CA: Sage, 1975.

———Research for policy's sake: The enlightenment function of social research. *Policy Analysis,* 1977, *4,* 531-543.(a)

_____*Using social research in public policy making*. Lexington, MA: Lexington Books, 1977.(b)

_____The many meanings of research utilization. *Public Administration Review*, 1979, *39*, 477-482.

_____Knowledge creep and decision accretion. *Knowledge: Creation, Diffusion, Utilization*, 1980, *1*, 381-404.

_____& Bucuvalas, M. J. The challenge of social research to decision-making. In C. H. Weiss (Ed.), *Using social research*. Lexington, MA: Lexington Books, 1977.

Weiss, R. S., & Rein, M. The evaluation of broad aim programs: Experimental design, its difficulties, and an alternative. *Administrative Science Quarterly*, 1970, *15*, 97-109.

Whitebread, C. H., & Bonnie, R. J. *The marijuana conviction: A history of marijuana prohibition in the United States*. Charlottesville, VA: University of Virginia Press, 1974.

Wholey, J. S., Scanlon, J. W., Duffy, H. G., Fahumoto, J. S., & Vogt, L. M. *Federal evaluation policy: Analyzing the effects of public programs*. Washington, DC: Urban Institute, 1970.

Whyte, W. *Street corner society*. Chicago, IL: Chicago University Press, 1955.

Williams, W., & Evans, J. W. The politics of evaluation: The case of Head Start. *The Annals of the American Academy of Political and Social Science*, 1969, *385*, 118-132.

Windle, C., & Woy, J. R. Implications of the community mental health center amendments of 1975 for program evaluation. In W. Neigher, R. J. Hammer, and G. Landsberg (Eds.), *Emerging developments in mental health program evaluation*. New York: Argold, 1977.

Winer, B. J. *Statistical principles in experimental design*. New York: McGraw-Hill, 1966.

Wortman, C. B., & Rabinowitz, V. C. Random assignment: The fairest of them all. In L. Sechrest, S. G. West, M. A. Phillips, R. Render, and W. Yeaton (Eds.), *Evaluation studies review annual, Vol. 4*. Beverly Hills, CA: Sage, 1979.

Wortman, P. M. Evaluation research: A psychological perspective. *American Psychologist*, 1975, *30*, 562-575.

_____& Saxe, L. *Methods for medical technology assessment*. Paper presented for the Office of Technology Assessment, U.S. Congress, 1981.

Zuniga, R. B. The experimenting society and radical social reform: The role of the social scientist in Chile's Unidad popular experience. *American Psychologist*, 1975, *30*, 99-115.

AUTHOR INDEX

SUBJECT INDEX

About the Authors

LEONARD SAXE is Assistant Professor of Psychology at Boston University. He formerly served as a Fellow at the Congressional Office of Technology Assessment (OTA) and during 1981-1982 will serve as a Fulbright-Hays Senior Lecturer at Haifa University, Israel. His interests concern the role of applied problems in psychological research and the use of research in the development of social policy. He was the study director of an OTA report on the efficacy and cost-effectiveness of psychotherapy and is the co-editor of *The Social Psychology of Education: Theory and Research*. He is on the editorial boards of the *Personality and Social Psychology Bulletin* and *New Directions in Program Evaluation*. He also serves as a Council member of the Evaluation Research Society.

MICHELLE FINE is Assistant Professor of Psychology at the University of Pennsylvania, in the Interdisciplinary Studies in Human Development program. Formerly, she was Research Director of the Industrial Social Welfare Center at Columbia University and Research Associate on the Vietnam Era Research Project. Her research focuses on women's responses to injustice; the influence of work, social class, and mental health; and the influence of "meritocracy" and victim-blaming in education and child care.